Fearless Cooking Against The Clock

Michele Evans

PUBLISHED BY POCKET BOOKS NEW YORK

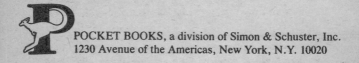
POCKET BOOKS, a division of Simon & Schuster, Inc.
1230 Avenue of the Americas, New York, N.Y. 10020

ISBN: 0-671-47641-6

First Pocket Books printing October, 1983

10 9 8 7 6 5 4 3 2 1

POCKET and colophon are registered trademarks
of Simon & Schuster, Inc.

Printed in the U.S.A.

IF YOU CAN SPARE 15 MINUTES . . .

Here is a tempting, delectable delight you can prepare in a quarter of an hour—*with* salad and dessert—and get rave reviews!

BUTTER SAUTÉED CHICKEN FILLETS serves 4

4 boneless chicken breasts, cut into 1–inch pieces lengthwise
salt and freshly ground pepper to taste
5 tablespoons butter
juice of 1 lemon
2 tablespoons of fresh chopped parsley

Pat the chicken pieces dry and season them lightly with salt and pepper. Heat the butter in a large skillet and sauté the chicken over medium heat about 5 minutes per side, until lightly browned and cooked. Transfer the fillets to a warmed serving dish. Add the juice of lemon and parsley. Stir and cook for 1 minute over medium-high heat. Pour over the chicken.

———————

Michele Evans, noted food consultant and author, received her formal training at the London Cordon Bleu, Le Cordon Bleu in Paris, and studied with James Beard, Jacques Pepin, and Simone Beck. She helped organize and operate the New York Times Cooking School, and was the resident gourmet on NBC's "Today" show.

"LAVISHLY GENEROUS . . . A BROAD SPECTRUM OF APPEALING MEALS . . ."

—*Publishers Weekly*

ACKNOWLEDGMENTS

To the following friends and acquaintances who generously contributed their ideas, recipes, and/or menus, many many thanks: Amanda Urban Auletta, Nancy Dussault, Nora Ephron, Sheila Ginsberg, Bob Gonko, Cindy Hubbard, Dinie James, Maryann Lopinto, Tamara Newell, Betty Pappas, Irene Patton, and Earlyne Rodriguez.

Special thanks go to my editor, Catherine Shaw, for her wisdom, patience and guidance, and to my perspicacious agent, Esther Newberg, for her friendship and for always being there.

I am indebted to Tully Plesser for the title, his ever-present humor and encouragement, and his delicious recipe.

For my father,
Gilbert Warren Evans

Contents

Introduction

Life today dictates that *time* is an essential ingredient in most of the plans we make, and meal-planning is certainly no exception. Ask anyone who cooks and loves good food to rank their kitchen priorities, and speed of preparation will be at the top of every list.

Time is our most valuable resource. America's busy working men and women are often less able to afford the time it can take to prepare gourmet meals than the costs of some expensive ingredients or of dining out. With 51 percent of all women in the United States, sixteen years of age and older, working today, and with increased appreciation of good food among men and women of all ages and economic means, learning how to prepare good meals quickly has become a national imperative.

Time is one element that does not expand with the economy. Regardless of how high salaries, interest rates, real estate values, or gold prices climb, the time available to shop for quality ingredients, plan delicious meals, and prepare first-rate menus remains unchanged. The temptation to compromise lurks in every corner of the supermarket and in the kitchen and on the highway when we approach the fast food restaurants' neon lights. Admittedly, frozen TV dinners, canned goods, and fast food can tempt us when the thought of spending over an hour in the kitchen after a long day seems out of the question. Yet frozen foods aren't always "fast" because they might require 50 minutes or more of heating time. And what these foods do save in preparation time, they sacrifice in quality: they are never as nourishing as fresh foods and they seldom taste very good.

The crucial question is what quality of food do we serve to ourselves and our families. Although Barbara Tuchman wasn't speaking specifically about food, she wrote, "Creating quality is self-nourishing. Quality, however, can be attained without genius." Her accurate and encouraging theory aptly applies to food; it *is* possible to cook excellent

1

quality fresh meals without being a professional chef and without exhausting the limited time that most of us have available.

The recipes in this book cover a broad spectrum of menus that take 15 minutes, 30 minutes, and 1 hour. Each menu is designed for quick and easy preparation. A sample 15-minute menu is Pan Sautéed Tournedos with Roquefort Sauce, Broccoli with Black Olives, and Chocolate Ice Cream with Tiny Chocolate Morsels and Crème de Menthe; a 30-minute menu could be Sea Scallops and Apples with Calvados Cream, Fresh Asparagus Salad, and Scrambled Fruit; and a 1 hour menu might be Chicken and Leek Sauté, Artichoke and Tomato Salad, and Fresh Cantaloupe Tart with Apricot and Pepper Glaze.

Because holiday meals combine the pleasures of entertaining with the extraordinary time pressures on a busy household, one chapter is devoted exclusively to holiday menus. Many of the dishes in these dinners are either partially or totally prepared the night before, or days before, the event. A New Year's Eve menu for six includes Raclette, Bouillabaisse with Rouille, Arugula and Endive Salad, and a Raspberry Crepe Cake. This particular meal requires only about 45 minutes of preparation just before sitting down to dine.

There are also two more chapters with menus and some of the recipes are designed for night before or "do ahead" preparation; these include five seasonal cocktail parties and a summer and winter children's birthday party.

In the 15-minute, 30-minute, and 1-hour meal chapters each recipe has also been timed, so that the cook can plan accordingly. The recipes in each menu are given in the order in which they should be cooked. Of course, several dishes may be cooking at the same time.

Cooking quickly is not as one might suspect—On Your Mark, Get Set . . . Go cooking. It is simply a result of organization and of cooking the right food in the right menus. Cooks of all levels can prepare these recipes with what I call common sense cooking skills.

Most of the ingredients used in the recipes are fresh, but good quality frozen and canned products are not overlooked. There are also recipes and menus for every pocketbook.

I hope that these menus and recipes will inspire imaginative cooks to create new, quick, quality recipes, and, therefore, a new quality of fast food.

MICHELE EVANS

2

CHAPTER ONE

The Larder

A well-stocked larder is essential for convenient and efficient quick cooking. My grandmother compared her well-supplied pantry to the laces in shoes: when laces are frayed buy a pair of new ones. She added an item to her shopping list when its container was three-quarters empty.

Most of these ingredients have good shelf life: herbs and spices, canned and bottled products, frozen food, and liqueur.

Dairy products spoil if not used within a few days or weeks, so it is helpful to remember that milk, cream, and butter or margarine can be frozen.

Oils become rancid unless used within a few weeks, so keep oil that isn't used often stored in the refrigerator.

Fresh foods, such as parsley, will also last a few days, so consider what you have on hand when menu planning. Add generous amounts of parsley to salads, dressings, soups, or vegetables to avoid waste. If there are several lemons left over, squeeze them over vegetables and make fresh lemonade.

Garlic can be chopped and preserved in vegetable or olive oil in a tightly sealed jar kept in the refrigerator. The mixture will keep for weeks.

Stock your larder according to your own tastes and needs.

HERB AND SPICE SHELF

Basil	Cream of tartar
Bay leaves	Cumin
Caraway seeds	Curry powder
Cayenne pepper	Dillweed
Celery seeds	Fennel seeds
Chili powder	Ginger
Chives	Mint
Cinnamon	Dry mustard
Coriander	Nutmeg (whole)

Oregano
Sweet paprika
Peppercorns (black and white)
Hot pepper flakes
Poppy seeds
Rosemary
Saffron

Sage
Salt
Seasoned salt (quality brand)
Sesame seeds
Tarragon
Thyme
Turmeric

NOTE: Keep herbs and spices in tightly covered containers away from direct light and heat.

CANNED PRODUCTS

Anchovies
Beef and chicken broth
Beef and chicken consommé
Chick-peas
Chopped clams
Salmon

Sweetened condensed milk
Tomato paste
Tomato sauce
Tomatoes (whole)
Tuna fish

MISCELLANEOUS BAKING, BOTTLED, AND PACKAGED INGREDIENTS

Baking powder
Baking soda
Barbecue sauce (Open Pit excellent brand)
Bread crumbs (plain and herbed)
Capers
Chili sauce
Chocolate (semisweet bars and morsels and unsweetened dark chocolate)
Chutney
Clam juice
Coffee (decaffeinated, too)
Cornichon pickles
Cornmeal
Cornstarch
Crackers
Flour (all-purpose)
Gelatin (plain)
Gherkins
Hoisin sauce
Honey

Horseradish
Ketchup
Lentils
Maple syrup
Mayonnaise
Mushroom caps (marinated)
Mustard (Dijon)
Nuts (whole and slivered almonds, walnuts, and pecans)
Olive oil
Olives (black and green stuffed with pimientos)
Pasta (a variety)
Pimientos
Preserves (apricot, strawberry, and red currant)
Rice (long-grain and wild)
Sesame seed oil
Soy sauce
Sugar (granulated, brown, and confectioners')
Tabasco sauce

Tea
Vanilla extract
Vegetable oil

Vinegar (white, red wine, and
  tarragon)
Walnut oil
Worcestershire sauce

DAIRY PRODUCTS

Butter and/or margarine
Cheese (Cheddar, Swiss, and
  Parmesan in whole pieces)
Heavy cream

Eggs
Milk
Sour cream
Yogurt

FRESH FOODS

Garlic
Lemons
Limes
Onions (yellow, red, scallions,
  and shallots)

Parsley
Potatoes (baking, boiling, and
  sweet)

FROZEN FOODS

Ice cream and sherbet (a
  variety of your choice)
Pattie shells
Puff pastry
Phyllo pastry leaves
Raspberries in syrup

Strawberries in syrup
Vegetables (chopped broccoli,
  corn, green peas, baby or
  regular lima beans, and
  chopped spinach)

WINES, SPIRITS, AND LIQUEURS

This list is solely for cooking. Check the index under the Bar for
entertaining. Liqueurs and/or cordials are fine additions to ice
creams, sherbets, or fruit.

Amaretto
Bourbon
Cointreau
Crème de menthe
Grand Marnier
Kahlua
Madeira

Marsala
Dark rum
Dry sherry
Red and white dry vermouth
Irish whiskey
Dry red and white wine

KITCHEN SUPPLIES

Aluminum foil
Plastic bags
Plastic containers (varied sizes
   for freezing foods, and ice
   cube trays with removable
   individual sections)

Plastic wrap
Kitchen string
Toothpicks (wooden)
Wax paper

CHAPTER TWO

Cooking Equipment

Nothing will speed up cooking faster than good quality cooking equipment—implements, pots, pans, baking dishes, knives, and some electrical appliances. Each item, designed to perform a specific function, is worth investing in for accuracy as well as speed. If well cared for, cooking equipment lasts for years. The next time you're in an antique shop, notice how many cooking implements line the shelves.

Since organization is vital to quick cooking, keep cooking utensils and all equipment in easily accessible and convenient locations and work areas.

There are five time-saving electrical appliances that I consider to be valuable "extra hands" in the kitchen: food processor, blender, electric mixer, toaster, and can opener. A good quality food processor is an expensive appliance, but it is multitalented. It slices, shreds, blends, purees, grinds, and mixes in seconds. Some brands offer attachments which act as juicers, french fry cutters, and so on. A food processor is certainly the most time-saving cooking device invented in recent years.

What the food processor can't do, the blender or electric mixer can. The blender purees and liquifies. Remember never to fill the blender container more than half full, and always use the lid. The electric mixer beats and whips cream, egg whites, and batters, a function neither the food processor nor the blender accomplishes well.

The toaster and can opener deserve honorable mention for the duties they perform fast and efficiently.

Not all the equipment listed below is necessary. Several items are multipurpose; a strainer can act as a sifter. The four-sided grater can serve as a nutmeg grater; however, the nutmeg grater contains a little compartment which holds 2 or 3 whole nutmegs, thereby saving a step.

Select what is convenient, affordable, and necessary for your kitchen, cooking preferences, and habits.

IMPLEMENTS AND EQUIPMENT

Bottle opener
Cake and cookie racks
Cake tester
Can opener
Canister set
Cherry pitter
Double-edged chopper
Small chopping board (hard wood or plastic)
Large chopping board (hard wood or plastic 16 × 18 inches)
Chopping bowl
Cleaver
Colander
Corkscrew
Egg slicer
Food mill
Long-handled fork
Funnel
Grapefruit knife
Garlic press
Four-sided grater
Ice cream scoop
Kitchen shears
Lemon juicer
Set of 4 dry measuring cups
2-cup liquid measuring cup
1-quart liquid measuring cup
Set of 4 measuring spoons
Meat pounder

Melon-ball cutter
Set of mixing bowls (small, medium, and 2 large)
Mouli grater
Nutmeg grater
Pastry blender
Pastry brush
Pepper mill (if desired, 1 for black pepper and 1 for white pepper)
Potato masher
Ricer
Rolling pin
Salad fork and spoon
Salad spinner
Sifter
6- and 8-inch wooden skewers
10-inch metal skewers
Skimmer
Spatula (cake, metal, and rubber)
Large spoon
Large slotted spoon
Wooden spoons (3)
Steamer (free-standing)
Strainers (small, medium, and large)
Tongs
Vegetable peeler
Wire whisks (small, medium, and balloon)

POTS AND PANS

1½-quart heavy saucepan with lid
2½-quart heavy saucepan with lid
3½-quart heavy saucepan with lid
5-quart Dutch oven or pot with lid
Double boiler
8- to 10-quart pot with lid

7- to 8-inch crepe pan (French iron)
7- to 8-inch omelet pan (French iron or nonstick)
10-inch curved-sided skillet with lid
14-inch straight-sided skillet with lid
Heavy cast iron skillet
Heavy cast iron ridged skillet

French fryer with basket
Large steamer
Broiling pan with rack (medium and large)
Rectangular baking dishes (12 and 14 inches)
Large au gratin oven-proof baking dish (16 inches)
Meat loaf pan
Bread pans (2)
Muffin pans (2)
Miniature muffin pans (2)
9-inch square cake pan

10-inch tube cake pan
9-inch spring form pan
Ring mold
Pie plates (2)
Baking sheets (2)
2½-, 5½-, and 8-quart casserole dishes with lids
Individual soufflé dishes (½-cup capacity)
2-quart soufflé dish
9-inch tart pan with removable bottom

MISCELLANEOUS

Fish poacher
Copper bowl
Coffeepot

Teapot
Espresso coffeepot

KNIVES (Carbon-steel or stainless steel)

Small sharp-pointed paring knife
7- to 8-inch cutting knife
10-inch chopping or chef's knife
14-inch carving knife

10-inch serrated knife
Chef's fork
Steel to sharpen knives (or small Zip Zap)
Clam opener
Oyster knife

SERVING ESSENTIALS

Hot pads
Trivets
Butter dish
Saltcellars
Pepper mills
Sauce boat and small ladle
Vegetable serving dishes (2)
Large oval serving dish
Large serving platters (2)
Soup tureen
Bread baskets (small, medium, and large)

Steak knives
Serving spoons and forks
Salad bowls (1 medium and 1 large)
Salad servers
Individual dessert bowls
Large dessert bowl
Sugar bowl
Creamer
Large pitcher

CHAPTER THREE

Strategies for Quick Cooking

1. Select a menu.
2. Make a shopping list of those ingredients not in supply. Keep an ongoing shopping list in the kitchen.
3. Shop for first-quality ingredients at a convenient time.
4. Set table in advance, if possible, and have serving dishes, coffee cups and saucers, etcetera ready for immediate serving.
5. Read each recipe thoroughly before starting to cook.
6. Set out all the ingredients needed for each dish on the menu, unless they require refrigeration or freezing.
7. Set out all pots, pans, cooking equipment and utensils needed for preparing meal.
8. Work at a steady pace; don't poke or race. If there are others present who can help by washing and drying lettuce or chopping vegetables, welcome their assistance.
9. Keep waste basket near the work area and clean up as you work, when possible.
10. When it is convenient, serve main courses and vegetable in same serving dish or platter.

RECIPES FOR FOUR

All of the recipes in the book, unless otherwise indicated, are for four servings.

Desserts

Some of the menus that follow suggest desserts of fruit and cheese, or of ice creams, sherbets or yogurts. No recipes are provided for these easy yet elegant desserts, because they are self-explanatory. These desserts will take no more than five or ten minutes to prepare. Vary the size of portions according to individual appetites.

Special Recipe and Menu Instructions for Timing

Each recipe of all the following menus is given in the order in which it should be cooked to insure the best timing. This has been determined not only by the length of time each recipe requires, but also by whether the dish can be held until serving time. For instance, a salad and dressing should be prepared first because they can be refrigerated until serving time, when they are quickly combined and tossed. The quick-cooking fish dish should be started later, because it would not remain hot while you prepared the salad. Naturally, several recipes may be in preparation or cooking at the same time. For this reason it is vital to read each recipe thoroughly before beginning a menu to properly orchestrate the meal. It won't take long! In keeping with the time-saving goals of this book, I've designed each recipe to be as clear and quickly read as possible.

The length of time listed with each individual recipe has been rounded off to the nearest 5 minutes, frequently giving the cook 3 or 4 minutes to work with.

For fearless cooking against the clock, remember to work at an even, steady pace.

CHAPTER FOUR

15-Minute Meals

Seafood

•

MENU

Madrilene Matisse
Herb Broiled Scallops
Pureed Lima Beans with Corn
Chocolate Ice Cream with
Semisweet Chocolate Shavings

•

PUREED LIMA BEANS WITH CORN   *15 minutes*

 1 10-ounce package frozen baby lima beans
 1 10-ounce package frozen corn
 3 tablespoons butter
 salt and freshly ground pepper

Cook the lima beans and corn in separate saucepans, according to the package directions. Drain. Puree the lima beans with the butter in a food processor fitted with the steel blade or force through a food mill. Season with salt and pepper and stir in the corn.

HERB BROILED SCALLOPS   *10 minutes*

 4 tablespoons melted butter
 1 tablespoon fresh lemon juice
 ½ teaspoon tarragon
 ½ teaspoon dill
 1 tablespoon fresh chopped parsley
 1½ pounds scallops
 4 slices toast, crust trimmed

Preheat the broiler. Combine the butter, lemon juice, and herbs. Toss the scallops in the mixture and place in a shallow baking dish. Cook under the broiler for 5 minutes until the scallops are lightly browned. Serve on the toast.

MADRILENE MATISSE   *5 minutes*

    1 small green pepper, seeded and diced
    2 scallions, thinly sliced
    1/2 cup diced tomatoes
    1/2 cup diced cucumber
    2 10-ounce cans jellied madrilene, well chilled
    1 cup sour cream
    freshly ground pepper

Cut up the vegetables. Spoon the madrilene in equal amounts into 4 soup bowls. Top with equal amounts of the sour cream and vegetables. Sprinkle with pepper.

•

MENU

Butter Sautéed Scallops
Hot Cooked Green Beans with Rosemary
Sliced Bananas in Apricot Yogurt

•

HOT COOKED GREEN BEANS
WITH ROSEMARY   *10 minutes*

    salt
    1 pound fresh green beans, ends cut off
    2 tablespoons butter
    1/2 teaspoon rosemary
    freshly ground pepper

In a saucepan bring 3 cups of water to a boil. Season lightly with salt. Drop the beans into the water and cook them over medium heat for exactly 5 minutes. Drain well. Return to the pan and add the butter and rosemary and season with salt and pepper; toss. Cover until ready to serve.

BUTTER SAUTÉED SCALLOPS

10 minutes

5 tablespoons butter
1¼ pounds bay scallops
salt and freshly ground pepper
flour
juice of 1 lemon
2 tablespoons fresh chopped parsley
4 slices firm white toast, crusts trimmed

Heat the butter in a large skillet. Season the scallops with salt and pepper. Dust with flour. Sauté the scallops over medium heat for 2 minutes. Shake the pan and sauté until golden, about 3 minutes. Sprinkle with the lemon juice and parsley, shake the pan and remove from the heat. Place a slice of toast on 4 dinner plates. Spoon equal amount of the scallops and sauce over the toast. Serve immediately.

•

MENU

Broiled Scrod with Lime Hollandaise
Asparagus with Garlic
Sliced Peaches in Cinnamon Cream

•

BROILED SCROD WITH
LIME HOLLANDAISE

15 minutes

1¼ pounds scrod fillet, cut into 4 equal-size pieces
½ cup dry white wine
2 tablespoons melted butter

LIME HOLLANDAISE:

3 large egg yolks
1 tablespoon fresh lime juice
¼ teaspoon salt
pinch cayenne pepper
1 stick (8 tablespoons) hot melted butter

Preheat the broiler. Place the scrod pieces in a buttered shallow baking dish, add the wine, and brush with the melted butter. Cook under the broiler for about 12 minutes until the fish is tender.

Meanwhile, 5 minutes before the fish is cooked, prepare the Lime Hollandaise. Put the egg yolks, lime juice, salt, and cayenne pepper in a blender and turn on to medium. Open the lid opening and slowly pour in the hot butter. Spoon the sauce over the broiled scrod.

ASPARAGUS WITH GARLIC   *10 minutes*

> 1 pound asparagus, cut into 1-inch lengths
> 2 tablespoons butter
> 1 garlic clove, crushed
> salt and freshly ground pepper

Cook the asparagus in 3 cups of boiling water for 5 minutes. Meanwhile, heat the butter in a skillet; add the garlic and cook over low heat for 3 minutes. Drain the asparagus and add to the skillet. Toss and season to taste with salt and pepper.

SLICED PEACHES
IN CINNAMON CREAM   *10 minutes*

> 4 ripe peaches, peeled and sliced
> 1 cup heavy cream, whipped
> ½ teaspoon cinnamon or to taste
> ½ cup sugar
> ½ teaspoon vanilla
> bakery cookies

Place the peaches in a bowl. Whip the cream until it thickens slightly. Add the cinnamon, sugar, and vanilla and beat until stiff. Pour the cream over the peaches and toss. Refrigerate until served. Toss before serving and accompany with bakery cookies.

•

MENU

Broiled Scrod with Shallots and Wine
Carrots Vichy
Sautéed Pears

•

BROILED SCROD WITH SHALLOTS
AND WINE
15 minutes

¼ cup sliced shallots
1¼ pounds scrod fillet, cut into 4 equal-size pieces
½ cup dry white wine
paprika
2 tablespoons butter

Line an au gratin dish with the shallots. Place the scrod on top. Pour the wine into the dish. Sprinkle the fish with paprika and dot with the butter. Cook under the broiler for approximately 12 minutes, until the fish flakes easily, and the top is golden brown.

CARROTS VICHY
10 minutes

1 pound carrots, peeled and thinly sliced
2 tablespoons butter
1 teaspoon sugar
salt and freshly ground pepper
1 tablespoon fresh chopped parsley

Cook the carrots in 3 cups of boiling water for 6 minutes. Drain. Heat the butter in a saucepan; add the carrots and sprinkle with the sugar, toss and cook for 1 minute. Season to taste with salt and pepper and sprinkle with the parsley.

SAUTÉED PEARS
10 minutes

4 fresh ripe firm pears, peeled, halved, and cored
sugar
3 tablespoons butter

Lightly coat each pear half with sugar. Heat the butter in a skillet and sauté the pears over medium-high heat until the pears are browned on each side, about 4 minutes per side.

●

MENU

Braised Cod with Pernod
Zucchini Patties
Sliced Peaches Georgia

●

BRAISED COD WITH PERNOD

15 minutes

3 tablespoons butter
2 medium onions, thinly sliced
1½ pounds cod fillet, cut into 4 equal-size pieces
1 cup bottled clam juice
2 tablespoons Pernod
2 tablespoons fresh chopped parsley
salt and freshly ground pepper

Heat the butter in a large skillet and cook the onions for 3 minutes over medium heat. Top the onions with the fish pieces and pour in the clam juice and Pernod. Sprinkle with the parsley and season with salt and pepper to taste. Cover and simmer for 12 minutes.

SLICED PEACHES GEORGIA

10 minutes

4 fresh ripe peaches, peeled, pitted, and sliced
1 cup whipped heavy cream
4 tablespoons brown sugar
4 tablespoons chopped pecans

Divide the peaches into 4 dessert bowls. Spoon equal amounts of the whipped cream over the peaches and sprinkle with the brown sugar and pecans. Refrigerate until served.

ZUCCHINI PATTIES

10 minutes

1¾ cups fresh grated zucchini
1 tablespoon flour
½ teaspoon seasoned salt
freshly ground pepper to taste
2 tablespoons butter
2 tablespoons vegetable oil

In a bowl combine the zucchini, flour, seasoned salt, and pepper. Heat the butter and oil in a skillet and spoon the zucchini, in equal portions, onto 4 areas of pan. Pat the tops down with the back of a fork. Cook over medium-high heat until browned. Turn and brown on the other side.

•

MENU

Sweet and Sour Mustard Shrimp
Poached Zucchini Slices with Scallions
Three Minute Fried Bananas

•

SWEET AND SOUR MUSTARD SHRIMP   *15 minutes*

16 large shrimp, shelled and deveined, with tails intact
6 tablespoons butter
1/3 cup Dijon mustard
3 tablespoons honey
1 tablespoon fresh lemon juice
2 scallions, minced
1/4 cup dry sherry

Preheat the broiler. Cut the shrimp from tail end to the other, but don't cut all the way through to the other side. Place the shrimp, tail side up, side by side in shallow broiling or au gratin pan. In a bowl combine the remaining ingredients and spoon the mixture over the shrimp. Cook under a broiler for about 6 minutes until the shrimp sizzle and are tender.

POACHED ZUCCHINI SLICES
WITH SCALLIONS   *10 minutes*

1/2 cup chicken broth
2 tablespoons dry white wine
2 medium zucchini, thinly sliced
6 scallions, cut into 1/2-inch pieces·
2 teaspoons butter
1/2 teaspoon seasoned salt
freshly ground pepper to taste

Bring the chicken broth to a boil with the wine. Add the zucchini, scallions, butter, salt, and pepper. Toss. Cover and cook for 5 minutes.

THREE-MINUTE FRIED BANANAS *5 minutes*

    4 slices white bread
    1 large egg
    4 bananas
    2 tablespoons butter
    4 tablespoons vegetable oil

Prepare this dessert right before serving. Trim the crusts from the bread and make bread crumbs using the steel blade in a food processor or a blender. Place the bread crumbs in a plate. Beat the egg in a wide shallow soup bowl or similar shaped dish. Peel the bananas. Coat each with the beaten egg and roll in the bread crumbs. Heat the butter and oil in a large skillet; add the bananas and cook over medium-high heat for 1½ minutes; turn and cook 1½ minutes until crisp. Serve hot.

•

MENU

Quick Shrimp with Lemon and Dill Butter Sauce
Spinach au Gratin
Chocolate Ice Cream with Spiked Vanilla Yogurt

•

SPINACH AU GRATIN *15 minutes*

    1 10-ounce package frozen chopped spinach, cooked and
      well-drained
    ½ cup sour cream
    salt and freshly ground pepper to taste
    ¾ cup grated Cheddar cheese
    3 tablespoons plain dry bread crumbs
    2 tablespoons melted butter

Preheat the broiler. In a bowl combine the spinach and sour cream. Season with salt and pepper. Place in an au gratin dish and sprinkle with the combined cheese and bread crumbs. Drizzle with the butter and cook under the broiler until the top sizzles.

QUICK SHRIMP WITH LEMON AND
DILL BUTTER SAUCE   *10 minutes*

    4 tablespoons butter
    1 pound medium shrimp, shelled and deveined
    2 scallions, thinly sliced
    1 tablespoon fresh chopped dill, or 1 teaspoon dried dill
    2 tablespoons fresh lemon juice
    salt and freshly ground pepper

Heat the butter in skillet. Add the shrimp and scallions.
Cook, stirring frequently, for 5 minutes over medium heat.
Sprinkle with the dill and lemon juice; season with salt and
pepper and toss.

CHOCOLATE ICE CREAM
WITH SPIKED VANILLA YOGURT   *5 minutes*

    1½ pints chocolate ice cream
    1 cup vanilla yogurt
    2 tablespoons Kahlua

Place the scoops of ice cream in 4 dessert bowls. Combine
the yogurt and Kahlua. Spoon over the ice cream.

•

MENU

Stir-Fried Shrimp and Peanuts with Snow Pea Pods
Five Minute Rice
Fresh Pineapple Slices with Pineapple Sherbet

•

STIR-FRIED SHRIMP AND PEANUTS
WITH SNOW PEA PODS
10 minutes

3 tablespoons vegetable oil
1 pound medium shrimp, shelled and deveined
1 clove garlic, crushed
½ cup unsalted peanuts
½ cup chicken broth
1½ tablespoons soy sauce
2 tablespoons dry sherry
1 tablespoon cornstarch dissolved in 2 tablespoons chicken
broth
⅓ pound snow pea pods, trimmed

Heat the oil in a wok or large skillet. Add the shrimp and stir-fry for 2 minutes over medium-high heat. Remove the shrimp. Add the garlic; stir and cook for 30 seconds. Add the peanuts, and stir-fry for 1 minute. Return the shrimp to the pan with the chicken broth, soy sauce, and sherry. Stir-fry for 1 minute. Add the cornstarch dissolved in the chicken broth and stir-fry for 1 minute. Add the snow pea pods, toss, and cook for 1 minute.

FIVE MINUTE RICE

Cook the rice according to the package directions for 4.

●

MENU

Sautéed Soft-Shelled Crabs
Butter-Parmesan Toast
Corn on the Cob
Quick Marinated Strawberries

●

CORN ON THE COB
10 minutes

1 tablespoon salt
1 cup milk (optional)
6 to 8 ears of fresh corn, shucked
butter
freshly ground pepper

30

In a large pot bring 4½ quarts of water to a boil. Add the salt and milk. Stir and add the corn. Bring back to a boil, cover, and cook over medium heat for exactly 3 minutes. Turn off the heat and don't remove lid for 5 minutes. Drain well and serve with plenty of butter, salt, and pepper.

SAUTÉED SOFT-SHELLED CRABS   *10 minutes*

    8 soft-shelled crabs, cleaned
    salt and freshly ground pepper
    flour
    6 tablespoons butter
    fresh chopped parsley
    1 lemon, cut into wedges

Season the crabs with salt and pepper. Dust with flour. Heat the butter in a large skillet and sauté the crabs over medium heat until golden on each side, about 4 minutes per side. Sprinkle with parsley. Serve with the lemon wedges.

BUTTER-PARMESAN TOAST   *5 minutes*

    8 slices French bread
    2 tablespoons melted butter
    2 tablespoons fresh grated Parmesan cheese

Under the broiler toast one side of the bread, turn, and brush with the butter. Sprinkle with the cheese and toast until golden.

QUICK MARINATED STRAWBERRIES   *5 minutes*

    1 quart fresh strawberries, hulled
    ⅓ cup Cointreau
    1 cup heavy cream
    sugar

Place the strawberries in a colander. Pour 1 cup of boiling water over the strawberries and immediately place them in a bowl. Sprinkle the Cointreau over the strawberries, and toss. Refrigerate until served. Serve with the cream and sugar.

•

MENU

Sole with Tarragon Cream Sauce
French-Style Peas
Cantaloupe Wedges with Port

•

SOLE WITH TARRAGON CREAM SAUCE   *15 minutes*

4 sole fillets
salt and freshly ground pepper
flour
4 tablespoons butter
1 tablespoon vegetable oil

TARRAGON CREAM SAUCE:

½ cup dry white wine
1 teaspoon tarragon
1 cup heavy cream

Season the sole fillets with salt and pepper. Coat with flour.
Heat the butter and oil in a large skillet and sauté the fillets,
browning on both sides, about 4 minutes per side. Transfer
the fillets to serving dish and keep warm in a low oven.

Pour off all but 1 tablespoon of the fat from the skillet. Add
the wine to the pan and cook over high heat until the liquid is
reduced to half, stirring and scraping bottom of the pan to
release any of the food particles. Stir in the tarragon and
cream and bring to a boil. Cook, whisking constantly, for
about 4 minutes until the sauce thickens. Pour over the fish.

FRENCH-STYLE PEAS   *10 minutes*

2 10-ounce packages frozen peas
4 leaves Boston lettuce, cut into thin strips
1 small onion, thinly sliced
¼ cup chicken broth
2 tablespoons butter
salt and freshly ground pepper

Cook the peas according to the package directions with the
lettuce and onion. Drain. Heat the chicken broth and butter
and add the peas and onion. Bring to a boil and season with
salt and pepper.

32

CANTALOUPE WEDGES WITH PORT   *5 minutes*

    1 large ripe cantaloupe
    8 tablespoons port

Quarter the cantaloupe and remove the seeds. Spoon 2
tablespoons of the port over each quarter and refrigerate
until served.

•

MENU

Sautéed Swordfish
Endive Strips and Mushroom Salad
Vanilla Ice Cream with Marron Glacé

•

SAUTÉED SWORDFISH   *10 minutes*

    4 5-ounce swordfish steaks
    salt and freshly ground pepper
    flour
    3 tablespoons butter
    2 tablespoons olive oil
    1 lemon, cut into 4 wedges

Season the swordfish with salt and pepper. Coat with flour.
Heat the butter and oil in a large skillet and sauté the fish
until golden brown on each side, about 4 minutes per side.
Serve with the lemon.

ENDIVE STRIPS AND
MUSHROOM SALAD   *10 minutes*

    3 large Belgian endives
    8 fresh mushrooms, very thinly sliced

DILL DRESSING:

    ½ cup olive oil
    1 tablespoon white wine vinegar
    ½ teaspoon dry mustard
    salt and freshly ground pepper to taste
    1 tablespoon fresh chopped dillweed

Slice the endives lengthwise in ¼-inch-thick slices and cut

33

off the root ends. Separate the leaves into a salad bowl. Add the mushrooms. Combine the dressing ingredients well and pour over the salad. Toss.

VANILLA ICE CREAM
WITH MARRON GLACÉ   *5 minutes*

    1 quart vanilla ice cream
    1 12-ounce jar marrons in syrup, chopped*

Place the ice cream in small scoops into 4 dessert bowls. Spoon equal amounts of the marrons and syrup over the ice cream.

●

MENU

Swordfish Steaks with Walnut Topping
Snow Pea Pods with Mushrooms
Orange Slices and Banana with Raisin Whip

●

SWORDFISH STEAKS
WITH WALNUT TOPPING   *15 minutes*

    4 tablespoons butter
    ½ cup finely chopped walnuts
    1½ pounds swordfish steak, cut into 4 equal portions
    1 onion, thinly sliced
    ⅓ cup dry white wine

Preheat the broiler. Melt 2 tablespoons of the butter in a small saucepan and mix with the walnuts. Spread the butter and nut mixture over one side of the pieces of fish. Heat the remaining 2 tablespoons butter in an ovenproof shallow au gratin or baking dish. Spread the onion slices over the bottom of the pan. Top with the fish pieces and add the wine. Bring to a boil on top of the stove. Immediately remove and place in the broiler under a medium flame and cook for about 8 minutes until crisp, golden, and tender.

---

* Marrons (chestnuts) in syrup can be found in specialty food shops.

ORANGE SLICES AND BANANA
WITH RAISIN WHIP
5 minutes

2 navel oranges
1 large banana, mashed
¼ cup raisins
¾ cup sour cream
1 teaspoon fresh lemon juice
2 tablespoons honey

Peel the oranges including the outer skins and white pith of the oranges and slice crosswise into ¼-inch slices. Cover and refrigerate. Combine the remaining ingredients and cover and refrigerate. When ready to serve the dessert, spoon the mixture over the oranges divided onto 4 dessert plates.

SNOW PEA PODS WITH MUSHROOMS   *10 minutes*

10 ounces fresh snow pea pods, or 1 10-ounce package
   frozen snow pea pods
3 tablespoons butter
¼ pound fresh mushrooms, halved
salt and freshly ground pepper

Trim the ends from the snow pea pods and remove the strings. Drop into enough rapidly boiling lightly salted water to cover them; cook for 1 minute. Drain. If using frozen snow pea pods, drop them into rapidly boiling lightly salted water and cook for 1 minute or until just thawed and drain. Heat the butter in a skillet. Add the mushrooms and cook over medium-high heat for 3 minutes, shaking pan. Add the snow pea pods and season with salt and pepper. Toss and cook for 1 minute.

•

MENU

Broiled Swordfish with Tomato Dill Butter
Sautéed Cucumbers
Fresh Bing Cherries with Hazelnut Ice Cream

•

BROILED SWORDFISH WITH TOMATO DILL BUTTER
15 minutes

4 swordfish steaks
1 tablespoon olive or vegetable oil
1 tablespoon fresh lemon juice
paprika
⅔ cup dry white wine

TOMATO DILL BUTTER:

6 tablespoons softened butter
1½ tablespoons tomato paste
1 teaspoon fresh chopped dill or 1 teaspoon dried dill
freshly ground pepper to taste

Prepare the Tomato Dill Butter first by combining the ingredients in a small bowl. Place in the freezer until ready to serve with the fish so that the mixture will harden slightly. Preheat the broiler. Place the fish steaks in a foil-lined shallow baking dish and turn up the edges of the foil. Brush the fish with the combined oil and lemon juice; sprinkle with paprika and pour the wine into area surrounding the fish. Broil under medium heat until the fish is tender, about 10 to 12 minutes. Top each fish steak with equal amount of the Tomato Dill Butter.

SAUTÉED CUCUMBERS
10 minutes

2 large cucumbers, peeled
salt
2 tablespoons butter
1 tablespoon fresh chopped parsley

Cut the cucumbers in half lengthwise. Scoop out the seeds with a teaspoon and cut into 1-inch lengths. Bring 1 quart of water to a boil in a saucepan. Season lightly with salt and drop the cucumber pieces into water. Cook for 2 minutes. Drain. Heat the butter in a large skillet and sauté the cucumbers over medium heat for 5 minutes, shaking the pan to turn them several times. Sprinkle with the parsley and serve immediately.

FRESH BING CHERRIES WITH
HAZELNUT ICE CREAM
10 minutes

½ pound Bing cherries, pitted
1½ pints vanilla ice cream
½ cup finely chopped hazelnuts

Divide the ice cream in scoops into 4 dessert bowls and top with the cherries and hazelnuts. (Chop the hazelnuts in a food processor fitted with the steel blade or chop in a Mouli grater.)

•

MENU

Cucumber and Carrot Nests with
Feta Cheese and Olives
Oyster Stew
Toasted Datenut Bread with Vanilla Ice Cream

•

CUCUMBER AND CARROT NESTS WITH
FETA CHEESE AND OLIVES
10 minutes

4 romaine lettuce leaves
1 large cucumber, peeled and shredded
2 carrots, peeled and grated
8 ounces feta cheese, cut into 4 equal-size cubes
16 Greek or plain black olives
6 tablespoons olive oil
1½ tablespoons red wine vinegar
½ teaspoon rosemary
½ teaspoon oregano
1 tablespoon minced scallion greens
freshly ground pepper

Place a lettuce leaf on each of four plates. Combine the shredded cucumber and carrots and divide into equal amounts. Make a nest with a hole in the center on each of the lettuce leaves with the cucumbers and carrots. Place a cube of feta cheese in the center of the hole. Place 4 black olives at the corners of each cheese cube. Combine the oil, vinegar, rosemary, oregano, scallion greens, and pepper with a wire whisk. Spoon in equal amounts over the cheese.

OYSTER STEW   *10 minutes*

    6 tablespoons butter
    1 medium onion, minced
    2 cups milk
    2 cups heavy cream
    ¼ cup dry white wine
    1 pint fresh oysters and their liquid
    salt and freshly ground white or black pepper
    oyster crackers

Heat 2 tablespoons of the butter in a large saucepan. Sauté
the onions for 5 minutes, stirring often. Pour in the milk,
cream, and wine with the oysters. Bring to a boil and simmer
for 1 minute. Season with salt and pepper to taste. Ladle into
4 soup bowls and top each bowl of stew with 1 tablespoon of
butter. Serve with oyster crackers.

•

MENU

Fried Oysters
Succotash
Sliced Bananas in Raspberry Yogurt

•

FRIED OYSTERS   *15 minutes*

    vegetable oil
    2 eggs
    2 tablespoons water
    24 shucked oysters
    flour
    plain bread crumbs
    salt and freshly ground pepper

Heat 1 inch of oil in a large skillet. Beat the eggs in a bowl
with the water. Dust the oysters with flour, dip in the egg
mixture, and roll in bread crumbs that have been seasoned
well with salt and pepper. Fry in the oil until golden, about 2
minutes per side. Drain on absorbent paper.

SUCCOTASH

10 minutes

1 10-ounce package frozen whole kernel corn
1 10-ounce package frozen baby lima beans
2 tablespoons butter
¼ cup chopped pimientos
salt and freshly ground pepper

Cook the corn and lima beans in separate saucepans according to package directions. Drain each well. Heat the butter in a saucepan and add the corn, lima beans, and pimientos. Season to taste with salt and pepper. Toss.

•

MENU

Fresh Fish Cakes
Corn with Cream
Lettuce and Cabbage Slaw
Papaya Halves with Pineapple Ice Cream

•

FRESH FISH CAKES

15 minutes

2 eggs, beaten
3 tablespoons mayonnaise
1 teaspoon Worcestershire sauce
freshly ground pepper
¼ teaspoon salt
⅓ cup flour
1 pound sole or flounder, coarsely chopped
bread crumbs
vegetable oil

Mix together the eggs, mayonnaise, Worcestershire sauce, pepper, salt, and flour. Fold in the chopped fish. Divide into 4 equal portions. Shape into 4 patties and coat with bread crumbs. Pour ⅛ inch depth of oil into medium-size skillet and heat. Sauté the fish cakes until golden brown on each side, approximately 4 minutes per side.

CORN WITH CREAM

10 minutes

2 10-ounce packages frozen whole kernel corn
½ cup heavy cream
salt and freshly ground pepper

Cook the corn according to the package directions and drain. Place in a saucepan with the heavy cream and heat thoroughly. Season with salt and pepper to taste.

LETTUCE AND CABBAGE SLAW

5 minutes

2 cups shredded cabbage
2 cups shredded romaine lettuce
1 carrot, peeled and grated
½ cup mayonnaise
1 tablespoon white wine vinegar
1 teaspoon celery seeds

Place the cabbage, lettuce and carrot in a bowl. Combine the remaining ingredients in a separate bowl, then pour over the salad. Toss well.

•

MENU

Avocado Stuffed with Salmon Salad
Bakery Croissants
Apples and Brie

•

AVOCADO STUFFED WITH
SALMON SALAD

15 minutes

1 12-ounce can salmon, drained
2 hard-cooked eggs, chopped
1 small onion, minced
1 tablespoon fresh chopped parsley
¼ cup chopped dill pickle
1 teaspoon fresh lemon juice
½ cup mayonnaise

salt and freshly ground pepper to taste
2 medium firm ripe avocados

Pick over the salmon, discarding all the skin and bones. Fold the salmon with the remaining ingredients, except for the avocados. Halve the avocados lengthwise. Remove the pits. Place equal amounts of the salmon salad in the avocado halves.

NOTE: If a garnish is desired, use crumbled crisp cooked bacon, capers, and lemon slices sprinkled with paprika.

●

MENU

Tuna Salad Ciga
Zucchini and Cabbage Slaw
Raspberry and Lemon Sherbet

●

ZUCCHINI AND CABBAGE SLAW   *5 minutes*

1 large zucchini, grated
2 cups shredded cabbage
½ cup sour cream
¼ cup mayonnaise
½ teaspoon celery seeds
salt and freshly ground pepper

Combine the ingredients in a bowl.

TUNA SALAD CIGA   *10 minutes*

½ cup crumbled crisp cooked bacon
2 7-ounce cans white meat tuna, drained and flaked
2 scallions, thinly sliced
½ cup thinly sliced celery
1 cup fresh diced tomato
½ teaspoon basil
½ teaspoon dill
1 cup mayonnaise
2 tablespoons fresh lemon juice
2 tablespoons fresh chopped parsley
salt and freshly ground pepper
4 slices whole wheat bread, crusts trimmed

Cook the bacon while preparing the rest of the salad. In a bowl place the tuna, scallions, celery, and tomato. Toss. In a small bowl combine the remaining ingredients except for the bread. Spoon the mixture over the tuna salad and combine well. Add the bacon and toss. Toast the bread and place 1 large scoop of the mixture over each slice.

Poultry

•

MENU

Butter Sautéed Chicken Fillets
Artichoke Hearts with Wilted Watercress
Mango and Kiwi Fruit Slices with Peach Ice Cream

•

BUTTER SAUTÉED CHICKEN FILLETS   *15 minutes*

    4 boneless chicken breasts, cut into 1-inch pieces lengthwise
    salt and freshly ground pepper to taste
    5 tablespoons butter
    juice of 1 lemon
    2 tablespoons fresh chopped parsley

Pat the chicken pieces dry and season them lightly with salt
and pepper. Heat the butter in a large skillet and sauté the
chicken over medium heat about 5 minutes per side, until
lightly browned and cooked. Transfer the fillets to a warmed
serving dish. Add the juice of lemon and parsley. Stir and
cook for 1 minute over medium-high heat. Pour over the
chicken.

ARTICHOKE HEARTS WITH
WILTED WATERCRESS   *10 minutes*

    2 10-ounce packages frozen artichoke hearts
    2 tablespoons olive oil
    1 garlic clove, crushed
    1 cup watercress leaves
    salt and freshly ground pepper to taste

Cook the artichoke hearts according to the package directions, but only until tender. Meanwhile, heat the olive oil in a saucepan and add the garlic. Cook over low heat for 4 minutes. Add the watercress, stir, and cook for 1 minute. Add the drained artichokes and season to taste with salt and pepper. Toss and serve immediately.

•

MENU

Chicken Brochettes with Honey Mustard
Five Minute Rice
Tomato and Mushroom Salad
Fresh Peaches and Plums with Camembert Cheese

•

CHICKEN BROCHETTES WITH
HONEY MUSTARD   *15 minutes*

    4 chicken breasts, skinned, boned, and halved
    ½ cup honey
    ¼ cup Dijon mustard
    2 tablespoons soy sauce
    2 tablespoons hot water
    ½ teaspoon coriander
    ½ teaspoon ginger

Preheat the broiler. Cut each breast half into pieces crosswise. Combine the remaining ingredients in a large bowl and add the chicken pieces. Toss until each piece is evenly coated. Prepare the 4 skewers by slipping 4 pieces of the chicken on each of the skewers. Cook under a hot broiler basting with the marinade 2 or 3 times during cooking time until the chicken is golden and tender, about 8 to 10 minutes.

FIVE MINUTE RICE

Cook the rice according to the package directions for 4.

TOMATO AND MUSHROOM SALAD   *5 minutes*

    2 medium tomatoes, thinly sliced
    10 mushrooms, thinly sliced
    1 small red onion, thinly sliced
    ⅓ cup olive oil

44

1 tablespoon red wine vinegar
½ teaspoon basil
salt and freshly ground pepper to taste

Place the tomatoes, mushrooms, and red onion in a bowl. Combine the remaining ingredients in a separate bowl, then pour over the salad. Toss.

•

MENU

Chicken Breasts Piccata
Broccoli and Tomatoes
Grilled Peaches

•

CHICKEN BREASTS PICCATA   *15 minutes*

4 medium chicken breasts, skinned, boned, and halved
salt and freshly ground pepper
flour
5 tablespoons butter
2 tablespoons vegetable oil
1 tablespoon fresh lemon juice
1 lemon, peeled, thinly sliced, and seeded
fresh chopped parsley

Place each piece of the chicken between 2 pieces of wax paper and flatten them to ⅛-inch thickness, taking care not to break the flesh. Season the chicken with salt and pepper and dust with flour on each side. Heat 2 tablespoons of the butter and oil in a large skillet and cook the chicken, 2 pieces at a time, until golden brown on each side. Transfer to a serving dish and keep warm in a low oven as the other pieces of chicken are being cooked. Add a little extra butter and oil, if necessary. When all of the chicken is cooked, pour off all but 1 tablespoon of the fat from the pan. Add 3 tablespoons of the butter and the lemon juice. Cook over high heat for 1 minute, stirring. Add the lemon slices and cook for 30 seconds. Arrange the lemon slices over the chicken and spoon the sauce over the top. Sprinkle with parsley.

BROCCOLI AND TOMATOES   *5 minutes*

 1 10-ounce package frozen chopped broccoli
 1 large ripe tomato
 2 tablespoons butter
 salt and freshly ground pepper

Cook the broccoli according to the package directions, but
only for 3 minutes. Meanwhile, cube the tomato and heat the
butter in a saucepan. Drain the broccoli and add to the
saucepan with the tomato. Stir and season to taste with salt
and pepper. Heat thoroughly.

GRILLED PEACHES   *5 minutes*

 4 large fresh ripe peaches, halved, peeled, and pitted
 3 tablespoons melted butter
 2 tablespoons brown sugar

Preheat the broiler. Brush the peach centers with the melted
butter and sprinkle with the brown sugar. Refrigerate until
dessert time. Place the peaches on a baking sheet under the
broiler and cook until the tops sizzle, for about 5 minutes.

•

MENU

Instant Borscht
Chunky Chicken Marsala
Sautéed Snow Pea Pods
Bel Paese Cheese with Grannie Smith Apples

•

INSTANT BORSCHT   *5 minutes*

 1 16-ounce can sliced beets and liquid, chilled
 1 tablespoon fresh lemon juice
 3 tablespoons tomato paste
 1 teaspoon sugar
 3 cups buttermilk
 salt and freshly ground pepper to taste
 2 scallions, thinly sliced

In a blender puree the beets, lemon juice, tomato paste, and sugar. Pour the mixture into a bowl and combine with the buttermilk. Season with salt and pepper and garnish with the scallions.

CHUNKY CHICKEN MARSALA   *15 minutes*

  3 boneless chicken breasts, cut into 1-inch pieces
  salt and freshly ground pepper
  flour
  7 tablespoons butter
  1 medium onion, thinly sliced
  1/2 pound mushrooms, sliced
  1/2 cup Marsala

Season the chicken pieces with salt and pepper and dust with flour. Heat 4 tablespoons of the butter in a skillet and over medium-high heat brown the chicken pieces on each side. Remove to a side dish and add the remaining 3 tablespoons of butter to the pan. Add the onion and mushrooms and cook for 5 minutes, stirring often. Return the chicken to the pan and pour in the Marsala. Cook over high heat for 1 minute. Season to taste.

SAUTÉED SNOW PEA PODS   *5 minutes*

  2 tablespoons butter
  1 tablespoon olive or vegetable oil
  1 garlic clove, crushed
  1/2 pound fresh snow pea pods, trimmed
  salt and freshly ground pepper to taste

Heat the butter and oil with the garlic and cook, stirring, over medium heat for 2 minutes. Add the snow pea pods and toss for 3 minutes. Add salt and pepper to taste before serving.

●

MENU

Chicken Supreme with Crisp Mustard Topping
Zucchini Roesti
Fresh Cucumber Salad
Lemon Sherbet with Pomegranate Pieces

●

CHICKEN SUPREME WITH CRISP MUSTARD TOPPING

15 minutes

4 small chicken breasts, skinned, boned, and halved
2 tablespoons Dijon mustard
4 slices white bread
2 tablespoons melted butter
½ cup dry white wine

Preheat the broiler. Place the chicken halves in a shallow baking pan. Brush each piece of the chicken with the mustard. Trim the crusts from the bread and make bread crumbs in a food processor fitted with the steel blade or in a blender. Sprinkle the crumbs over the mustard and then sprinkle the melted butter over the crumbs. Pour the wine into the pan and bring to a boil on top of stove. Immediately place under the broiler for approximately 7 minutes, until the top is golden brown and the chicken is cooked.

FRESH CUCUMBER SALAD

5 minutes

1 large cucumber, peeled
2 tablespoons grated onion

VINAIGRETTE SAUCE:

⅓ cup olive or vegetable oil
1 tablespoon white wine vinegar
1 teaspoon tarragon
1 tablespoon fresh chopped parsley
salt and freshly ground pepper

Slice the cucumber in half lengthwise. Scoop out the seeds with a teaspoon and slice the cucumbers very thin in a food processor fitted with the slicing disk, or by hand. Mix together the sauce ingredients in a small bowl with a wire whisk. Pour the sauce over the cucumbers and onion. Toss.

ZUCCHINI ROESTI

10 minutes

2 medium zucchini
salt and freshly ground pepper
2 tablespoons butter
2 tablespoons vegetable oil

Grate the zucchini and season with salt and pepper to taste. Heat the butter and oil in a large skillet and add the zucchini.

Pat down to cover bottom of pan. Fry over medium-high heat until golden brown on one side, and carefully turn over and brown on the other side.

•

MENU

Chicken Breast Strips with
Green Peppercorn Sauce
Carrot Logs
Vanilla Ice Cream with Amaretto and
Whole Smoked Almonds

•

CHICKEN BREAST STRIPS WITH GREEN PEPPERCORN SAUCE   *15 minutes*

3 chicken breasts, skinned and boned
salt and freshly ground pepper
3 tablespoons butter
1 tablespoon vegetable oil
2 tablespoons Cognac or brandy
¼ cup chicken broth
1 small onion, minced
1 cup heavy cream
2 tablespoons drained green peppercorns

Cut each breast in half and cut each half into 4 pieces lengthwise. Season the pieces with salt and pepper. Heat the butter with the oil in a large skillet and brown the chicken on each side, about 8 minutes. Meanwhile, heat the Cognac, broth, and onions in a small saucepan over high heat until reduced by half. Remove the cooked chicken pieces to a warmed serving dish. Pour out all of the fat in skillet, except for 1 tablespoon, and add Cognac mixture, stirring to release food particles in the pan. Add the heavy cream and cook over high heat, stirring with a wire whisk until the sauce thickens. Stir in the green peppercorns and taste for seasoning. Spoon over the chicken.

CARROT LOGS
10 minutes

2½ cups chicken broth
1 pound carrots, peeled and cut into 1-inch lengths
2 tablespoons butter
1 tablespoon fresh chopped parsley

Bring the chicken broth to a boil in a saucepan. Add the carrots and cook over medium heat for 8 minutes or until tender. Drain the carrots, reserving ½ cup of broth. (Use remaining broth for another time.) Bring the broth and butter to a boil and add the carrots and parsley. Toss.

VANILLA ICE CREAM WITH AMARETTO
AND WHOLE SMOKED ALMONDS
5 minutes

1½ pints vanilla ice cream
8 tablespoons Amaretto
¾ cup smoked almonds

Place scoops of the ice cream in 4 dessert bowls and spoon 2 tablespoons of the Amaretto over each. Top with equal portions of the almonds and serve.

CHICKEN SALADS

Cooked chicken lends itself beautifully to salad making. For 15 minute meals either use "extra" chicken from a previous meal or poach boneless chicken breasts in slow boiling water with a chopped onion and chopped celery and/or carrot for about 12 minutes. Prepare the other ingredients in the recipe while the chicken is cooking.

Cooked turkey can be substituted for chicken in any chicken salad recipe.

Accompany chicken salads with your choice of bread, rolls, or crackers with sweet butter.

For dessert select a seasonal fruit with a complementary cheese, or ice cream or sherbet.

CHICKEN AND CANTALOUPE SALAD
WITH MINT DRESSING
10 minutes

2 cups cubed cooked chicken
2 cups peeled, seeded, and cubed cantaloupe

MINT DRESSING:

½ cup vegetable oil
2 tablespoons white wine vinegar
1 tablespoon fresh chopped mint, or 1 teaspoon dried mint,
  plus whole leaves for garnish
1 teaspoon sugar
salt and freshly ground pepper

Place the chicken and cantaloupe in a bowl. In a small bowl beat together the Mint Dressing ingredients with a wire whisk and pour over the chicken and cantaloupe. Toss. Garnish with fresh mint leaves.

CHICKEN SALAD WITH ALMONDS   *10 minutes*

3 cups chopped cooked chicken
1 cup thinly sliced celery
¾ cup toasted almond slivers
1 cup mayonnaise
1 tablespoon fresh lemon juice
2 tablespoons fresh chopped parsley
salt and freshly ground pepper
4 large romaine lettuce leaves
cherry tomatoes

Combine all ingredients well, except for the lettuce leaves and tomatoes. Spoon equal amounts of the salad on each lettuce leaf and garnish with tomatoes.

CHICKEN SALAD IN A BREAD LOAF   *15 minutes*

3 cups chopped cooked chicken
1 cup seedless green grapes
1 16-ounce can pineapple chunks, drained but reserve ¼
  cup of liquid
½ cup roasted peanuts
½ cup raisins
1 medium red onion, chopped
1 cup mayonnaise
1 tablespoon fresh lime or lemon juice
salt and freshly ground pepper to taste
1 large round loaf or I large loaf Vienna bread
fresh chickory leaves

In a large bowl combine the chicken, grapes, pineapple,

peanuts, raisins, and onion. In a medium bowl beat together the mayonnaise, pineapple juice, and lemon juice. Pour the mixture over the salad and toss. Add salt and pepper to taste. Cut off the top quarter of the bread and set aside. Pull out the soft bread inside of the loaf and fill the bread shell with the chicken salad. Place the top back on the loaf at an angle. Garnish bread with chickory.

WALDORF CHICKEN SALAD   *10 minutes*

    2 cups cubed cooked chicken
    2 Delicious apples, cored and cut into ½-inch cubes
    ½ cup chopped walnuts
    ½ cup raisins
    1 cup seedless green grapes
    ¾ cup mayonnaise
    2 teaspoons fresh lemon juice
    Boston lettuce leaves
    cherry tomatoes

Gently combine all the ingredients except for the lettuce and tomatoes in a large bowl. Arrange the lettuce leaves on a platter or on individual plates and spoon the salad onto the lettuce. Garnish with cherry tomatoes.

DORSET COBB SALAD   *15 minutes*

    1 medium head romaine lettuce, torn into bite-size pieces
    8 strips cooked bacon, crumbled
    2½ cups thinly sliced cooked chicken breast
    1 large avocado, peeled, pitted, and cubed
    2 medium tomatoes, cut into 8 wedges each

LEMON VINAIGRETTE:

    ½ cup olive oil
    2 tablespoons fresh lemon juice
    1 teaspoon Dijon mustard
    1 large garlic clove, crushed
    2 tablespoons fresh chopped parsley
    ½ teaspoon tarragon
    ½ teaspoon salt or to taste
    freshly ground pepper

Combine the ingredients for the Lemon Vinaigrette in a bowl with a wire whisk and set aside. Place the lettuce pieces in a salad bowl and top with the remaining salad ingredients. Pour the dressing over the salad and gently toss.

CHICKEN BREAST AND FENNEL SALAD   *10 minutes*

    2½ cups cubed cooked chicken breast
    ¾ cup sliced fennel stalks
    2 tablespoons fresh chopped parsley
    2 scallions, thinly sliced

DRESSING:

    ½ cup olive oil
    2 tablespoons fresh lemon juice
    1 teaspoon Dijon mustard
    ½ teaspoon tarragon
    salt and freshly ground pepper

Place the chicken, fennel, parsley, and scallions in bowl. In a separate small bowl beat together the dressing ingredients with a wire whisk. Pour over the chicken mixture and toss.

CHINESE CHICKEN SALAD   *15 minutes*

    3 cups diced cooked chicken
    ½ cup chopped water chestnuts
    ½ cup diced cornichon or sour pickles
    ½ cup chopped watercress
    1 cup bean sprouts
    ½ cup sesame oil
    2 tablespoons fresh lemon juice
    1 tablespoon soy sauce
    1 tablespoon fresh chopped parsley
    1 teaspoon fresh grated ginger (optional)
    freshly ground pepper

Place the chicken, water chestnuts, pickles, watercress, and bean sprouts in a bowl and gently toss. Beat together the remaining ingredients in a bowl with a wire whisk. Pour over the salad and toss. Serve immediately or cover and refrigerate.

•

MENU

Turkey Tonnato
Green Bean Salad
Fresh Chilled Cherries and Gorgonzola Cheese

•

TURKEY TONNATO   *15 minutes*

  1 ½ pounds breast of turkey, thinly sliced
  3 tablespoons well-drained capers

  TONNATO SAUCE:

  1 7-ounce can white meat tuna, drained and flaked with fork
  6 anchovy fillets, chopped
  1 large garlic clove
  1 cup mayonnaise
  ½ cup olive oil
  2 teaspoons fresh lemon juice or to taste

Prepare the Tonnato Sauce by putting all of the ingredients in
a food processor fitted with the steel blade, or in a blender,
and pureeing. Taste for seasoning. On a serving platter
arrange the sliced turkey in overlapping layers. Spoon the
Tonnato Sauce over the border of turkey and sprinkle the
sauce with capers. Dish can be chilled until served, if time
permits.

Serves 6.

GREEN BEAN SALAD   *10 minutes*

  2 10-ounce packages frozen Italian green beans
  ⅓ cup olive oil
  ¼ cup thinly sliced scallions
  1 tablespoon red wine vinegar
  ½ teaspoon oregano
  ½ teaspoon Dijon mustard
  salt and freshly ground pepper

Cook the green beans according to the package directions,
but just until tender. Meanwhile, in a bowl combine the
remaining ingredients. Drain the beans and immediately
pour the dressing over them. Toss.

FRESH CHILLED CHERRIES AND GORGONZOLA CHEESE

5 minutes

A simple and delightful Italian summertime traditional dessert is a bowl of fresh cherries with stems intact, accompanied by a bowl of water with ice cubes in it. Diners immerse their cherries in the ice water to refresh and chill them.

Serve the cherries with Gorgonzola cheese and crusty Italian bread.

Beef

•

MENU

Pan-Sautéed Tournedos with Roquefort Sauce
Broccoli with Black Olives
Chocolate Ice Cream with Tiny Chocolate Morsels and
Crème de Menthe

•

PAN-SAUTÉED TOURNEDOS WITH ROQUEFORT SAUCE
15 minutes

½ teaspoon salt
4 1½-inch-thick tournedos

ROQUEFORT SAUCE:

1 cup heavy cream
¼ pound Roquefort cheese, crumbled
1 teaspoon cracked black pepper

Sprinkle the salt in a heavy iron skillet and heat until the salt turns light brown. Add the meat and cook over high heat for 5 minutes. Turn and cook for 4 or 5 minutes on the other side for rare. Meanwhile, bring the cream to a boil in a saucepan. Let it boil, whisking often, until the cream thickens, about 4 minutes. Whisk in the cheese and black pepper. Stir and cook for 1 minute. Spoon the sauce over the tournedos.

BROCCOLI WITH BLACK OLIVES
10 minutes

2 10-ounce packages frozen chopped broccoli
2 tablespoons butter

½ cup pitted black olives
salt and freshly ground pepper

Cook the broccoli according to the package directions, but only until tender. Drain. Heat the butter in a saucepan and add the olives and broccoli. Toss over medium heat and season with salt and pepper.

•

MENU

Broiled Delmonico Steaks with Parsley-Lemon Butter
Cauliflower with Dill
Peach Melba

•

CAULIFLOWER WITH DILL   *15 minutes*

1 medium cauliflower
3 tablespoons butter
1 teaspoon chopped dillweed
salt and freshly ground pepper

In a large saucepan bring 2½ cups water to a boil. Meanwhile, cut the cauliflower into flowerets. Cook the cauliflower in the boiling water, covered, for 8 minutes. Heat the butter in a saucepan with the dillweed and add the drained cauliflower. Season to taste with salt and pepper and toss.

BROILED DELMONICO STEAKS WITH
PARSLEY-LEMON BUTTER   *15 minutes*

4 1-inch-thick Delmonico steaks
seasoned salt
freshly ground pepper

HOT PARSLEY-LEMON BUTTER:

3 tablespoons lemon juice
¼ pound (1 stick) sweet butter
⅓ cup fresh chopped parsley

Preheat the broiler. Sprinkle both sides of the steaks lightly with the seasoned salt and pepper. Place on a rack in a broiling pan and cook 5 to 6 inches under the hot broiler for 5 minutes; turn and cook for 5 minutes for rare, or cook to desired doneness. Meanwhile, prepare the Parsley-Lemon Butter. Heat the lemon juice in a small heavy saucepan over high flame until reduced to half. Lower the heat and add the butter in pieces; stir until melted. Add the parsley and stir. Serve the sauce with the steaks.

PEACH MELBA   *5 minutes*

    1½ pints vanilla ice cream
    4 canned peach halves*
    1 10-ounce package frozen raspberries in syrup, pureed

Place 1 large scoop of ice cream in each of 4 dessert bowls. Top each with an inverted peach half and spoon the pureed raspberry sauce over peaches.

•

MENU

Cold Beet, Tomato, and Orange Puree
Kansas Fried Steaks
Mama's Sautéed Potatoes
Butter Pecan Ice Cream with Chopped Candied Ginger

•

MAMA'S SAUTÉED POTATOES   *15 minutes*

    3 tablespoons vegetable oil
    3 tablespoons butter
    3 medium potatoes, peeled and thinly sliced
    salt and freshly ground pepper

Heat the oil and butter in a large skillet and add the potatoes. Cook over medium-high heat until slightly browned; turn and lower heat to medium. Cook until brown. Season with salt and pepper.

---

* If time permits and fresh peaches are in season, poach the two ripe fresh peeled peaches in simmering water with ¼ cup of sugar for about 10 minutes. Drain the peaches, cut in half, and pit.

KANSAS FRIED STEAKS
15 minutes

2 eggs
2 tablespoons milk or water
4 cube steaks, scored
flour
½ teaspoon salt
freshly ground pepper
2 tablespoons butter
2 tablespoons vegetable oil

In a shallow dish beat the eggs with the milk. Dip the steaks in the mixture and coat with flour seasoned with salt and pepper. Heat the butter and oil in a large skillet and quickly brown the steaks on each side over medium-high heat.

NOTE: To make milk gravy, after cooking the steaks, pour out all but 1 tablespoon of the fat from the skillet. Sprinkle with 1 tablespoon of flour and stir over medium-high heat. Pour in 1 cup of milk or light cream and stir with a wire whisk until thickened and smooth. Taste for seasoning. Cooking time is about 5 minutes.

COLD BEET, TOMATO, AND
ORANGE PUREE
5 minutes

1 16-ounce can beets with juice, chilled
1 16-ounce can whole tomatoes with juice, chilled
1 cup orange juice, chilled
1 small onion, chopped
1 garlic clove, crushed
¾ cup sour cream
freshly ground pepper
1½ tablespoons finely grated orange rind

In a large bowl combine the beets, tomatoes, orange juice, onion, and garlic. Puree two cupsful at a time in a blender until smooth. Strain and refrigerate the soup until ready to serve. Garnish each serving with a dollop of the sour cream sprinkled with pepper and the orange rind.

•

MENU

Beef à la Lindstrøm
Broiled Tomato Halves with Fresh Basil
Grapes Holbrook

•

BEEF À LA LINDSTRØM   *15 minutes*

> 1½ pounds lean ground beef
> 2 eggs
> 1 medium onion, minced
> 2 tablespoons drained capers
> ¼ cup heavy cream
> salt and freshly ground pepper
> 2 tablespoons butter
> 2 tablespoons vegetable oil

In a bowl mix together the first 6 ingredients. Shape into 4 patties. Heat the butter and oil in a large skillet and cook the patties over medium-high heat until browned on each side, about 5 minutes per side.

BROILED TOMATO HALVES
WITH FRESH BASIL   *10 minutes*

> 2 medium-large fresh ripe tomatoes, halved crosswise
> 2 tablespoons fresh chopped basil
> salt and freshly ground pepper
> 4 tablespoons fresh bread crumbs
> 2 tablespoons melted butter

Preheat the broiler. With a teaspoon, scoop out the tomato pulp from the tomato halves and chop. Add the basil and season with salt and pepper to taste. Spoon the mixture back into the tomato shells and sprinkle each with 1 tablespoon of the bread crumbs and drizzle with the butter. Place on a baking sheet and cook under the broiler until the tops are golden brown.

GRAPES HOLBROOK   *10 minutes*

> 1¼ pounds seedless green grapes, stemmed
> 1½ cups sour cream
> 1 tablespoon chopped candied ginger
> ⅓ cup light brown sugar
> ½ teaspoon vanilla
> ½ cup almond slivers

Place the grapes in a bowl. Combine the remaining ingredients in a separate bowl and spoon the mixture over the grapes. Toss and refrigerate until ready to serve.

•

MENU

Pan-Fried Ground Beef Steaks and Onion Cream Sauce
Sugar Snap Beans
Bubbling Brown Bananas

•

PAN-FRIED GROUND BEEF STEAKS
AND ONION CREAM SAUCE   *15 minutes*

> 1½ pounds ground beef
> 1 tablespoon Worcestershire sauce
> 1 small onion, grated
> 2 tablespoons vegetable oil

ONION CREAM SAUCE:

> 2 tablespoons butter
> 1 medium onion, very thinly sliced
> 1½ tablespoons flour
> 2 tablespoons dry sherry
> 1 cup heavy cream
> salt and freshly ground pepper

Combine the ground beef, Worcestershire sauce, and grated onion. Shape into 4 oval steaks, each about 1 inch thick. Heat the oil in a large skillet and cook over medium-high heat about 5 minutes per side for medium-rare. Meanwhile, for the sauce, heat the butter in a saucepan and add the onion. Cook for 5 minutes, stirring often. Sprinkle with the flour and stir. Cook 1 minute. Add the combined sherry and heavy cream and bring to a boil, whisking continuously until

61

thickened. Taste for salt and pepper. Spoon the sauce over the steaks.

BUBBLING BROWN BANANAS   *15 minutes*

> 4 medium bananas
> 1/4 cup orange juice
> 1/4 cup dark rum
> 1/2 teaspoon cinnamon
> 1/4 teaspoon nutmeg
> 1/4 cup dark brown sugar
> 2 tablespoons butter

Preheat the oven to 425°F. Peel the bananas and cut into 1-inch lengths. Place in a lightly buttered baking dish just large enough to hold the bananas. Combine the orange juice, rum, cinnamon, and nutmeg. Pour over the bananas and sprinkle with the brown sugar. Dot with the butter. Cook for 10 minutes until the mixture bubbles.

SUGAR SNAP BEANS   *5 minutes*

> salt
> 1 pound sugar snap beans, trimmed
> 2 tablespoons butter
> 1 tablespoon fresh chopped parsley
> freshly ground pepper

Bring 1 quart of water to a boil. Add a little salt and drop the beans into the boiling water. Cook for exactly 3 minutes. Drain. Heat the butter in a skillet and add the beans with parsley. Toss and cook for 1 minute. Season with pepper.

NOTE: For variety, substitute the parsley with 1 teaspoon of chopped fresh mint or basil.

Liver

•

MENU

Calf's Liver Meunière
Carrots and Grapes
Instant Lime Pudding

•

INSTANT LIME PUDDING   *10 minutes*

1 14-ounce can sweetened condensed milk
juice of 2 fresh limes
2 teaspoons grated lime rind
1 egg yolk, beaten
1 cup heavy cream, whipped
bakery cookies (optional)

In a large bowl combine the sweetened condensed milk, lime juice, and grated lime rind. Stir until the mixture thickens and is smooth. Beat in the egg yolk and fold in the whipped cream. Spoon into 4 dessert bowls and chill until served.

Serve with bakery cookies of your choice.

CARROTS AND GRAPES   *10 minutes*

1 pound carrots, peeled and thinly sliced
2 tablespoons butter
3 tablespoons heavy cream
1/4 teaspoon rosemary
1 cup seedless green grapes
salt and freshly ground pepper

Cook the carrots in boiling water for 6 minutes. Drain. Heat the butter in a skillet with the heavy cream and rosemary and bring to a boil. Add the carrots and grapes. Toss and season with salt and pepper.

CALF'S LIVER MEUNIÈRE   *10 minutes*

1½ pounds calf's liver
flour
3 tablespoons butter
1 tablespoon olive or vegetable oil
1 tablespoon fresh lemon juice
2 tablespoons fresh chopped parsley
salt and freshly ground pepper

Coat the liver with flour. Heat the butter and oil in a large skillet and sauté the liver quickly over medium-high heat for 4 minutes per side until lightly browned. Remove to a warmed serving dish. Add the lemon juice and parsley to the pan and stir over high heat. Season to taste with salt and pepper. Immediately pour over the liver and serve.

Veal

•

MENU

Paillards of Veal
Glazed Carrots
Raspberry Fool with Chocolate Ice Cream

•

GLAZED CARROTS   *15 minutes*

    1 teaspoon salt
    1 pound carrots, peeled and cut into ½-inch diagonal slices
    2½ tablespoons butter
    2 tablespoons sugar

In a saucepan bring 3½ cups of water to a boil. Add the salt
and carrots. Cook over medium heat for 5 minutes or until
tender. Drain. Heat the butter and sugar in a skillet, whisking constantly until the mixture begins to turn light brown.
Immediately add the carrots, toss until well coated. Serve
immediately.

PAILLARDS OF VEAL   *10 minutes*

    4 4- to 5-ounce veal scallops
    olive oil
    salt and freshly ground pepper
    1 lemon, cut into 8 wedges
    2 tablespoons fresh chopped parsley

Flatten each veal scallop between 2 sheets of wax paper to
⅛-inch thickness. Brush with oil and sprinkle with salt and
pepper. Heat a heavy ridged iron grill pan and brush with a
little oil. When the pan is hot, quickly grill 2 of the scallops at

a time for 20 seconds and turn each scallop to form a crisscross pattern on the meat from the ridges on the pan. Turn the scallops over and grill for 20 seconds. Transfer the scallops to a heated serving platter. Repeat procedure with the remaining 2 veal scallops. Dust each lemon wedge with parsley and serve with the scallops. Serve immediately.

RASPBERRY FOOL WITH CHOCOLATE ICE CREAM

10 minutes

1 10-ounce package frozen raspberries in syrup, thawed
1 cup heavy cream
1 pint chocolate ice cream

Puree the raspberries in the blender and set aside. Whip the cream in a blender or by hand and add the raspberry puree. Stir in a circle twice. Refrigerate. When ready to serve, place the ice cream scoops into 4 balloon wineglasses or dessert bowls and spoon the raspberry mixture over the ice cream.

Lamb

•

MENU

*Roast Lamb Chops with Parsley and
Bread Crumb Crust
Sliced Beefsteak Tomatoes with Onions and
Roquefort Cheese
Honey and Orange Glazed Doughnuts*

•

ROAST LAMB CHOPS WITH PARSLEY
AND BREAD CRUMB CRUST   *15 minutes*

    vegetable oil
    8 1-inch-thick lamb chops

PARSLEY AND BREAD CRUMB CRUST:

    4 slices white bread, crusts trimmed
    2 tablespoons butter
    1 garlic clove, crushed
    ¼ cup fresh chopped parsley
    salt and freshly ground pepper

Preheat the oven to 425°F. Lightly oil a roasting pan and cook the chops for 5 minutes in the oven. Meanwhile, make the bread crumbs in a food processor fitted with the steel blade or in a blender. Heat the butter in a saucepan with the garlic and cook for 1 minute. Remove from the heat. Stir in the parsley and bread crumbs; add salt and pepper to taste. Remove the chops from the oven and turn them. Press equal amounts of the parsley mixture on top of each chop. Return to the oven and cook for 5 minutes, then cook the chops under the broiler until the tops are golden.

SLICED BEEFSTEAK TOMATOES WITH
ONIONS AND ROQUEFORT CHEESE   *5 minutes*

    2 large ripe firm beefsteak tomatoes, cut into ½-inch slices
    1 large Bermuda onion, thinly sliced
    ½ pound Roquefort cheese
    4 tablespoons olive oil
    freshly ground pepper

On 4 salad plates overlap equal amounts of the tomato and
onion slices. Crumble the cheese and top each salad with
equal amounts. Sprinkle 1 tablespoon of the olive oil and a
little pepper over each salad.

HONEY AND ORANGE GLAZED
DOUGHNUTS   *5 minutes*

    4 plain bakery doughnuts
    6 tablespoons honey
    2 tablespoons fresh orange juice
    ¼ teaspoon cinnamon
    1½ tablespoons fresh grated orange rind
    4 tablespoons chopped almonds or walnuts

Place the doughnuts on a cookie rack. Combine the honey,
orange juice, and cinnamon. Brush the mixture over the
doughnuts. Sprinkle with the grated orange rind and nuts.
Warm doughnuts for 3 minutes.

•

MENU

Lamb Chops Parmesan
Curried Corn and Tomatoes
Cantaloupe and Honeydew with
Pureed Strawberries

•

LAMB CHOPS PARMESAN   *15 minutes*

    8 1-inch-thick loin lamb chops
    3 tablespoons melted butter
    ½ cup fresh grated Parmesan cheese

68

½ cup plain dry bread crumbs
salt and freshly ground pepper

Preheat the broiler. Brush the lamb chops with the butter. Coat the chops with the combined cheese and bread crumbs. Season with salt and pepper. Cook under the broiler for about 6 minutes per side, or to desired doneness.

CURRIED CORN AND TOMATOES

10 minutes

1 16-ounce can whole tomatoes, drained
1 10-ounce package frozen whole kernel corn, cooked and
    drained
2 tablespoons butter
1½ teaspoons curry powder
salt and freshly ground pepper

Chop the tomatoes and place in a saucepan with the corn, butter, and curry powder. Bring to a boil and season with salt and pepper to taste.

CANTALOUPE AND HONEYDEW WITH
PUREED STRAWBERRIES

10 minutes

1 ripe medium cantaloupe
1 ripe small honeydew melon
1 package frozen strawberries, thawed

Cut the melons in half lengthwise. Remove the seeds. Peel the halves and cut into ½-inch-thick slices. On 4 individual plates, arrange alternating slices of the melons in equal amounts. Puree the strawberries in a blender, and spoon equal amounts across the center of the melon slices.

NOTE: Melons should be the same size.

•

MENU

Sliced Figs, Kiwi Fruit, and Prosciutto
Broiled Noisettes of Lamb with Herbs
Sautéed Cherry Tomatoes
Stilton Cheese, Fresh Pears, and Crackers

•

BROILED NOISETTES OF LAMB WITH HERBS

15 minutes

8 1-inch-thick lamb chops
8 strips of bacon
1 teaspoon rosemary
1 teaspoon thyme
½ teaspoon freshly crushed black pepper
¼ teaspoon salt

Have a butcher bone the lamb chops or do it yourself by cutting away the meat from bone with a small sharp knife. Preheat the broiler. Roll up each lamb chop and wrap a strip of bacon around each chop; secure it with a piece of kitchen string. Combine the rosemary, thyme, pepper, and salt. Sprinkle evenly on each side of the lamb. Cook 6 to 8 inches under broiler about 6 minutes per side for pink, or cook a few moments longer to desired doneness. Remove the strings.

SLICED FIGS, KIWI FRUIT, AND PROSCIUTTO

5 minutes

4 fresh rip figs, peeled and quartered
4 kiwi fruit, peeled and cut into ¼-inch-thick slices
16 thin slices prosciutto

Arrange 1 fig and 1 kiwi fruit on each of 4 first course plates. Top each with 4 slices of the prosciutto.

SAUTÉED CHERRY TOMATOES

5 minutes

1 pint cherry tomatoes, at room temperature, washed and stemmed
3 tablespoons olive oil
salt and freshly ground pepper
1 tablespoon fresh chopped parsley

Thoroughly dry the tomatoes. Heat the oil in large skillet and add the tomatoes. Cook over medium-high heat, shaking the pan frequently, for 2 minutes. Sprinkle with salt, pepper, and parsley; toss and serve immediately.

NOTE: For variations, toss in 1 tablespoon fresh chopped dill, basil, or mint in place of the parsley.

•

MENU

Honey-Basted Broiled Lamb Chops
Minted Peas
Tamara's Strawberries

•

HONEY-BASTED BROILED LAMB CHOPS   *15 minutes*

> 8 1-inch-thick loin lamb chops
> salt and freshly ground pepper
> ½ cup honey

Preheat the broiler. Season the lamb chops with salt and pepper on both sides. Place on a rack over a roasting pan. Brush each with the honey and cook under broiler for 5 minutes. Turn, brush with the honey, and cook for 5 minutes for pink, or to desired doneness.

MINTED PEAS   *10 minutes*

> salt
> 2 10-ounce packages frozen peas
> 2 tablespoons butter
> freshly ground pepper
> 1 teaspoon dried mint

Cook the peas in lightly salted boiling water according to the package directions until just thawed. Drain and return to the pan. Add the butter, salt and pepper to taste, and mint. Toss and cover until ready to serve.

TAMARA'S STRAWBERRIES   *5 minutes*

> 2 cups sour cream
> 1½ cups lightly tossed brown sugar
> 2 pints fresh large strawberries with stems

Place the sour cream and sugar in separate bowls on a serving dish. Surround the bowls with the strawberries. Diners dip each strawberry in the sour cream and coat with the brown sugar.

Pasta

•

MENU

Peaches with Prosciutto
Fresh Uncooked Tomato Sauce with Spaghetti
Italian Bread
Raspberry Sherbet with Bakery Butter Cookies

•

FRESH UNCOOKED TOMATO SAUCE WITH SPAGHETTI

15 minutes

3½ pounds fresh ripe tomatoes
¼ cup olive oil
2 tablespoons tomato paste
1 large garlic clove, crushed
2 scallions, thinly sliced
3 tablespoons fresh chopped parsley
¼ cup chicken broth
6 fresh basil leaves, chopped, or 1 teaspoon dried basil
½ teaspoon oregano
2 teaspoons fresh lemon juice
salt and freshly ground pepper
1 pound spaghetti or other pasta
¼ cup fresh grated Parmesan cheese

In a saucepan bring 6 cups of water to a boil. Immerse the tomatoes, one at a time, for 8 seconds. Remove with a slotted spoon. Peel the tomatoes with a small sharp knife and cut out the stem ends. Cut the tomatoes in half crosswise; squeeze out the seeds into strainer over a large bowl to catch the juice. Discard the seeds. Chop the tomatoes in a blender, or a food processor using the steel blade. Place the tomatoes into the bowl with the remaining ingredients, except for the pasta and Parmesan cheese. Stir with a wire whisk and leave at room temperature. Drop the spaghetti into 4½ quarts of lightly salted boiling water and cook for about 6 minutes until just tender. Drain well and turn into a bowl. Spoon the sauce over the spaghetti and toss. Serve with the fresh grated Parmesan cheese.

PEACHES WITH PROSCIUTTO   *5 minutes*

    4 ripe peaches
    16 very thin slices prosciutto
    1 fresh lime, cut into 4 wedges

Cut the peaches in half and pit. Place 2 halves each on 4 first course plates, cut side up, and top each half with 2 slices of the prosciutto. Garnish each with a wedge of the lime.

•

MENU

Fettuccine Alfredo
Tomato, Cucumber, and Black Olive Salad
Fresh Strawberries with Hot Cream and Marsala

•

FETTUCCINE ALFREDO   *15 minutes*

    1 tablespoon salt
    1 pound fettuccine
    5 tablespoons butter
    1 cup heavy cream
    ¾ cup fresh grated Parmesan cheese
    salt and freshly ground pepper

Bring 4½ quarts of water to a boil. When water boils, add the salt and fettuccine and cook for 6 minutes or until just tender. Meanwhile, melt the butter in a saucepan. Add the cream and bring to a boil. Stir in the cheese and immediately remove from the heat. Season to taste with salt and pepper. Drain the cooked pasta well and turn into a bowl. Pour the cream mixture over the pasta and toss.

TOMATO, CUCUMBER, AND
BLACK OLIVE SALAD
5 minutes

2 medium tomatoes, cut into 8 wedges each
1 medium cucumber, peeled and thinly sliced
1 cup pitted black olives
1 tablespoon fresh chopped parsley
olive oil
red wine vinegar
salt and pepper mill

Toss the tomatoes, cucumbers, black olives, and parsley in a salad bowl. Serve with oil, vinegar, and salt and peppermill.

FRESH STRAWBERRIES WITH
HOT CREAM AND MARSALA
10 minutes

1 quart fresh strawberries, hulled
1 cup heavy cream
1/3 cup Marsala

Divide the strawberries into 4 large balloon wineglasses. Bring the heavy cream to a boil and cook, stirring for 4 minutes until slightly thickened. Stir in the Marsala, whisk for 1 minute. Spoon over the strawberries.

Cheese Dishes

•

MENU

Holly's Black Bean Soup
Quesadillas
Fresh Papayas with Lemon Sherbet

•

QUESADILLAS   *15 minutes*

½ pound Monterey Jack cheese, grated
1 3-ounce can green chilies, peeled, seeded, and chopped
8 flour tortillas

Preheat the oven to 400°F. Place equal amounts of the cheese and chilies in the center of each tortilla and fold in half. Place on a lightly greased baking sheet and cook in the oven for about 8 minutes, until the cheese melts and the tortillas are light brown.

HOLLY'S BLACK BEAN SOUP   *15 minutes*

2 16-ounce cans Goya black bean soup
3 tablespoons dry sherry
3 tablespoons olive oil
½ cup chopped onion
1 green pepper, seeded and chopped
1 teaspoon cumin
salt and freshly ground pepper
8 tablespoons sour cream
1 hard-cooked egg, thinly sliced

Place the soup and sherry in a large saucepan and bring it to a boil; reduce heat and simmer. In a skillet heat the oil and

cook the onion and green pepper for 8 minutes, stirring
often. Add the onion mixture to the soup with the cumin and
stir. Taste for seasoning. Ladle the soup into 4 soup bowls
and garnish each with 2 tablespoons of the sour cream and
top with 2 slices of the egg.

•

MENU

Welsh Rarebit Mary Alice
Watercress and Bean Sprout Salad
Strawberry Ice Cream with Toasted Almond Slivers

•

WELSH RAREBIT MARY ALICE   *15 minutes*

    2 tablespoons butter
    4 cups grated Cheddar cheese
    2 egg yolks
    ½ cup beer
    1 tablespoon Worcestershire sauce
    1 teaspoon Dijon mustard
    dash or 2 of Tabasco sauce
    salt and freshly ground pepper
    8 1-inch-thick slices toasted French bread
    ½ pound thinly sliced roast beef, cut into narrow strips

In the top of a double boiler melt the butter over simmering
water. Add the cheese, stir and cook until melted. Combine
the egg yolks and beer and gradually stir into the cheese,
whisking constantly. Add the Worcestershire sauce, mustard, and Tabasco. Cook until the mixture thickens. Taste for
seasoning. Arrange 2 slices of the toast on each dinner plate
and top with equal amounts of the roast beef. Spoon the
Welsh Rarebit over the top of the meat in equal amounts.

WATERCRESS AND
BEAN SPROUT SALAD   *5 minutes*

    1 large bunch watercress, washed and dried
    2 scallions, thinly sliced
    2 cups bean sprouts
    ½ cup olive oil
    1 tablespoon red wine vinegar

76

½ teaspoon sugar
½ teaspoon Dijon mustard
salt and freshly ground pepper

Place the watercress, scallions, and bean sprouts in a bowl.
Combine the remaining ingredients in a separate bowl, then
pour over the salad. Toss.

Eggs

•

MENU

Scrambled Eggs in Avocado Halves
French Bread
Rum Raisin Ice Cream

•

SCRAMBLED EGGS IN
AVOCADO HALVES

10 minutes

2 medium-size ripe avocados
1 lime, quartered
6 eggs
1 tablespoon water
½ teaspoon seasoned salt
freshly ground pepper
2 tablespoons butter
¼ cup drained diced pimientos

Cut the avocados in half lengthwise. Remove the pits. Squeeze a lime quarter over each avocado and discard the pieces of the lime. Brush the lime juice over the avocado surface. In a bowl beat together the eggs, water, seasoned salt, and pepper. Heat the butter in a large skillet and add the egg mixture. Cook over medium-low heat, turning the eggs with a tablespoon. When they begin to set, sprinkle them with pimientos and turn a few times with spoon until cooked to desired doneness. Spoon equal amounts of the scrambled eggs into the avocado halves.

RUM RAISIN ICE CREAM

5 minutes

  ½ cup dark rum
  ½ cup raisins
  1½ pints vanilla ice cream

Heat the rum in a saucepan with the raisins. Refrigerate until serving time. Spoon the rum and raisins over the ice cream in individual bowls.

Sandwiches

•

MENU

Caesar's Hero Sandwiches
Jiffy Ambrosia

•

CAESAR'S HERO SANDWICHES   *10 minutes*

   butter
   4 Italian hero rolls, halved lengthwise
   4 large romaine lettuce leaves
   8 thin slices prosciutto or ham
   8 anchovy fillets
   8 thin slices provolone cheese
   ¼ pound thinly sliced Italian salami
   1 medium onion, thinly sliced and broken into rings
   olive oil
   fresh lemon juice
   Worcestershire sauce

Preheat the broiler. Spread butter on each roll half. Toast
under the broiler. On the bottom half of each roll place 1
lettuce leaf, 2 slices of the prosciutto and provolone cheese,
and equal amounts of the anchovies, salami, and onion rings.
Sprinkle with olive oil, lemon juice, and Worcestershire
sauce. Top each with a roll top. Cut in half crosswise.

JIFFY AMBROSIA   *5 minutes*

   1 8-ounce can crushed pineapple and liquid
   1 10-ounce can mandarin oranges, drained
   1 cup whole pitted dates

1 cup seedless green grapes
¾ cup shredded coconut
¼ cup Grand Marnier

Combine the ingredients in a bowl and refrigerate until served.

●

MENU

Uitsmijters
Garnitures
Iced Beer
Delicious Apples and Gouda Cheese

●

UITSMIJTERS   *15 minutes*

butter, as needed for frying eggs
8 eggs
8 slices pumpernickel
1 pound thinly sliced roast beef
salt and freshly ground pepper

With about 1 tablespoon of butter, fry 4 eggs at a time in a large skillet to desired doneness. Meanwhile, for each uitsmijter, place 2 slices of the bread side by side on each of the 4 dinner plates and top with equal amounts of the roast beef slices, overlapping slices. Place 2 of the fried eggs on each of 2 plates, and cook the remaining 4 eggs. When cooked, place them on the 2 remaining sandwiches. Season with salt and pepper and serve immediately.

GARNITURES

Garnish the sandwich with any of the following foods: pickles, pickled onions, cherry tomatoes, pickled peppers, radishes, carrots, or olives.

CHAPTER FIVE

30-Minute Meals

Seafood

•

MENU

Butter Broiled Cod
New Potato Slices with Watercress
Romaine and Tomato Salad with
Thousand Island Dressing
Quick Zabaglione

•

QUICK ZABAGLIONE   *5 minutes*

1 package instant vanilla pudding mix
⅔ cup Marsala
1 cup heavy cream, whipped
chocolate or lemon wafers (optional)

In a bowl beat together the pudding and Marsala until
smooth. Fold in the whipped cream. Refrigerate until
served. Serve with chocolate or lemon wafers.

NEW POTATO SLICES
WITH WATERCRESS   *20 minutes*

1½ pounds new potatoes, peeled and thinly sliced
2 tablespoons melted butter
salt and freshly ground pepper
1 cup chopped watercress leaves

Cook the potato slices in boiling water for about 15 minutes
until tender. Drain. Place in a bowl and top with the butter,
salt and pepper to taste, and watercress leaves. Toss.

BUTTER BROILED COD   *15 minutes*

    1½ pounds cod fillet, cut into 4 equal-size pieces
    ½ cup dry white wine
    3 tablespoons melted butter
    1 tablespoon fresh lemon juice
    1 tablespoon grated onion
    ½ teaspoon paprika

Place the pieces of cod in a baking dish with the wine.
Combine the butter, lemon juice, onion, and paprika. Brush
the cod with mixture and broil for about 12 minutes until the
fish flakes easily with a fork.

ROMAINE AND TOMATO SALAD WITH
THOUSAND ISLAND DRESSING   *10 minutes*

    1 medium head romaine lettuce, washed, dried, and torn into
      bite-size pieces
    2 medium tomatoes, cut into 8 wedges each

THOUSAND ISLAND DRESSING:

    ½ cup mayonnaise
    2 tablespoons chili sauce
    2 teaspoons fresh lemon juice
    2 tablespoons diced green pepper
    2 tablespoons minced cornichon pickle
    1 scallion, minced

Place equal portions of the lettuce and tomatoes in 4 individual salad bowls. Combine the Thousand Island Dressing
ingredients and spoon over the salads.

•

MENU

Cod and Tomatoes au Gratin
Baby Lima Beans and Carrots
Romaine Lettuce and Crouton Salad
Lemon Sherbet with Mandarin Oranges

•

COD AND TOMATOES AU GRATIN   *20 minutes*

4 ripe firm tomatoes, peeled and thinly sliced
¼ cup olive oil
¼ cup dry white wine
1 garlic clove, crushed
¼ teaspoon rosemary
½ teaspoon basil
salt and freshly ground pepper
1 pound cod fillet, cut into 4 pieces
¼ cup plain bread crumbs
¼ cup fresh grated Parmesan cheese

Preheat the oven to 400°F. In a greased shallow baking dish arrange the tomato slices overlapping in rows, completely covering bottom of the dish. Combine the oil with wine, garlic, rosemary, basil, salt and pepper. Place the cod over tomatoes and pour the oil mixture over the top. Sprinkle with the combined bread crumbs and cheese and drizzle a little oil over the top. Cook for 15 minutes until the fish flakes easily. Pass under the broiler for a few seconds for the final browning.

BABY LIMA BEANS AND CARROTS   *10 minutes*

1 10-ounce package frozen lima beans
salt
1 pound carrots, peeled and thinly sliced
2 tablespoons butter
¼ cup chicken broth
freshly ground pepper
fresh chopped parsley

In saucepan cook the lima beans in 2 cups of lightly salted boiling water for 8 minutes. Drain. Meanwhile, cook the carrots in another saucepan in lightly salted boiling water for 6 minutes. Drain both of the vegetables and place into a saucepan with the heated butter and chicken broth. Gently toss. Season to taste with salt and pepper and sprinkle with parsley.

ROMAINE LETTUCE AND
CROUTON SALAD

10 minutes

1 medium head romaine lettuce, washed and dried
6 tablespoons olive oil
5 slices white bread, crusts trimmed and cut into ½-inch
  cubes

FRENCH DRESSING:

½ cup olive oil
2 tablespoons white wine vinegar
½ teaspoon dry mustard
salt and freshly ground pepper

Cut the lettuce leaves into ½-inch slices and place in a bowl.
Heat the olive oil in a skillet and fry the bread cubes until
golden, about 3 minutes. Drain. Combine the ingredients for
the dressing. Pour the dressing over the lettuce and toss.
Add the croutons and toss.

•

MENU

Yogurt and Mint Cucumber Soup
Crisp Fried Cod with Curry Sauce
Hot Fluffy Rice
Toasted Pita Bread
Fresh Figs with Goat Cheese

•

HOT FLUFFY RICE

25 minutes

Cook 1 cup of long-grain rice according to the package
directions.

YOGURT AND MINT CUCUMBER SOUP

10 minutes

2 cups plain yogurt
1 medium cucumber, peeled, seeded, and thinly sliced
1 tablespoon finely chopped mint or 1 teaspoon dried mint
1½ cups cold club soda
2 teaspoons fresh lemon juice
salt and freshly ground pepper to taste
½ cup chopped walnuts

Combine all of the ingredients in a bowl, except for the walnuts. Chill the soup until ready to serve and garnish with the walnuts.

CRISP FRIED COD WITH CURRY SAUCE   *20 minutes*

    3 tablespoons butter
    1 medium-large onion, very thinly sliced
    1 tablespoon curry powder
    2 tablespoons flour
    1½ cups heated chicken broth
    1 teaspoon fresh lemon juice or to taste
    1 cup chopped and drained canned tomatoes
    salt and freshly ground pepper
    ¾ cup vegetable oil
    1¾ pounds cod fillet, cut in 4 equal-size portions
    1 tablespoon fresh chopped parsley

Heat the butter in a saucepan and cook the onion for 5 minutes, stirring often. Add the curry and flour and combine quickly with a wire whisk. Stir in the heated broth and cook until thickened and smooth. Add the lemon juice, and tomatoes, and season with salt and pepper. Simmer over very low heat while the fish is being cooked. Heat the oil in a skillet and coat the cod pieces with flour. Fry the fish over medium-high heat until crisp and golden on each side. Drain. Place in a serving dish and spoon sauce over the fish. Garnish with parsley.

•

MENU

Sautéed Flounder and Bananas
Lime Yogurt and Chutney Sauce
Mashed Buttered Yams with Pecans
Grated Zucchini and Tomato Salad
Cherry Vanilla Ice Cream with Cherry Heering

•

LIME YOGURT AND CHUTNEY SAUCE   *5 minutes*

    1 cup yogurt
    ¾ cup chutney
    1 tablespoon fresh lime juice

Place the ingredients in a blender container and turn machine on for the few seconds it takes to chop the chutney.

SAUTÉED FLOUNDER AND BANANAS   *20 minutes*

1¾ pounds flounder fillets, cut into 2-inch pieces
salt and freshly ground pepper
flour
4 eggs, beaten
bread crumbs
7 tablespoons butter
5 tablespoons vegetable oil
4 bananas, peeled and cut into 3-inch pieces

Season the fish pieces with salt and pepper. Coat with flour and dip in the eggs. Coat with bread crumbs. Heat 3 tablespoons of the butter and 2 tablespoons of the oil in a large skillet and cook the fish pieces until golden brown on each side, about 4 minutes per side. Drain. In a separate skillet heat the remaining 4 tablespoons of the butter and 3 tablespoons of oil. Dip the bananas in the eggs and coat with bread crumbs. Brown in the fat about 1½ minutes per side.

Serve the flounder and bananas with Lime Yogurt and Chutney Sauce.

GRATED ZUCCHINI AND
TOMATO SALAD   *10 minutes*

2 medium zucchini, grated
1 pint cherry tomatoes, halved
1 scallion, thinly sliced
1 tablespoon fresh chopped parsley
½ cup olive oil
2 tablespoons red wine vinegar
½ teaspoon Dijon mustard
salt and freshly ground pepper to taste

Place the zucchini, tomatoes, scallion, and parsley in a bowl. Mix together the remaining ingredients and pour over the salad. Toss.

MASHED BUTTERED YAMS
WITH PECANS
10 minutes

    2 10-ounce cans yams
    2 tablespoons butter
    2 tablespoons heavy cream
    salt and freshly ground pepper
    ½ cup chopped pecans

Heat the yams in saucepan in liquid. Drain. Mash with the butter and cream to creamy consistency. Add a little more of the cream, if necessary. Add the pecans and combine.

•

MENU

Haddock Chowder
Crunchy Vegetable Salad with Herb Dressing
Blueberry-Nut Muffins

•

BLUEBERRY-NUT MUFFINS
30 minutes

    ½ cup sugar
    ¼ cup vegetable oil
    1 egg
    1½ cups plus 2 tablespoons all-purpose flour
    2 teaspoons baking powder
    ½ teaspoon salt
    1½ cups fresh blueberries
    ½ cup chopped pecans

Preheat the oven to 400°F. Beat together the sugar, oil, and egg. Add 1½ cups of the flour, baking powder, and salt. Mix well. Toss the blueberries with remaining 2 tablespoons of flour and fold into the batter with the pecans. Grease 12 muffin cups and fill each a little over half full. Bake in the oven about 20 minutes, or until done.

HADDOCK CHOWDER

25 minutes

- ¼ cup diced salt pork
- 4 tablespoons butter, plus butter for garnish
- ¾ cup chopped onion
- 3 stalks celery, thinly sliced
- salt and freshly ground pepper
- 2 tablespoons flour
- 2½ cups diced peeled potatoes
- 2 8-ounce bottles clam juice
- 3 cups water
- 1½ pounds haddock fillet, cut into 1-inch cubes or pieces
- 2 cups heavy cream
- butter
- fresh chopped parsley

Cook salt pork in a Dutch oven for about 5 minutes over medium heat. Remove the pork pieces. Add the butter and heat. Cook the onions and celery for 5 minutes, stirring often, over medium-low heat. Season with salt and pepper to taste and sprinkle with the flour. Stir. Add the potatoes, clam juice, and water. Bring to a boil, reduce heat, and cook over medium heat for 10 minutes. Add the fish and cream. Simmer for 5 minutes. Season to taste. Top each bowl of the soup with 1 pat of butter and fresh chopped parsley.

CRUNCHY VEGETABLE SALAD WITH HERB DRESSING

15 minutes

- 1 medium head romaine lettuce, washed, dried, and torn into bite-size pieces
- 8 radishes, sliced
- 1 medium green pepper, seeded and cut into thin strips
- 1 cucumber, skin scored with fork and thinly sliced
- 2 celery stalks, sliced

HERB DRESSING:

- ½ cup olive oil
- 2 tablespoons red wine vinegar
- 1 teaspoon Dijon mustard
- ½ teaspoon tarragon
- ½ teaspoon basil
- ½ teaspoon dillweed
- salt and freshly ground pepper

In a salad bowl place the first 5 ingredients and toss. Combine the Herb Dressing ingredients and pour over the salad. Toss.

●

MENU

Mussels Marinières à la Crème
Toasted French Bread
Arugula and Bibb Salad
Raspberries with Kirsch

●

MUSSELS MARINIÈRES À LA CRÈME   *30 minutes*

3 pounds fresh mussels
1½ cups dry white wine
¼ cup chopped shallots
½ teaspoon thyme
1 cup heavy cream
3 tablespoons flour
3 tablespoons butter
salt and freshly ground pepper
fresh chopped parsley

Wash and scrub the mussels in cold water. Pull out the beards. Place the mussels in a large pot with the wine, shallots, and thyme. Bring to a boil, reduce the heat to medium, cover, and cook for 5 minutes. Remove the mussels and discard any that do not open. Place the mussels into 4 serving bowls. Strain the liquid from the pot through a fine mesh strainer into a saucepan. Bring to a boil and cook for 5 minutes. Add the cream and reboil. Meanwhile, mash the flour with the butter and stir it into the sauce. Season to taste with salt and pepper, and cook for 2 minutes. Pour the sauce over the mussels and sprinkle with parsley.

ARUGULA AND BIBB SALAD   *5 minutes*

    1 bunch arugula, washed and dried
    2 Bibb lettuce, washed, dried, and torn into bite-size pieces
    1 small red onion, thinly sliced
    olive oil
    red wine vinegar
    salt and freshly ground pepper

Combine the arugula, Bibb lettuce, and onion in a bowl.
Toss. Divide the mixture into 4 salad bowls and serve with
oil, vinegar, salt, and pepper.

•

MENU

Broiled Salmon Steaks
Curried Rice Ring
Avocado Sesame Salad
Toasted Pound Cake Slices with Coconut Ice Cream

•

CURRIED RICE RING   *30 minutes*

    2½ cups chicken broth
    1 tablespoon curry powder
    1 cup long-grain rice
    2 tablespoons melted butter
    ½ cup raisins
    ½ cup pine nuts or almond slivers
    1½ cups watercress leaves

In a saucepan bring the chicken broth to a boil; add the curry
powder and rice. Stir and simmer for 20 minutes, covered.
Turn off the heat and leave covered for 5 minutes. Add the
butter, raisins, and pine nuts. Toss gently and turn into a
lightly oiled ring mold. Press the rice mixture down with the
back of a tablespoon. Let it rest for 1 minute and place a
serving dish over mold and invert. Release the rice from
mold and garnish center with the watercress.

AVOCADO SESAME SALAD   *10 minutes*

> 2 medium ripe avocados, peeled, pitted, and cubed
> 1 scallion, thinly sliced
> ¼ cup pimiento, diced
> 2 tablespoons vegetable oil
> 2 tablespoons sesame oil
> 1 tablespoon fresh lemon juice
> 1 tablespoon sesame seeds
> salt and freshly ground pepper to taste

Place the avocado cubes in a bowl with the scallion and pimiento. Combine the remaining ingredients and pour over the salad; toss lightly.

BROILED SALMON STEAKS   *15 minutes*

> 4 1-inch-thick salmon steaks
> 3 tablespoons melted butter
> ½ teaspoon dillweed
> 1 tablespoon fresh lemon juice
> salt and freshly ground pepper

Preheat the broiler. Place the salmon steaks in a broiling pan and brush with the combined butter, dillweed, and lemon juice seasoned with salt and pepper. Cook under the broiler for 5 minutes, turn, and baste with the butter mixture. Cook for about 5 minutes until tender.

•

MENU

Salmon Steaks Poached with Vegetables and Wine
Buttered Noodles with Cream and
Parmesan Cheese
Honeydew Melon Balls with Kirsch and Macaroons

•

SALMON STEAKS POACHED WITH
VEGETABLES AND WINE   *30 minutes*

4 1-inch-thick fresh salmon steaks
2 carrots, peeled and cut into julienne strips
1 medium zucchini, cut into julienne strips
⅓ cup dry white wine
4 tablespoons butter
1 teaspoon tarragon
salt and freshly ground pepper to taste

Preheat the oven to 400°F. Place the salmon steaks in a shallow baking dish. Top with the cut vegetables. Pour the wine into the dish and place 1 tablespoon of the butter over each piece of the salmon. Sprinkle with the tarragon, salt, and pepper. Cover tightly with foil and cook for 25 minutes.

BUTTERED NOODLES WITH CREAM
AND PARMESAN CHEESE   *20 minutes*

8 ounces egg noodles
salt
3 tablespoons softened butter
½ cup heavy cream
½ cup fresh grated Parmesan cheese
salt and freshly ground pepper

Bring 3½ quarts of water to a boil in a pot. Add 2 teaspoons of the salt, stir, and drop in the noodles. Stir and cook until done, about 8 minutes. Drain well and turn into a bowl. Add the butter, cream, and cheese immediately and toss. Sprinkle with salt and pepper to taste and toss again.

HONEYDEW MELON BALLS WITH
KIRSCH AND MACAROONS   *15 minutes*

1 ripe honeydew melon, cut into balls with melon-ball cutter
3 tablespoons kirsch
8 macaroon cookies

Place the melon balls in a bowl and sprinkle with the kirsch. Refrigerate until served. Place equal portions of the melon balls in 4 dessert bowls and garnish each with 2 macaroons.

·

MENU

Sea Scallops and Apples with Calvados Cream
Fresh Asparagus Salad
Scrambled Fruit

·

FRESH ASPARAGUS SALAD   *10 minutes*

1½ pounds fresh asparagus, peeled and cut into 1-inch
    diagonal lengths, stalk ends trimmed
½ cup olive oil
1 tablespoon white wine vinegar
1 teaspoon Dijon mustard
salt and freshly ground pepper

In a saucepan cook the asparagus in boiling water for exactly
5 minutes. Meanwhile, combine the remaining ingredients in
a small bowl with a wire whisk. Drain the asparagus and
place in a serving bowl. Pour the sauce over the asparagus
and toss. Let rest at room temperature until served. Toss
again before serving.

SCRAMBLED FRUIT   *15 minutes*

1 tablespoon butter
2 tablespoons water
2 tablespoons Cointreau
1 tablespoon sugar
1 cantaloupe, seeded and cut into balls with a melon-ball
    cutter
1 pint strawberries, hulled and dried
1 8-ounce can pineapple chunks, drained
bakery cookies (optional)

Heat the butter, water, Cointreau, and sugar in a large
skillet. Add the fruit and gently toss over high heat for 3
minutes. Serve with bakery cookies.

SEA SCALLOPS AND APPLES WITH
CALVADOS CREAM   *15 minutes*

    1½ pounds sea scallops, sliced into ⅓-inch slices, crosswise
    1 tablespoon fresh lemon juice
    7 tablespoons butter
    3 green apples, peeled, cored, and cut into ½-inch-thick
      wedges
    3 tablespoons Calvados
    1½ cups heavy cream
    salt and freshly ground pepper
    1 scallion, thinly sliced

Sprinkle the scallops with the lemon juice. Heat 4 tablespoons of the butter in a skillet and simmer the scallops in
the butter for 5 minutes, turning once during cooking time.
Meanwhile, in a separate skillet heat the remaining 3 tablespoons of butter and sauté the apples over medium heat for 3
minutes. Turn and cook for 3 minutes. Transfer the scallops
and apples to serving dish. Pour out all of the butter from the
skillet that the scallops cooked in and add the Calvados. Stir
and pour in the heavy cream. Bring to a boil and cook over
high heat until slightly thickened. Season to taste with salt
and pepper and pour over the scallops and apples. Toss, and
sprinkle with the scallions.

•

MENU

Bay Scallop and Cheese Ragout
Parsley Rice Ring
Hearts of Palm and Endive Salad
Dates Rolled in Toasted Coconut with
Lemon Sherbet

•

PARSLEY RICE RING   *30 minutes*

    2 cups long-grain rice
    3 tablespoons melted butter
    ½ cup fresh chopped parsley
    oil for the mold

Cook the rice according to the package directions. When
cooked, add the butter and parsley and toss. Lightly oil a

ring mold and spoon the rice into the mold. Pat the top of rice down with the back of a tablespoon and let it set for 2 minutes. Place a serving plate on top of the mold; holding both, invert and release the mold.

HEARTS OF PALM AND ENDIVE SALAD   *15 minutes*

1 14-ounce can hearts of palm, drained and cut into ½-inch slices.
3 Belgian endives, sliced into 1-inch lengths
1 small red onion, thinly sliced
½ cup imported olive oil
2 tablespoons white wine vinegar
1 teaspoon Dijon mustard
½ teaspoon salt
freshly ground pepper

Place the hearts of palm slices and endive leaves with the onion in a bowl. Combine the remaining ingredients with a wire whisk and pour over the salad. Toss. If desired, refrigerate until served, at which time, toss again.

BAY SCALLOP AND CHEESE RAGOUT   *15 minutes*

2 tablespoons butter
2 tablespoons flour
1 cup chicken broth
1 cup light cream
¾ cup grated Cheddar cheese
½ teaspoon thyme
½ teaspoon tarragon
salt and freshly ground pepper
6 tablespoons butter
1½ pounds bay scallops

Heat 2 tablespoons of the butter in a saucepan and stir in the flour with a wire whisk. Stir and cook for 1 minute. Stir in the broth and cream and cook until smooth and thickened. Add the cheese and herbs and stir until the cheese melts. Season to taste with salt and pepper. Remove from the heat and cover. Heat the 4 remaining tablespoons of the butter in a skillet and add the scallops. Cook the scallops over medium-high heat, shaking the pan for 3 or 4 minutes. Remove the scallops with a slotted spoon and add to the cheese sauce. Combine. Spoon the ragout into the center of the rice ring.

·

MENU

Salmon Croquettes
Butter Braised Endives
Carrot and Raisin Salad with Orange Dressing
Blueberries with Vanilla Yogurt

·

BUTTER BRAISED ENDIVES   25 minutes

¾ cup chicken broth
3 tablespoons butter
12 Belgian endives, halved lengthwise and ends trimmed
salt and freshly ground pepper

Preheat the oven to 400°F. Heat the chicken broth with the butter in a saucepan. Place the endives in a lightly buttered shallow baking dish, cut side down. Pour the broth mixture over the endives and bake in the oven for 20 minutes. Season with salt and pepper to taste.

SALMON CROQUETTES   20 minutes

1 15-ounce can salmon, drained, bones and skins removed
¾ cup plain dry bread crumbs plus bread crumbs for
    breading
2 large eggs
1 medium onion, grated
1 teaspoon dillweed
¼ teaspoon salt
freshly ground pepper
2 tablespoons water
flour
2 tablespoons butter
4 tablespoons vegetable oil

In a bowl combine the salmon, ¾ cup bread crumbs, 1 egg, onion, dillweed, salt and pepper. Shape the mixture into 8 equal-size patties. Beat the remaining egg with 2 tablespoons of water. Coat the patties in flour, dip in egg mixture, and coat with bread crumbs. Heat the butter and oil in a large skillet and fry the patties until golden brown on each side, about 4 minutes per side.

100

CARROT AND RAISIN SALAD WITH ORANGE DRESSING

10 minutes

2½ cups grated carrots
½ cup golden raisins
½ cup mayonnaise
¼ cup sour cream
2 tablespoons fresh grated orange rind
1 tablespoon orange juice
1 tablespoon white wine vinegar
salt and freshly ground pepper

Place the grated carrots and raisins in a bowl. Combine the remaining ingredients and pour over the salad. Toss.

●

MENU

Shrimp Meunière
Mushrooms with Garlic and Parsley Butter
Vegetable Stuffed Tomatoes with
Creamy Pepper Dressing
Brie with Almond Slices and Apricots

●

MUSHROOMS WITH GARLIC AND PARSLEY BUTTER

15 minutes

6 tablespoons softened butter
1 large garlic clove, crushed
½ cup fresh chopped parsley
1 teaspoon fresh grated lemon rind
freshly grated pepper
24 fresh medium-size mushrooms, stemmed
4 slices white toast, crusts trimmed

Preheat the broiler. Beat together the butter, garlic, parsley, lemon rind, and pepper. Place the mushrooms, stem ends up, on a lightly greased baking sheet with sides. Dot the mushrooms with about 1 teaspoon of the garlic butter. Set the mushrooms aside until 5 minutes before serving. Cook under a hot broiler for about 5 minutes until the butter sizzles. Place 6 mushrooms on each slice of the toast.

VEGETABLE STUFFED TOMATOES
WITH CREAMY PEPPER DRESSING   *10 minutes*

3 stalks celery, very thinly sliced
2 carrots, peeled and grated
2 tablespoons capers, drained
4 medium-large ripe tomatoes, tops cut off and pulp removed
4 romaine lettuce leaves, cut into ½-inch-thick strips

CREAMY PEPPER DRESSING:

¼ cup mayonnaise
¼ cup sour cream
½ teaspoon basil
1 tablespoon red wine vinegar
salt to taste
1 teaspoon crushed pepper

In a bowl combine the celery, carrots, and capers. Mix
together the Creamy Pepper Dressing ingredients in a separate bowl. Pour over the vegetables and capers and toss.
Stuff the tomatoes with equal portions. Serve each tomato
on a salad plate surrounded by equal portions of the lettuce.

SHRIMP MEUNIÈRE   *15 minutes*

20 large shrimp, shelled and deveined
flour
5 tablespoons butter
2 tablespoons olive oil
juice of 1 lemon
2 tablespoons fresh chopped parsley
salt and freshly ground pepper

Coat the shrimp with flour. Heat 2 tablespoons of the butter
and oil in a large skillet. Brown the shrimp quickly on both
sides over medium-high heat. Transfer the shrimp to a
warmed serving dish. Add the remaining 3 tablespoons of
butter and the lemon juice. Sprinkle with the parsley and
cook for 1 minute; season with salt and pepper. Pour the
butter sauce over the shrimp.

MENU

*Native-Style Snapper
Hot Cooked Rice
Hearts of Palm and Tomato Salad with Rum Dressing
Papaya, Banana, and Coconut Compote*

●

HOT COOKED RICE   *30 minutes*

Cook 1 cup of long-grain rice according to the package
directions.

NATIVE-STYLE SNAPPER   *25 minutes*

3 tablespoons butter
¾ cup thinly sliced celery
1 cup chopped onion
1 cup chopped canned tomatoes
1 large garlic clove, quartered
2 tablespoons fresh chopped parsley
½ teaspoon oregano
½ teaspoon thyme
½ cup dry white wine
½ cup chicken broth
1 teaspoon Bovril
salt and freshly ground pepper
½ cup vegetable oil
1¾ pounds snapper fillets, cut into 2-inch pieces
1 tablespoon cornstarch

Heat the butter in a skillet and add the vegetables; cook for 5
minutes, stirring often. Add the remaining ingredients, except for the oil, fish, and cornstarch. Bring to a boil, reduce
the heat, and simmer for 10 minutes. Meanwhile, heat the oil
in a separate skillet and brown the pieces of fish on each
side. Transfer to a serving dish. Dissolve the cornstarch in a
little water and stir into the vegetable mixture. Stir and cook
over high heat until the sauce thickens slightly. Spoon the
mixture over the fish.

PAPAYA, BANANA, AND
COCONUT COMPOTE
10 minutes

    2 ripe papayas, peeled, seeded, and cubed
    2 large bananas, sliced
    ½ cup flaked coconut
    3 tablespoons Grand Marnier
    1 tablespoon fresh lime juice
    bakery coconut cookies (optional)

Place the papayas, bananas, and coconut in a bowl. Toss.
Add the Grand Marnier and lime juice and toss. Refrigerate
until served. Serve with bakery coconut cookies.

HEARTS OF PALM AND TOMATO SALAD
WITH RUM DRESSING
10 minutes

    1 14-ounce can hearts of palm, thinly sliced
    1 pint cherry tomatoes, halved
    1 tablespoon fresh chopped parsley

RUM DRESSING:

    ½ cup olive oil
    2 tablespoons white wine vinegar
    1 tablespoon light rum
    salt and freshly ground pepper

Place the hearts of palm, tomatoes, and parsley in a salad
bowl and toss. Combine the Rum Dressing ingredients in a
bowl and pour over the salad. Toss. Refrigerate until served.
Toss again before serving.

•

MENU

Baked Sole Rolls with Herbs
Braised Scallions
Cherry Tomatoes Provençal
Toasted Raisin Bread with Cream Cheese and
Kiwi Fruit

•

BAKED SOLE ROLLS WITH HERBS

30 minutes

5 tablespoons fresh chopped parsley
½ teaspoon tarragon
½ teaspoon thyme
3 tablespoons plain bread crumbs
½ teaspoon salt
¼ teaspoon freshly ground pepper
4 sole fillets
1 tablespoon butter
½ cup dry white wine
butter

Preheat the oven to 350°F. In bowl combine the parsley, tarragon, thyme, bread crumbs, salt, and pepper. Cut the fillets in half lengthwise. Sprinkle equal amounts of the herb mixture over the fillets and roll up. Butter a shallow baking dish just large enough to hold the fish comfortably. Place the rolls, cut side up, in the dish. Pour in the wine, cover with buttered wax paper, and cook for 20 minutes.

BRAISED SCALLIONS

20 minutes

3 tablespoons olive oil
1 garlic clove, crushed
6 bunches scallions, root ends trimmed, leaving 2 inches of
   green intact
3 tablespoons dry white wine
¾ cup chicken broth
salt and freshly ground pepper
2 tablespoons fresh chopped parsley

In a large skillet heat the oil and cook garlic over medium-low heat for 5 minutes. Add the scallions, turning to coat evenly with oil. Pour the wine and broth over the scallions. Cover and simmer for 10 minutes. Season with salt and pepper to taste and sprinkle with the parsley.

CHERRY TOMATOES PROVENÇAL   *5 minutes*

    2 tablespoons olive oil
    2 tablespoons butter
    1 pint cherry tomatoes, stemmed
    ½ cup drained cocktail onions
    3 anchovy fillets, chopped
    2 tablespoons drained capers
    1 tablespoon fresh chopped parsley
    salt and freshly ground pepper

Heat the olive oil and butter in a skillet. Add the tomatoes, onions, anchovies, and capers. Cook over medium-high heat, shaking the pan often, for 3 minutes. Sprinkle with the parsley and season with salt and pepper to taste. Serve immediately.

•

MENU

Goujonettes of Sole
Tartar Sauce
Tomato and Chive Salad
Broiled Glazed Grapefruit

•

TARTAR SAUCE   *5 minutes*

    1¼ cups mayonnaise
    1 tablespoon white wine vinegar
    ¼ cup chopped gherkins
    1 tablespoon fresh chopped parsley
    1 small onion, minced
    1 teaspoon Dijon mustard

Combine the ingredients well.

GOUJONETTES OF SOLE   *20 minutes*

    1½ pounds sole fillets, cut into ½-inch-thick strips
    flour
    2 large eggs
    2 tablespoons water
    bread crumbs

oil for deep frying
salt and freshly ground pepper
2 lemons, halved crosswise and seeded

Dust each sole strip with flour and dip into the eggs beaten with 2 tablespoons of water. Coat with bread crumbs. Heat the oil in fryer or skillet and fry the goujonettes, a few at a time, until golden, about 4 minutes. Drain. Season with salt and pepper. Serve with the lemon pieces and the Tartar Sauce.

TOMATO AND CHIVE SALAD   *10 minutes*

1½ pints cherry tomatoes, halved
3 tablespoons fresh snipped chives
½ cup olive oil
1 tablespoon red wine vinegar
1 teaspoon Dijon mustard
salt and freshly ground pepper

Toss the tomato halves and chives in a bowl. Combine the remaining ingredients and pour over the salad. Toss.

BROILED GLAZED GRAPEFRUIT   *10 minutes*

4 generous tablespoons thick natural honey
2 large grapefruits, halved, seeded and cut into sections in shells
4 tablespoons brown sugar

Preheat the broiler. Spread the honey over the tops of the grapefruit and sprinkle with the brown sugar. Broil for a few minutes until tops are golden brown and sizzling.

Poultry

●

MENU

*Chicken Breasts à la Neige with
Lemon Tartar Sauce
Vegetable Melange
Sliced Oranges with Strawberry Puree*

●

CHICKEN BREASTS À LA NEIGE
WITH LEMON TARTAR SAUCE   *30 minutes*

LEMON TARTAR SAUCE:

¾ cup mayonnaise
1 tablespoon fresh lemon juice
1 teaspoon fresh grated lemon rind
2 teaspoons capers
1 tablespoon fresh chopped parsley
1 tablespoon chopped sweet gherkins
1 tablespoon chopped shallots or scallions
freshly ground pepper to taste

Combine the ingredients in a small bowl, cover and refrigerate until ready to use.

CHICKEN BREASTS À LA NEIGE:

2 chicken breasts, boned
juice of 1 lemon
½ cup fresh bread crumbs*

---

* To make fresh bread crumbs, trim the crusts from 10 slices of day-old white bread. Tear the pieces and place in the bowl of a food processor fitted with the steel blade. Turn on and run until the crumbs are smooth, about 20 seconds.

1 stick (8 tablespoons) butter
2 large egg whites

Halve the chicken breasts lengthwise, then cut each half in half lengthwise. Flatten each piece to ¼-inch thickness between 2 pieces of wax paper. Squeeze the lemon juice over the chicken and rub evenly to coat all of the pieces. Place the bread crumbs in a flat plate next to the stove. Heat the butter in a large skillet. Meanwhile, beat the egg whites in a large bowl until frothy, but not stiff. Immediately dip each chicken piece in the egg whites and roll in the bread crumbs and put in the pan, cooking 2 or 3 pieces at a time. Cook over medium-low heat for 10 minutes, turn, and cook until golden brown. Keep cooked pieces in a warm oven until all are cooked. Serve with the Lemon Tartar Sauce.

VEGETABLE MELANGE   *10 minutes*

    1 cup chicken broth
    ½ teaspoon oregano
    2 tablespoons butter
    1 tablespoon fresh chopped parsley
    1 medium zucchini, thinly sliced
    8 mushrooms, thinly sliced
    2 tomatoes, cut into wedges
    salt and freshly ground pepper to taste

Heat the chicken broth with the oregano, butter, and parsley. Bring it to a boil. Add the remaining ingredients, cover, and simmer for 5 minutes.

SLICED ORANGES WITH
STRAWBERRY PUREE   *5 minutes*

    4 navel oranges, peeled, including white pith, and thinly
      sliced
    1 10-ounce package frozen strawberries in syrup
    2 tablespoons kirsch

Place 1 sliced orange across each of 4 dessert plates. Puree the strawberries in a blender with the kirsch. Spoon equal amounts of the sauce over one side of the oranges. Refrigerate until served.

•

MENU

Puree of Green Pea Soup
Chicken Breasts Amandine
Pear, Celery, and Walnut Salad
Frozen Lemon Yogurt with Macaroons

•

CHICKEN BREASTS AMANDINE · *25 minutes*

4 chicken breasts, boned
salt and freshly ground pepper
flour
5 tablespoons butter
3 tablespoons vegetable oil
1 cup sliced almonds

Evenly trim the chicken breasts and season with salt and pepper. Coat with flour and heat 3 tablespoons of the butter and the oil in a large skillet. Cook the chicken over medium heat until browned and cooked on both sides, about 7 minutes per side. Transfer the chicken to a warmed serving dish. Pour all of the fat out of the pan except for 1 tablespoon and add the remaining 2 tablespoons of the butter. Add the almonds and cook until golden brown, turning often. Spoon over the chicken breasts.

PEAR, CELERY, AND WALNUT SALAD · *10 minutes*

3 fresh ripe pears, peeled, cored, and thinly sliced
3 stalks celery, sliced very thin diagonally
½ cup raisins
½ cup walnut halves
4 large romaine lettuce leaves

WALNUT CREAM DRESSING:

½ cup mayonnaise
2 tablespoons walnut oil
1 teaspoon fresh lemon juice
salt and freshly ground pepper to taste

Place the salad ingredients, except for the lettuce, in a bowl. Combine the Walnut Cream Dressing ingredients in a sepa-

110

rate bowl and spoon over the salad. Toss. Spoon equal portions of the salad over each lettuce leaf on salad plates.

PUREE OF GREEN PEA SOUP · · · · · · · · · · · *10 minutes*

    1 10-ounce package frozen green peas
    3½ cups chicken broth
    1 small onion, thinly sliced
    ¼ teaspoon oregano
    ¼ teaspoon thyme
    ½ cup light cream or milk
    salt and freshly ground pepper
    ½ cup sour cream

Place the peas and broth in a saucepan with onion. Bring to a boil and simmer for 5 minutes. Add the oregano, thyme, and cream. Puree the mixture, a few cupsful at a time, in a blender. Return to the pan and heat thoroughly. Season to taste with salt and pepper. Garnish each bowl of soup with a dollop of the sour cream.

•

MENU

Sautéed Chicken Breasts with Dill Cream Sauce
Braised Whole Baby Carrots
Chocolate Ice Cream Tartuffe

•

SAUTÉED CHICKEN BREASTS WITH
DILL CREAM SAUCE · · · · · · · · · · · · · · *30 minutes*

    4 small chicken breasts, boned
    salt and freshly ground pepper
    2 tablespoons butter
    1 tablespoon vegetable oil
    ½ cup chicken broth
    ¼ cup dry white wine
    1 tablespoon fresh lemon juice
    1 cup heavy cream
    1 tablespoon fresh chopped dillweed
    8 small sprigs dill

Season the chicken breasts with salt and pepper. Heat the butter and oil in a large skillet and brown the chicken on the

111

skin side. Turn and add the broth and wine and simmer, partially covered, for 10 minutes. Turn and cook for 10 minutes. Remove the chicken from the pan to a heated serving dish. Add the lemon juice to the liquid in the pan and bring to a boil. Cook for 1 minute. Add the cream, stirring, and cook for 2 minutes. Stir in dillweed and cook for 1 minute. Spoon the sauce over the chicken and garnish each breast with the dill sprigs.

CHOCOLATE ICE CREAM TARTUFFE   *5 minutes*

1½ pints softened chocolate ice cream
4 ounces semisweet chocolate morsels
2 tablespoons butter

Melt the butter in a saucepan and stir in the chocolate morsels. Remove from the heat and stir until melted. Set aside. Pack one quarter of the ice cream into each of 4 small soufflé dishes or ramekins. Pour equal amounts of the chocolate over the ice cream and freeze until served.

BRAISED WHOLE BABY CARROTS   *15 minutes*

1½ cups chicken broth
1 small onion, thinly sliced
1 pound baby carrots, peeled and left whole
2 tablespoons butter
1 teaspoon sugar
salt and freshly ground pepper

Bring the chicken broth with onion to a boil in a saucepan. Add the carrots, butter, and sugar. Cover and simmer for 7 minutes. Season to taste with salt and pepper.

•

MENU

Roasted Oysters
Boneless Chicken Breasts Madeira
Steamed Broccoli with Lemon Butter
Kiwi Fruit, Peaches, and Strawberries with
Creamy Apricot Sauce

•

KIWI FRUIT, PEACHES, AND STRAWBERRIES
WITH CREAMY APRICOT SAUCE   *10 minutes*

3 kiwi fruit, peeled and sliced
3 large fresh peaches, peeled, pitted, and sliced
1 pint strawberries, hulled and sliced

CREAMY APRICOT SAUCE:

½ cup heavy cream, whipped
½ cup sour cream
½ cup apricot preserves

Place the fruit in a bowl. Fold together the sauce ingredients and pour over the fruit. Refrigerate until served.

BONELESS CHICKEN BREASTS
MADEIRA   *20 minutes*

4 chicken breasts, boned, halved, and trimmed
salt and freshly ground pepper
flour
4 tablespoons butter
2 tablespoons vegetable oil
½ cup Madeira

Season the chicken pieces with salt and pepper. Coat with flour. Heat 2 tablespoons of the butter and oil in the skillet and sauté the chicken until evenly browned and cooked on both sides, about 5 minutes per side. Remove to a warmed serving dish. Pour out all the fat in the pan and add 2 tablespoons of the butter and the Madeira. Cook, stirring for 2 minutes. Pour the sauce over the chicken.

STEAMED BROCCOLI WITH
LEMON BUTTER   *15 minutes*

1 bunch fresh broccoli, ends trimmed, cut into spears
3 tablespoons melted butter
2 tablespoons fresh lemon juice

Place the broccoli in a large steamer over boiling water and steam it for 12 minutes or until tender. Place in a serving dish and pour the combined butter and lemon juice over the broccoli.

ROASTED OYSTERS   *10 minutes*

rock salt
20 fresh shucked oysters in the half shell (have your fish
   store shuck the oysters)
5 tablespoons butter
juice of 1 lemon
3 tablespoons finely chopped fresh parsley

Preheat the oven to 450°F. Place the rock salt in a large
roasting pan and arrange the oysters in their shells in the
salt. Dot with the butter and sprinkle with the lemon juice.
Roast in the oven for exactly 5 minutes. Sprinkle with the
parsley and serve immediately.

•

MENU

Chicken Supreme with Creamed Spinach
Sautéed Whole Mushrooms
Strawberries and Orange Slices with
Coconut Whipped Cream

•

CHICKEN SUPREME WITH
CREAMED SPINACH   *25 minutes*

1 10-ounce package frozen spinach
2 chicken breasts, skinned, boned and halved
salt and freshly ground pepper
5 tablespoons butter
2 teaspoons olive or vegetable oil
1 medium onion, minced
¾ cup sour cream
dash of fresh grated nutmeg
4 ⅛-inch-thick fresh lemon slices

Cook the spinach according to the package directions. Drain
in a fine mesh sieve and press out as much water as possible.
Set aside. Flatten each breast half between 2 pieces of wax
paper to ¼-inch thickness. Season the breast halves with
salt and pepper. Heat 3 tablespoons of the butter and the oil
in a skillet and sauté the chicken over medium heat until
browned on each side. Transfer the cooked breasts to a
serving platter and keep warm in a low oven. Heat 2 table-

spoons of the butter in a saucepan and sauté the onion for 5 minutes. Add the spinach, and stir. Remove from the heat and stir in the sour cream and nutmeg. Season to taste with salt and pepper. Spoon in equal amounts over the chicken breasts and garnish each with a lemon slice.

STRAWBERRIES AND ORANGE SLICES
WITH COCONUT WHIPPED CREAM   *10 minutes*

  2 navel oranges, peeled, including white pith, and thinly
    sliced
  1 pint strawberries, hulled and sliced
  1 cup heavy cream
  1/4 cup coconut cream
  1/2 cup toasted almond slivers

Place the orange slices in a bowl and top with the strawberry slices. Whip the cream and fold in the coconut cream. Spoon over the fruit and sprinkle with the toasted almonds.

SAUTÉED WHOLE MUSHROOMS   *5 minutes*

  4 tablespoons olive oil
  1 pound whole fresh mushrooms, wiped clean and ends
    trimmed
  salt and freshly ground pepper to taste
  2 tablespoons fresh chopped parsley

Heat the oil in a large skillet and sauté the mushrooms over medium-high heat for 5 minutes, shaking the pan frequently until lightly browned. Sprinkle with salt and pepper and parsley.

•

MENU

Broiled Chicken Cap Estel
Confetti Rice
Sautéed Tomato Slices
Brandied Peaches with Whipped Cream

•

BROILED CHICKEN CAP ESTEL   *30 minutes*

    2 2½-pound broilers, halved, with backbones removed
    6 tablespoons olive oil
    2 tablespoons red wine vinegar
    ½ teaspoon paprika
    salt and freshly ground pepper
    ¾ cup fresh bread crumbs
    2 tablespoons melted butter

Preheat the broiler. Brush the chicken halves with the combined olive oil, vinegar, paprika, salt, and pepper to taste. Cook on a rack in a roasting pan under the broiler until golden and tender on each side, about 10 minutes per side. Baste with the oil mixture twice per side during the cooking time. On the skin side sprinkle with the bread crumbs and butter and cook under broiler until the crumbs are golden brown.

CONFETTI RICE   *25 minutes*

    1 cup long-grain rice
    1 cup fresh shelled green peas
    1 carrot, peeled and diced
    ½ cup black olive slivers
    2 scallions, thinly sliced
    1 tablespoon fresh chopped parsley
    salt and freshly ground pepper

Cook the rice according to the package directions, adding the peas and carrot with the rice to the boiling water. When the rice is cooked, toss with the olives, scallions, and parsley. Season to taste with salt and pepper.

SAUTÉED TOMATO SLICES   *10 minutes*

    2 tablespoons butter
    2 tablespoons olive or vegetable oil
    2 firm beefsteak tomatoes, cut into ⅓-inch slices
    herb-flavored dry bread crumbs
    salt and freshly ground pepper

Heat the butter and oil in a large skillet. Coat each side of the tomato slices with bread crumbs. Sauté the tomatoes over medium heat until browned on each side. Season with salt and pepper and serve immediately.

•

MENU

Fried Chicken with Hot Sauce
Stewed Tomatoes with Okra
Braised Vanilla Apples and Raisins with
Cinnamon Cream

•

FRIED CHICKEN WITH HOT SAUCE   *30 minutes*

8 serving pieces of chicken
salt and freshly ground pepper
flour
½ cup olive oil
½ cup vegetable oil

HOT SAUCE:

6 tablespoons olive oil
2 tablespoons red wine vinegar
¼ teaspoon Tabasco sauce
1 teaspoon fresh minced garlic
2 tablespoons fresh minced onion
1 teaspoon Dijon mustard

Season the chicken pieces with salt and pepper. Coat the chicken pieces with flour. Heat the olive and vegetable oil in a large skillet and fry the chicken until golden on each side, about 12 minutes per side. Meanwhile, in a small heavy saucepan heat all the ingredients for the Hot Sauce except for the mustard, and bring to a boil. Reduce the heat and simmer for a minute or two. Remove from the heat and beat in the mustard. Cover and set aside. Spoon the sauce over the cooked chicken.

BRAISED VANILLA APPLES AND RAISINS
WITH CINNAMON CREAM   *20 minutes*

  1 cup water
  ½ cup plus 2 tablespoons sugar
  1 teaspoon vanilla
  4 large Delicious apples, peeled, cored, and quartered
    lengthwise
  ½ cup raisins
  1 cup heavy cream
  ½ teaspoon cinnamon

Place the water, ½ cup sugar, and vanilla in a saucepan and
bring to a boil. Add the apples and raisins and simmer,
covered, for 10 minutes. Meanwhile, whip the cream with
the remaining sugar and cinnamon. Refrigerate both in separate bowls until ready to serve. At serving time, spoon the
whipped cream on individual servings of the apple and raisin
mixture and sprinkle with the cinnamon.

STEWED TOMATOES WITH OKRA   *15 minutes*

  1 16-ounce can stewed tomatoes
  1 10-ounce package frozen sliced okra
  salt and freshly ground pepper

Place the stewed tomatoes and okra in a saucepan and bring
to a boil. Separate the okra with a fork as it thaws, and stir.
Reduce the heat and simmer for 8 to 10 minutes. Season with
salt and pepper to taste.

•

MENU

Chicken and Chicken Liver Sauté
Poached Zucchini
Tomato and Red Pepper Salad
Blueberries in Raspberry Yogurt

•

CHICKEN AND CHICKEN LIVER SAUTÉ   *25 minutes*

5 tablespoons butter
2 tablespoons vegetable oil
2 chicken breasts, skinned, boned, and cut into bite-size
    pieces
½ pound chicken livers, quartered
¼ cup chopped shallots
1 garlic clove, crushed
¾ cup dry white wine
¼ cup fresh chopped parsley
1 tablespoon Dijon mustard
salt and freshly ground pepper

In a large skillet heat 3 tablespoons of the butter with the oil and sauté the chicken pieces over medium heat for about 10 minutes, until golden. Remove to a side dish. Add the livers, and cook for about 5 minutes, turning twice during the cooking time. Remove to a side dish. Pour off all but 2 tablespoons of the fat in the pan and sauté the shallots and garlic for 5 minutes stirring often. Pour in the wine and cook until reduced to ¼ cup. Stir in the parsley and mustard. Season with salt and pepper to taste, and whisk in the remaining 2 tablespoons butter. Add the chicken and livers, toss, and serve immediately.

TOMATO AND RED PEPPER SALAD   *10 minutes*

6 small tomatoes, sliced crosswise
2 medium red peppers, seeded and cut into thin strips
½ cup pimiento strips
1 medium red onion, thinly sliced
½ cup mayonnaise
3 tablespoons olive oil
1 teaspoon paprika
2 teaspoons red wine vinegar
few drops Tabasco sauce
salt and freshly ground pepper
2 tablespoons fresh chopped parsley

In a bowl place the tomato, red peppers, pimiento, and onion. Combine the mayonnaise, oil, paprika, vinegar, and Tabasco sauce; season with salt and pepper to taste. Spoon the mixture over vegetables and toss. Sprinkle with the parsley.

POACHED ZUCCHINI   *10 minutes*

1 pound fresh zucchini
1/2 teaspoon salt
1 tablespoon butter
2 teaspoons fresh chopped parsley

Bring 3 cups of water to a boil in a saucepan. Cut the
zucchini in half lengthwise and cut into 1-inch lengths. Add
the salt to boiling water. Drop the zucchini into water and
simmer for about 6 minutes until tender. Drain and return to
pan. Add the butter and parsley; toss gently and serve
immediately.

•

MENU

Mock Frog Legs Provençal
Zucchini with Herbs and Wine
Camembert and Raspberry Preserve-Filled Croissants

•

MOCK FROG LEGS PROVENÇAL   *30 minutes*

16 chicken wings, wing tips cut off
salt and freshly ground pepper
flour
3 tablespoons oil
4 tablespoons butter
2 large garlic cloves, minced
1 1/2 cups fresh chopped, peeled, and seeded tomatoes*
juice of 1 lemon
2 tablespoons fresh chopped parsley

Preheat the oven to 275°F. Season the wings with salt and
pepper. Dust with flour. Heat the oil and butter in a large
skillet. Sauté the wings eight at a time over medium heat
until golden brown on each side. Transfer the cooked wings
to a serving platter and keep warm in the oven. Cook the
remaining wings in the same manner. Place them in the
platter with the other cooked wings and return to the oven.

---

* To peel and seed fresh tomatoes, immerse them into rapidly boiling water
for 8 seconds. Remove them with a slotted spoon and cut off the stem ends.
Cut each tomato in half and squeeze out the seeds. Peel off the skins with the
aid of a small sharp knife.

Add the garlic to the skillet with the tomatoes and lemon juice. Stir and cook over medium heat, stirring often, for 4 minutes. Season with salt and pepper to taste. Spoon the tomato sauce over the chicken wings and sprinkle with parsley.

ZUCCHINI WITH HERBS AND WINE   *15 minutes*

    2 tablespoons olive or vegetable oil
    1 medium onion, chopped
    1 garlic clove, crushed
    1 pound zucchini, thinly sliced
    ½ teaspoon basil
    ¼ teaspoon oregano
    1 bay leaf
    ¼ cup dry white wine
    salt and freshly ground pepper to taste

Heat the olive oil and cook the onion and garlic for 5 minutes, stirring often. Add the zucchini, toss, and cook over medium heat for 3 minutes. Add the remaining ingredients, toss, cover and simmer for 5 minutes.

CAMEMBERT AND RASPBERRY
PRESERVE-FILLED CROISSANTS   *5 minutes*

    4 large bakery croissants
    4 ounces ripe Camembert cheese
    4 heaping tablespoons raspberry preserves

Cut pockets in the croissants, lengthwise, and spread equal portions of the cheese and raspberry preserves inside.

●

MENU

*Buffalo Chicken Wings with
Blue Cheese Dressing and Vegetables
Small Shells with Ricotta, Butter, and Herbs
Frozen Strawberry Yogurt and Bakery Cookies*

●

BUFFALO CHICKEN WINGS   *25 minutes*

24 chicken wings
salt and freshly ground pepper
oil for deep frying
6 celery stalks, cut into 8 sticks
6 large carrots, peeled and cut into 8 sticks

BLUE CHEESE DRESSING:

2 cups mayonnaise
½ cup sour cream
½ pound blue cheese, crumbled
2 tablespoons fresh lemon juice
2 tablespoons fresh chopped parsley

Prepare the dressing first by mixing all the ingredients together. Cover and refrigerate until ready to serve. Preheat
the oven to 300°F. Cut the chicken wings into 3 pieces each,
at joints. Discard the wing tips. Season the pieces well with
salt and pepper. Heat 3 inches of oil to 370°F in the fryer and
fry the wing pieces, 12 at a time, until golden, about 5
minutes. Drain. As the chicken wings are cooked place them
on a baking sheet and keep warm in the oven. Serve the
wings with the celery and carrot sticks and the Blue Cheese
Dressing.

SMALL SHELLS WITH RICOTTA, BUTTER, AND HERBS   *15 minutes*

1 tablespoon salt
8 ounces small shells
3 tablespoons softened butter
1½ cups ricotta cheese
1 tablespoon fresh chopped parsley
½ teaspoon oregano
½ teaspoon basil
freshly ground pepper
½ cup fresh grated Parmesan cheese

In a Dutch oven bring 3½ quarts of water to a rolling boil.
Add the salt, stir; add the shells and cook until tender, about
6 minutes. Drain well. Immediately place in a bowl with the
butter and toss. Add the ricotta, parsley, oregano, basil,
pepper, and Parmesan cheese. Toss well and serve immediately.

Beef, Veal, and Liver

•

MENU

Burgers Pojarsky
Potato Pancakes
Puree of Carrots with Maple Syrup
Coulommiers Cheese with Figs

•

BURGERS POJARSKY   *30 minutes*

    4 slices firm white bread, crusts trimmed, cubed
    ¼ cup milk
    ½ cup heavy cream
    2 pounds ground beef
    4 tablespoons softened butter, plus 3 tablespoons butter
    salt and freshly ground pepper
    few grates of nutmeg
    flour
    2 large eggs
    2 tablespoons water
    plain dry bread crumbs
    3 tablespoons vegetable oil

Soak the bread cubes in the combined milk and cream for 30
seconds. Squeeze out the excess liquid. In a bowl combine
the bread, beef, softened butter, salt, pepper, and nutmeg.
Shape into 6 loin chop shaped patties, about 1-inch thick.
Dust with flour and dip in the eggs beaten with water, and
coat with bread crumbs. Heat the butter and oil in a large
skillet and cook over medium heat for about 5 minutes per
side until crisp.

Serves 6.

POTATO PANCAKES   *20 minutes*

    4 medium potatoes, peeled
    1 medium onion, peeled
    1 whole egg
    1 rounded tablespoon flour
    1 teaspoon salt
    freshly ground pepper to taste
    6 tablespoons vegetable oil

Grate the potatoes and onion into a large bowl. Add the egg
and mix. Sprinkle the flour over the potatoes with salt and
pepper and combine. Heat the 4 tablespoons of the oil in a
large skillet. Drop a heaping tablespoon of the potato mixture into the hot fat in 4 places in the pan and flatten with the
back of the spoon into 4 pancakes. Fry over medium heat
until browned, about 5 minutes. Turn each pancake with a
spatula and brown on the other side. Remove the pancakes
and drain on paper towels. Add the remaining 2 tablespoons
of oil and make 4 more pancakes. After the pancakes are
drained, keep them warm in a low oven on a rack over a pan.

PUREE OF CARROTS WITH
MAPLE SYRUP   *15 minutes*

    1½ pounds carrots, peeled and sliced
    salt
    3 tablespoons butter
    3 tablespoons maple syrup
    freshly ground pepper

Cook the carrots in enough lightly salted boiling water to
cover them for 10 minutes. Drain and puree with the butter
and syrup in a food processor, fitted with the steel blade, or
force through a food mill. Beat well and season with salt and
pepper to taste.

•

MENU

Broiled London Broil with Steak Sauce
Sautéed Potatoes with Thyme and Garlic
Cherry Tomatoes, Swiss Cheese, and Watercress Salad
with Dill Dressing
Chocolate Chip Ice Cream with Fudge Sauce

•

BROILED LONDON BROIL
WITH STEAK SAUCE   *25 minutes*

    ½ cup sherry
    3 tablespoons vegetable oil
    1 medium onion, grated
    salt and freshly ground pepper to taste
    2 pounds London broil

    STEAK SAUCE:

    ¾ cup mayonnaise
    ⅓ cup ketchup
    2 tablespoons Dijon mustard
    2 tablespoons Worcestershire sauce
    1 teaspoon horseradish

Preheat the broiler. Combine the sherry, oil, onion, salt, and
pepper. Place the steak in a broiling pan and brush with the
sherry mixture. Cook for 5 minutes. Turn and brush with the
sherry mixture and cook for about 8 minutes for rare, or to
desired doneness, basting twice during cooking time. Meanwhile, in a bowl, combine the Steak Sauce ingredients with a
wire whisk. Serve the Steak Sauce with the thinly sliced
steak.

SAUTÉED POTATOES WITH
THYME AND GARLIC   *20 minutes*

    2 tablespoons butter
    ¼ cup olive oil
    4 medium potatoes, peeled and thinly sliced
    2 large garlic cloves, crushed
    ½ teaspoon thyme
    salt and freshly ground pepper

125

Heat the butter and oil in a large skillet. Add the potatoes and sprinkle with the garlic and thyme and season with salt and pepper to taste. Cover and cook over medium heat for 5 minutes. Turn the potatoes, re-cover, and cook for 5 minutes. Remove cover and cook for 5 or 6 minutes until browned and done.

CHERRY TOMATOES, SWISS CHEESE, AND WATERCRESS SALAD WITH DILL DRESSING

10 minutes

1 pint cherry tomatoes, halved
1 bunch watercress, washed and dried
2 ounces Swiss cheese, cut into thin strips
1 medium red onion, very thinly sliced

DILL DRESSING:

½ cup olive oil
2 tablespoons red wine vinegar
½ teaspoon dry mustard
1 teaspoon fresh dillweed
salt and freshly ground pepper

Place the tomatoes, watercress, cheese, and onion in a salad bowl. Combine the ingredients for the Dill Dressing. Pour the dressing over the salad and toss.

•

MENU

Broiled Sirloin with Mock Béarnaise
Brussels Sprouts with Mushrooms
Creamy Baked Potatoes
Raspberry Sherbet and Chocolate Mints

•

CREAMY BAKED POTATOES

30 minutes

1½ pounds new potatoes, peeled and thinly sliced
1 cup heavy cream
1 small onion, grated
salt and freshly ground pepper
paprika

In a saucepan, cook the potatoes covered with boiling water for 6 minutes. Preheat the oven to 375°F. Drain the potatoes and place in a lightly greased shallow baking dish. Combine the cream and onion and pour over the potatoes. Sprinkle the top with the salt, pepper, and paprika. Bake in the oven for 20 minutes.

BROILED SIRLOIN WITH
MOCK BÉARNAISE

20 minutes

3 tablespoons olive oil
1 tablespoon cracked black pepper
2 pounds 1½-inch-thick sirloin steak

MOCK BÉARNAISE:

1 cup mayonnaise
2 tablespoons tarragon wine vinegar
1 scallion, thinly sliced
½ teaspoon tarragon
1 tablespoon fresh chopped parsley

Preheat the broiler. Combine the oil and pepper and brush over the steak in a broiling pan. Cook under the broiler for 7 minutes. Turn and baste for about 8 minutes for medium-rare. Meanwhile, combine the ingredients for the Béarnaise Sauce. Thinly slice the steak and serve with the sauce.

BRUSSELS SPROUTS WITH
MUSHROOMS

20 minutes

1 pint Brussels sprouts
½ pound fresh mushrooms, quartered
2 tablespoons butter
salt and freshly ground pepper

In a saucepan cook the Brussels sprouts in 3 cups of boiling water for 8 minutes. Meanwhile, cook the mushrooms covered with boiling water in a separate saucepan for 3 minutes. Drain immediately. Place in a bowl with butter and toss. Drain the Brussels sprouts and add to the mushrooms with butter and season with salt and pepper to taste. Toss well.

•

MENU

Shell Steaks Italian-Style
Sautéed Broccoli with Garlic
Banana-Nut Muffins

•

BANANA-NUT MUFFINS   *30 minutes*

butter
⅔ cup sugar
2 eggs, beaten
⅓ cup vegetable oil
1 cup mashed bananas
1¾ cups sifted all-purpose flour
1 teaspoon baking soda
¼ teaspoon salt
½ cup chopped pecans or walnuts

Preheat the oven to 350°F. Butter 12 muffin tins. Beat the sugar and eggs until light yellow and creamy. Add the vegetable oil and bananas and combine. In a separate bowl add all dry ingredients, except for nuts, and mix. Add the banana mixture and combine well. Fold in the nuts. Fill each muffin hollow about half full and bake in the oven for about 18 to 20 minutes until done.

SHELL STEAKS ITALIAN-STYLE   *20 minutes*

3 tablespoons olive oil
¾ cup chopped onion
¾ cup diced red or green pepper
2 garlic cloves, crushed
¾ cup chopped zucchini
¼ cup dry white wine
¼ cup beef stock
3 tablespoons tomato paste
salt and freshly ground pepper
4 1-inch-thick shell steaks

Heat the olive oil in a large skillet and add the onion, pepper, and garlic. Cook over medium heat for 5 minutes. Preheat the broiler. Add zucchini to mixture in the skillet, stir, and cook 5 minutes. Stir in the wine, stock, and tomato paste over high heat. Season with salt and pepper to taste. Cover and simmer while cooking the steaks. Place the steaks on a rack in a roasting pan and broil to desired doneness, about 5 minutes per side for rare. Spoon equal amounts of the onion and pepper sauce over the steaks.

SAUTÉED BROCCOLI WITH GARLIC   *10 minutes*

    4 stalks fresh broccoli, cut into 2-inch lengths
    salt
    2 tablespoons butter
    2 tablespoons olive oil
    1 large clove garlic, minced
    freshly ground pepper

Drop the broccoli into lightly salted boiling water to cover. Cook over medium-high heat for 4 minutes. Drain. Heat the butter and oil in a large skillet with the garlic and sauté for 1 minute, stirring. Immediately add the broccoli and sauté for 3 minutes, gently stirring twice during cooking time. Season with pepper.

•

MENU

*Tournedos with Cognac and Black Peppercorn Sauce
Vegetable Kebobs
Fresh Raspberries and Blueberries with
Whipped Cream*

•

TOURNEDOS WITH COGNAC AND
BLACK PEPPERCORN SAUCE

30 minutes

2 tablespoons vegetable oil
1 tablespoon butter
4 1-inch-thick beef tournedos

BLACK PEPPERCORN SAUCE:

4 tablespoons butter
1/2 cup chopped shallots
1/2 cup Cognac or brandy
1/2 cup beef broth or stock
1 cup heavy cream
1 tablespoon Dijon mustard
1 tablespoon cracked black peppercorns
salt

Prepare the sauce first. Heat 2 tablespoons of the butter in a large saucepan and add the shallots, Cognac, and beef broth. Bring to a boil and reduce mixture to half. Strain. Return liquid to the pan; stir in the heavy cream and cook over high heat until the sauce thickens, about 5 minutes. Whisk in the mustard and peppercorns and remaining 2 tablespoons of butter. Season with salt to taste. Cover.

In a large skillet heat oil and butter and cook the tournedos over high heat for 5 minutes. Turn and cook for 5 minutes for rare, or cook to desired doneness. Spoon reheated sauce over the tournedos.

VEGETABLE KEBOBS

15 minutes

8 cherry tomatoes
1 large green pepper, seeded and cut into 8 pieces
1 large zucchini, cut into 8 slices
2 scallions, cut into 8 1-inch lengths
2 tablespoons melted butter
1 tablespoon soy sauce
3 tablespoons chicken broth

Preheat the broiler. Arrange alternating vegetables on 4 8-inch skewers. Place the kebobs in a broiling pan. Combine the butter, soy sauce, and chicken broth. Cook under the broiler for 4 minutes. Turn and cook for 5 minutes, basting with the pan juices.

FRESH RASPBERRIES AND BLUEBERRIES
WITH WHIPPED CREAM

5 minutes

1 pint fresh raspberries
1 pint blueberries, stemmed
1 cup heavy cream
2 tablespoons sugar

Place the raspberries and blueberries in a bowl and lightly toss. Whip the cream halfway and add the sugar. Beat until stiff. Refrigerate the berries and the whipped cream until dessert time. In individual dessert bowls, serve equal portions of the berries topped with the whipped cream.

•

MENU

Beef Stroganoff
Hot Cooked Noodles with Herbs
Green Goddess Salad
Mixed Fresh Fruit

•

BEEF STROGANOFF

25 minutes

6 tablespoons butter
1 medium-large onion, thinly sliced
½ pound fresh mushrooms, thinly sliced
2 tablespoons vegetable oil
1½ pounds sirloin, cut into strips ¼ inch thick and 2 inches
   in length
½ cup red wine
1 cup beef broth plus 2 tablespoons
½ teaspoon sweet paprika
2 tablespoons tomato paste
2 tablespoons flour
1 cup heavy cream
salt and freshly ground pepper

Heat 4 tablespoons of the butter in a large skillet and cook onion over medium heat for 5 minutes, stirring often. Add the mushrooms and cook 5 minutes, stirring twice during cooking time. Transfer the onions, mushrooms, and pan juices to a side dish. In a clean skillet, heat the remaining 2 tablespoons butter and oil. Quickly brown the beef strips over high heat, turning often. Transfer the browned beef to a side dish and pour the combined wine and 1 cup of broth into the pan. Bring it to a boil. Meanwhile, combine the paprika, tomato paste, flour, and 2 tablespoons of the beef broth and make a smooth mixture. Stir the mixture into the boiling liquid with a wire whisk and cook over high heat until thickened and smooth. Add the onions, mushrooms, beef, and heavy cream. Heat thoroughly and season to taste with salt and pepper. Serve over the Hot Cooked Noodles with Herbs.

HOT COOKED NOODLES WITH HERBS   *20 minutes*

    1/2 teaspoon basil
    1/2 teaspoon thyme
    1 tablespoon fresh snipped chives
    2 tablespoons fresh chopped parsley
    1 pound medium egg noodles
    salt
    4 tablespoons softened butter
    freshly ground pepper

Bring 4 1/2 quarts of water to a boil. Meanwhile, combine the herbs in a small bowl. Cook the noodles in salted rapidly boiling water until just tender, about 7 or 8 minutes, and drain well. Immediately place in a bowl and add the butter and herbs. Toss and season to taste with salt and pepper. Noodles should be lightly coated with the butter and herbs; add a little more butter, if necessary.

GREEN GODDESS SALAD   *10 minutes*

    2 Bibb lettuce, washed, dried, and torn into bite-size pieces
    1 small romaine lettuce, washed, dried, and torn into
       bite-size pieces
    1/2 cup mayonnaise
    1 tablespoon tarragon vinegar
    2 anchovy fillets, mashed
    1 garlic clove, crushed
    1 teaspoon tarragon
    salt and freshly ground pepper

Place the lettuce in a bowl, and toss. Combine the remaining ingredients and pour over the salad and toss.

•

MENU

Sliced Flank Steak with Peppers and Tomatoes
Hot Cooked Rice
Fried Zucchini Sticks
Gorgonzola Cheese, Apples, and Italian Bread

•

HOT COOKED RICE   *30 minutes*

Cook 1 cup of long-grain rice according to package directions.

SLICED FLANK STEAK WITH PEPPERS
AND TOMATOES   *25 minutes*

    1¼ pounds flank steak
    salt and freshly ground pepper
    3 tablespoons vegetable or peanut oil
    1 medium onion, thinly sliced
    1 large garlic clove, crushed
    2 tablespoons dry sherry
    1 cup beef broth or stock
    1 cup diced green pepper
    2 ripe firm tomatoes, peeled and cut into 8 wedges*
    1¼ tablespoons cornstarch
    3 tablespoons water
    1 tablespoon soy sauce

Cut the steak into thin slices and season with salt and pepper. In a large skillet, heat the oil, add the onion and garlic, and sauté for 3 minutes, stirring often. Add the meat and brown on all sides. Add the sherry, broth, and green pepper and bring to a boil. Reduce the heat, cover and simmer for 8 minutes. Add the tomatoes, cover and cook 3 minutes. Dissolve the cornstarch in 3 tablespoons of water and stir into the mixture along with the soy sauce. Cook until the sauce thickens, stirring frequently.

---

* To peel tomatoes: Dip each one in boiling water for 8 seconds, and remove the skins with the point of a small sharp knife.

FRIED ZUCCHINI STICKS   *15 minutes*

   3 large zucchini, ends cut off, cut into ½-inch by 2½-inch
      sticks
   flour
   oil for deep frying
   salt

Dust the zucchini sticks with flour. Heat the oil in a fryer to
370°F. Fry the zucchini sticks, a few at a time, until evenly
crisp and golden, about 3 or 4 minutes. Drain and cook the
remaining zucchini. Season with salt.

●

MENU

Clams on the Half Shell al Pesto
Veal Scallopini
Zucchini and Red Peppers with Parmesan Cheese
Fontina Cheese and Pears

●

VEAL SCALLOPINI   *25 minutes*

   12 veal scallops, thinly sliced
   salt and freshly ground pepper
   flour
   4 tablespoons vegetable oil
   ½ cup dry white wine
   3 tablespoons butter
   1½ tablespoons fresh chopped parsley

Season the scallops with salt and pepper and coat lightly
with flour. Heat the oil in a large skillet and brown the
scallops a few at a time on each side over high heat, about 3
minutes per side. Transfer to warmed serving dish as
cooked. When all of the scallops are browned and removed,
add the wine, stir, and cook for 2 minutes. Season to taste
with salt and pepper. Add the butter and parsley to the pan,
stir and pour over the browned scallops.

CLAMS ON THE HALF SHELL AL PESTO   *10 minutes*

2 dozen clams on the half shell (have fish store prepare
  them)
10 basil leaves, coarsely chopped
1¼ cups olive oil
2 garlic cloves, crushed
1½ tablespoons fresh lemon juice
salt and freshly ground pepper to taste

Place the clams on a shallow roasting pan. Add the remaining ingredients to a blender and puree. Spoon 1 tablespoon of the mixture over each clam. (At this point the clams can set at room temperature until ready to cook.) Heat the broiler. Place clams under the broiler and cook for exactly 5 minutes. Serve immediately.

ZUCCHINI AND RED PEPPERS
WITH PARMESAN CHEESE   *10 minutes*

2 tablespoons butter
1 tablespoon olive oil
2 medium zucchini, each halved crosswise then quartered
1 large red pepper, seeded and cut into thin strips
¼ cup chicken broth
salt and freshly ground pepper
⅓ cup fresh grated Parmesan cheese

Heat the butter and oil in a skillet. Add the zucchini and pepper and cook over high heat for 3 minutes, turning once. Reduce heat, add the broth, cover, and simmer for 5 minutes. Season to taste with salt and pepper and sprinkle with the Parmesan cheese and toss.

•

MENU

Veal Chops à la Crème
Fried Artichoke Hearts
Yellow Squash with Rosemary
Vanilla Ice Cream with Crushed Pineapple and
Almond Slices

•

VEAL CHOPS À LA CRÈME　　　　　*30 minutes*

　　6½ tablespoons butter
　　16 fresh mushrooms, quartered
　　1 tablespoon oil
　　4 veal chops
　　1 medium onion, chopped
　　½ cup dry white wine
　　3 tablespoons brandy
　　½ cup beef broth
　　1 cup heavy cream
　　salt and freshly ground pepper

Heat 3 tablespoons of the butter in a large skillet and sauté
the mushrooms over medium-high heat for 4 minutes. Remove to a side dish. Wipe out the skillet. Heat 1½ tablespoons of the butter and oil in a skillet and brown the chops
over medium-high heat for about 4 minutes per side. Transfer the veal to a side dish. Pour off all of the fat in the pan and
add the remaining 2 tablespoons butter. Saufe the onion for 4
minutes. Pour in the combined wine, brandy, and beef broth.
Bring to a boil, stirring to release the particles in the bottom
of the pan. Cook until liquid is reduced to ½ cup by boiling.
Meanwhile, preheat the broiler. Bring the heavy cream to a
boil in a saucepan and boil for 4 to 5 minutes, whisking often,
until thickened. Gradually stir in the reduced liquid into the
cream. Add the mushrooms and season to taste with salt and
pepper. Cover. Pass the chops under a hot broiler for 1
minute on each side. Spoon a small amount of the sauce over
each chop and serve the rest in a sauce boat.

FRIED ARTICHOKE HEARTS　　　　　*15 minutes*

　　1 10-ounce package frozen artichoke hearts
　　salt
　　2 eggs, beaten with 2 tablespoons water
　　plain dry bread crumbs
　　freshly ground pepper
　　1 cup peanut or vegetable oil

Cook the artichokes in 2 cups of lightly salted boiling water
for 3 minutes and immediately drain. Coat with flour and dip
in the eggs and water. Coat with the combined bread crumbs
seasoned with salt and pepper. Heat the oil in a large skillet

and fry the artichokes until browned on each side, approximately 2 minutes per side. (Cook half of the artichokes first and keep them warm in a low oven.)

YELLOW SQUASH WITH ROSEMARY   *10 minutes*

  1½ pounds yellow squash, cut into ¼-inch diagonal slices
  2 tablespoons butter
  ¼ cup chicken broth
  ½ teaspoon rosemary
  1 tablespoon fresh chopped parsley
  salt and freshly ground pepper

Bring 1½ cups of water to a boil. Add the squash and cook over medium heat for 6 minutes. Drain and place in saucepan with the butter, broth, rosemary, and parsley. Season with salt and pepper to taste and heat thoroughly.

•

MENU

Curried Herring
Calf's Liver with Orange Sauce
Green Beans and Scallions
Fresh Strawberries and Cream

•

CURRIED HERRING   *5 minutes*

  16-ounce jar herring in cream sauce
  1 tablespoon curry powder
  ½ cup sour cream
  thinly sliced pumpernickel bread

With a fork remove the herring pieces to a bowl. Pour the cream sauce into a separate bowl and combine with the curry powder and sour cream. Pour the curry sauce over the herring and toss several times to combine well. Serve with thinly sliced pumpernickel.

CALF'S LIVER WITH ORANGE SAUCE   *25 minutes*

1½ pounds thinly sliced calf's liver
flour
3 tablespoons butter
2 tablespoons vegetable oil
2 medium onions, thinly sliced
½ cup dry red wine
½ cup orange juice
2 teaspoons fresh grated orange rind
2 tablespoons brown sugar
½ teaspoon thyme
1 tablespoon cornstarch
salt and freshly ground pepper
1 tablespoon fresh chopped parsley

Dust the liver pieces with flour and heat the butter and oil in a large skillet. Quickly brown the liver over medium-high heat, about 5 minutes per side. Transfer to a side dish. Add the onions to the pan and cook over medium heat for 5 minutes, stirring often. Drain off all the fat in the pan but 1 tablespoon. Add the wine, orange juice, orange rind, brown sugar, and thyme to the pan and bring to a boil, stirring. Cook for 3 minutes. Dissolve the cornstarch in a little water and stir into the sauce. Taste for salt and pepper and cook for 1 minute. Return the liver to the pan, and turn each piece to coat it evenly. Place in a serving dish and sprinkle with parsley.

GREEN BEANS AND SCALLIONS   *15 minutes*

salt
1 pound fresh green beans, trimmed and cut into 1-inch
    lengths
3 tablespoons butter
1 bunch scallions, cut into 1-inch lengths
freshly ground pepper

In a saucepan bring 3½ cups of water to a boil. Season lightly with salt and stir. Drop the beans into water and cook over medium heat for 6 minutes. Meanwhile, heat the butter in a skillet and sauté the scallions for 5 minutes. Drain the beans and add them to the skillet. Toss and season to taste with salt and pepper.

Pork

•

MENU

Pork Strips Paprikash
Tomatoes au Gratin
Buttered Noodles with Caraway Seeds
Raspberries and Pineapple with Lemon Sherbet
and Macaroons

•

TOMATOES AU GRATIN   *20 minutes*

3 tablespoons butter, plus 2 tablespoons melted butter
2 medium onions, thinly sliced
4 medium-large tomatoes, cut into ½-inch-thick slices
salt and freshly ground pepper
⅓ cup fresh grated Parmesan cheese

Heat 3 tablespoons of the butter in a skillet and cook the onions over medium heat for 5 minutes, stirring often. Meanwhile, preheat the oven to 425°F and arrange the tomatoes in a lightly buttered shallow baking dish, overlapping in 2 rows. Spoon the sautéed onions over the tomatoes and sprinkle with salt, pepper, the Parmesan cheese, and melted butter. Cook in the oven for 12 minutes.

PORK STRIPS PAPRIKASH
20 minutes

    3 tablespoons butter
    1 tablespoon vegetable oil
    1½ pounds boneless pork, cut into thin strips
    1 large onion, cut into slivers
    1 large garlic clove, crushed
    ¼ cup dry white wine
    1 tablespoon sweet paprika
    1½ cups sour cream
    salt and freshly ground pepper

Heat the butter and oil in a large skillet and sauté the pork until lightly browned, over medium-high heat, stirring often. Remove to a side dish. Add the onion and garlic to the pan and cook for 5 minutes, stirring often. Pour the wine into the pan and sprinkle with paprika. Return the pork to the pan and stir. Heat thoroughly. Remove from the heat and stir in the sour cream. Season to taste with salt and pepper.

BUTTERED NOODLES WITH
CARAWAY SEEDS
15 minutes

    8 ounces medium egg noodles
    salt
    4 tablespoons softened butter
    1 teaspoon caraway seeds
    freshly ground pepper

Cook the noodles in 3½ quarts of lightly salted rapidly boiling water until tender, about 7 to 8 minutes. Drain and place in a bowl. Toss with the butter and caraway seeds. Season to taste with salt and pepper.

RASPBERRIES AND PINEAPPLE WITH
LEMON SHERBET AND MACAROONS
5 minutes

    1½ pints lemon sherbet
    1 8-ounce can crushed pineapple, drained
    1 pint raspberries
    1 cup crumbled macaroons

Combine the pineapple and raspberries in a bowl. Place 4 equal portions of the sherbet in 4 dessert bowls and top with the fruit mixture. Sprinkle with the macaroons.

·

MENU

Breaded Fried Pork Chops
Pureed Green Beans
Hot Red Cabbage and Potato Salad
Sliced Bananas with Vanilla Yogurt

·

BREADED FRIED PORK CHOPS   *30 minutes*

1 egg
2 tablespoons water
4 1-inch-thick loin pork chops
herbed bread crumbs
salt and freshly ground pepper
1 cup vegetable oil

Beat the egg with 2 tablespoons of water and coat the pork
chops. Roll in the bread crumbs seasoned with salt and
pepper. Heat the oil in a large skillet and fry the pork chops
over medium heat until browned; lower the heat and sauté
until browned and tender, about 25 minutes total cooking
time.

HOT RED CABBAGE AND
POTATO SALAD   *20 minutes*

1½ pounds potatoes, scrubbed, peeled, and cut into
    ¼-inch-thick slices
2 tablespoons butter
½ cup chicken broth
2 cups shredded red cabbage
¼ cup olive oil or as needed
1 tablespoon white wine vinegar
1 teaspoon Dijon mustard
salt and freshly ground pepper
1 teaspoon caraway seeds

Cook the potatoes in boiling water for about 15 minutes,
until tender. Meanwhile, heat the butter and chicken broth in
a saucepan and add the cabbage. Simmer for 12 minutes.
Mix together the oil, vinegar, and mustard and season well

with salt and pepper. Drain the potatoes and place in a bowl. Drain the cabbage and add to the potatoes with caraway seeds. Pour the oil mixture over the ingredients and toss lightly.

PUREED GREEN BEANS   *10 minutes*

> 2 10-ounce packages frozen green beans
> 2 tablespoons butter
> 3 tablespoons heavy cream
> salt and freshly ground pepper

Cook the green beans according to the package directions. Drain. Puree in a food processor fitted with the steel blade, with the butter and cream, or force through a food mill. Season to taste with salt and pepper. Serve immediately.

•

MENU

Pork Brochettes à l'Orange
Sautéed Sweet Potatoes
Steamed Spinach
Brie, Prunes, and French Bread

•

PORK BROCHETTES À L'ORANGE   *30 minutes*

> 2 pounds pork leg, cut into 1½-inch cubes
> 2 navel oranges, cut into wedges
> ¼ cup olive oil
> ¼ cup orange juice
> 1 tablespoon fresh grated orange rind
> 1 tablespoon red wine vinegar
> 1 tablespoon soy sauce

Preheat the broiler. Arrange 10-inch metal skewers with alternating pieces of the meat and orange wedges. Combine the remaining ingredients and brush the brochettes. Place in a roasting pan and cook under the broiler, basting frequently, until the pork is cooked evenly, about 18 minutes total cooking time.

SAUTÉED SWEET POTATOES

20 minutes

3 medium sweet potatoes
3 tablespoons butter
2 tablespoons vegetable oil
salt and freshly ground pepper

Peel the potatoes and cut them into ½-inch cubes. Heat the butter and oil in a large skillet and cook the potatoes over medium-high heat for about 7 minutes, until lightly browned. Turn the potatoes with a spatula and cook until golden brown on the other side, about 7 minutes. Immediately remove and season with salt and pepper.

STEAMED SPINACH

10 minutes

1½ pounds fresh spinach, washed and stemmed

Steam the spinach leaves in a large steamer over boiling water for 5 minutes. Serve immediately.

Lamb

●

MENU

*Lamb Patties with Cream of Curry and
Mushroom Sauce
Cauliflower with Snow Pea Pods
Banana Fritters*

●

LAMB PATTIES WITH CREAM OF CURRY
AND MUSHROOM SAUCE   *20 minutes*

1¾ pounds ground lamb
salt and freshly ground pepper
1 garlic clove, crushed
3 tablespoons vegetable oil
fresh chopped parsley

CREAM OF CURRY AND MUSHROOM SAUCE:

3 tablespoons butter
¼ pound coarsely chopped mushrooms
1 tablespoon fresh lemon juice
¼ cup dry white wine
1 cup chicken broth
1 cup heavy cream
1½ tablespoons cornstarch
2 tablespoons fresh chopped parsley
salt and freshly ground pepper

Combine the ground lamb, salt and pepper to taste, and
garlic. Shape into 4 equal-size patties. Heat the oil in a skillet
and cook the patties over medium heat, about 6 minutes per
side. Meanwhile, prepare the sauce. Heat the butter in a

saucepan and add the mushrooms. Cook for 5 minutes, stirring occasionally. Add the lemon juice, white wine, and broth and simmer for 5 minutes. Add the cream and bring to a boil. Dissolve the cornstarch in a little water and stir it into the sauce. Stir and cook until thickened. Add the parsley, taste for salt and pepper, and serve over the cooked lamb patties. Garnish with parsley.

CAULIFLOWER WITH SNOW PEA PODS *15 minutes*

1 small head cauliflower, separated into flowerets
salt
1/4 pound snow pea pods, ends trimmed, halved lengthwise
2 tablespoons melted butter
salt and freshly ground white or black pepper to taste

In a large saucepan bring 1 1/2 cups of lightly salted water to a boil. Add the cauliflower, cover, and cook for 8 minutes. Meanwhile, blanch the snow pea pods in 2 cups of boiling water for 1 minute. Drain. Drain the cauliflower and place in a bowl with the snow pea pods. Pour the butter over vegetables, season with salt and pepper, and toss.

BANANA FRITTERS *15 minutes*

4 medium bananas
1 cup flour
1 cup beer
2 tablespoons sugar
oil for deep frying
confectioners' sugar

Peel the bananas and cut into 3 pieces crosswise. In a bowl, beat together the flour, beer, and sugar. Heat oil to 370°F. Dip each piece of banana in the batter and gently drop into the fat. Cook for a few minutes until golden, cooking 3 or 4 fritters at a time. Drain and sprinkle with confectioners' sugar.

•

MENU

Roasted Double Lamb Rib Chops
Flageolets and Carrots
German Fries
Blue Cheese with Apples

•

ROASTED DOUBLE LAMB RIB CHOPS   *30 minutes*

4 double lamb rib chops
2 garlic cloves, crushed
3 tablespoons olive oil
½ teaspoon rosemary

Preheat the oven to 425°F. Combine the garlic, oil, and rosemary. Rub the chops with the mixture. Place in a roasting pan, fat side up, and cook for 20 minutes.

GERMAN FRIES   *25 minutes*

2 tablespoons butter
2 tablespoons vegetable oil
1½ pounds potatoes, peeled and thinly sliced
1 small onion, minced
½ teaspoon paprika
salt and freshly ground pepper

Heat the butter and oil in a skillet and add the potatoes. Cook over medium heat until browned, about 8 minutes. Turn and sprinkle with the onion and paprika. Cover and cook for 8 minutes. Season with salt and pepper to taste.

FLAGEOLETS AND CARROTS   *15 minutes*

1 pound carrots, peeled and thinly sliced
½ cup chicken broth
2 tablespoons butter
1 15-ounce can flageolets, drained and washed
1 tablespoon fresh chopped parsley
salt and freshly ground pepper

In a saucepan cook the carrots in boiling water for 5 minutes. Meanwhile, in a separate saucepan heat the broth and butter. Add the flageolets and simmer. Drain the carrots, and add to the saucepan with the flageolets. Add the parsley. Toss and season with salt and pepper to taste.

•

MENU

Lamb Chops Teriyaki
Pureed Green Peas
Wild Rice Mixture with Almonds
Carob Ice Cream with Toasted Sesame Seeds

•

WILD RICE MIXTURE WITH ALMONDS   *30 minutes*

1 package wild rice mixture
2 tablespoons butter
3 tablespoons almond slivers

Cook the rice according to the package directions. Meanwhile, heat the butter in a skillet and add the almond slivers. Cook over medium heat until lightly browned, stirring occasionally, about 4 minutes. Drain on paper towels. Stir the almonds into the cooked rice.

LAMB CHOPS TERIYAKI   *25 minutes*

¼ cup soy sauce
1 teaspoon fresh grated ginger
¼ cup dry sherry
1 garlic clove, crushed
8 1-inch-thick loin lamb chops

Preheat the broiler. Combine the soy sauce, ginger, sherry, and garlic. Baste the lamb chops in a roasting pan and cook under the broiler for 5 minutes. Turn and baste with the mixture. Cook for about 5 minutes or to desired doneness.

PUREED GREEN PEAS

10 minutes

2 10-ounce packages frozen peas
2 tablespoons melted butter
3 tablespoons heavy cream
salt and freshly ground pepper

In a saucepan bring 2 cups of water to a boil. Add the peas and separate with a fork. Cook for 5 minutes. Immediately drain and place in a food processor fitted with the steel blade with the butter and cream. Puree until smooth, or force through a food mill. Season to taste with salt and pepper and serve immediately.

•

MENU

Broiled Lamb Shank Steaks
Orange Flavored Rice with Raisins
Sautéed Mushrooms with Bacon
Watermelon Cubes with Litchis and Pineapple Juice

•

ORANGE-FLAVORED RICE WITH RAISINS

30 minutes

1 cup long-grain rice
1½ cups water
1 cup orange juice
1 tablespoon fresh grated orange rind
½ cup raisins
salt and freshly ground pepper

Cook the rice according to the package directions, but use 1½ cups of water and 1 cup of orange juice for the liquid. After the rice has cooked 20 minutes, add the orange rind and raisins; don't stir, re-cover, and let rest away from the heat for 5 minutes. Gently combine and season to taste with salt and pepper.

WATERMELON CUBES WITH LITCHIS
AND PINEAPPLE JUICE
10 minutes

    1 quart 1½-inch watermelon cubes, seeded
    1 11-ounce can litchis, drained
    ½ cup pineapple juice

Place the fruit in a bowl and pour the pineapple juice over it. Toss and refrigerate until serving time.

BROILED LAMB SHANK STEAKS
15 minutes

    4 6-ounce lamb shank steaks
    ½ cup dry red wine
    1 tablespoon Dijon mustard

Preheat the broiler. Cut edges of the steaks at 1½-inch intervals to prevent from curling during cooking. Combine the remaining ingredients. Place the steaks in a broiling pan and brush with the mixture. Broil for 4 minutes, turn, baste with the sauce, and cook for about 4 minutes for pink, or to desired doneness.

SAUTÉED MUSHROOMS WITH BACON
15 minutes

    8 strips bacon
    2 tablespoons butter
    1 pound fresh mushrooms, quartered
    1 garlic clove, crushed
    2 teaspoons fresh lemon juice
    salt and freshly ground pepper
    1 tablespoon fresh chopped parsley

In a large skillet cook the bacon until crisp, and drain on paper towels. Pour out all the bacon fat from the skillet except for 1 tablespoon. Add the butter, mushrooms, and garlic. Cook, stirring often, over medium-high heat for 4 minutes. Add the lemon juice, parsley, and bacon. Toss, season with salt and pepper, and serve.

Pasta

•

MENU

Cantaloupe and Prosciutto
Spaghetti Primavera
Crisp Italian Bread
Chocolate and Vanilla Ice Cream with Amaretto

•

SPAGHETTI PRIMAVERA   *30 minutes*

- ¼ pound snow pea pods, trimmed
- 2 cups fresh chopped broccoli
- 2 cups diced zucchini
- 1 cup frozen green peas
- 3 tablespoons olive oil
- ¼ cup pine nuts
- 2 large garlic cloves, crushed
- 1 medium-large onion, thinly sliced
- 1 tablespoon salt plus salt for seasoning
- 1 pound spaghetti
- ½ pound mushrooms, thinly sliced
- 12 cherry tomatoes, halved
- 3 tablespoons fresh chopped parsley
- 1 teaspoon basil
- 1 cup heavy cream
- 5 tablespoons softened butter
- ¾ cup fresh grated Parmesan cheese or to taste
- freshly ground pepper

Place 4½ quarts of hot water in a large pot and bring to a boil. Meanwhile, in a large saucepan bring 1½ quarts of water to a boil and blanch the snow pea pods, in a strainer, for 30 seconds. Drain and place in a large shallow dish. Add the broccoli to the water and cook for 4 minutes. Remove and drain. Place in the dish with the pea pods. Add the zucchini and green peas and cook in water for 3 minutes. Drain and place in a large dish with the other vegetables. Heat the oil in a large skillet and brown pine nuts, shaking pan over high heat, for 1 minute. Remove and add to dish with the vegetables. Add the garlic and onion to the skillet and sauté for 5 minutes, stirring often. Add salt to boiling water in large pot, stir, and add the spaghetti. Stir and cook until just tender, about 6 minutes.

Meanwhile, add the mushrooms to the skillet and cook for 3 minutes, stirring often. Add a little oil, if necessary. Add the tomatoes and cook for 1 minute. Cover and set aside. Sprinkle the vegetables and pine nuts with the parsley and basil. Slowly heat the cream in a saucepan. Drain the spaghetti well, and turn into a large bowl. Toss the spaghetti with the softened butter, heated cream, and Parmesan cheese. Add the vegetables and pine nuts, and mushroom mixture; toss. Season to taste with salt and pepper. Serve immediately.

CANTALOUPE AND PROSCIUTTO   *5 minutes*

    1 large cantaloupe, halved, seeded, and peeled
    16 thin slices prosciutto
    1 lime, cut into 4 wedges

Cut the cantaloupe halves into thin wedges and arrange in equal portions on 4 first course plates. Cover with equal amounts of the sliced prosciutto and garnish each with a wedge of lime.

•

MENU

Spiedini
Linguini with Spinach and Clam Sauce
Tomato and Fava Bean Salad
Softened Vanilla Ice Cream with Strawberries

•

TOMATO AND FAVA BEAN SALAD   5 minutes

> 1 cup cubed tomatoes
> 1 20-ounce can fava beans, drained
> 2 scallions, thinly sliced
> ⅓ cup olive oil
> 1 tablespoon red wine vinegar
> ½ teaspoon basil
> 1 tablespoon fresh chopped parsley
> salt and freshly ground pepper

Place the tomatoes, fava beans, and scallions in a bowl. Combine the remaining ingredients and pour over the salad. Toss and chill until served.

LINGUINI WITH SPINACH AND
CLAM SAUCE   25 minutes

> 1 10-ounce package frozen chopped spinach
> ¼ cup olive oil
> ¾ cup chopped onions
> ½ teaspoon minced garlic
> 2 8-ounce cans chopped clams and liquid
> 2 8-ounce bottles clam juice
> ¼ cup fresh chopped parsley
> salt and freshly ground pepper to taste
> 1 pound linguini
> fresh grated Parmesan cheese

Fill a pot with 4½ quarts of water and bring to a boil. Meanwhile, cook the spinach in a saucepan according to the package directions and drain well in a strainer. Heat the olive oil and sauté the onion and garlic over medium heat for 5 minutes. Add the clams, clam juice, parsley, salt, and pepper. Bring to a boil. Puree the spinach in a food processor fitted with the steel blade, or in a blender. Add to the clam sauce. Reduce the heat and simmer for about 6 minutes. Drop linguini into the lightly salted boiling water. Boil for about 6 minutes until just soft to the tooth (*al dente*). Drain the pasta and turn into a large bowl. Immediately pour the sauce over the pasta and toss. Sprinkle with the Parmesan cheese, toss again, and serve.

SPIEDINI

4 slices firm white bread, crusts trimmed
½ pound mozzarella cheese
2 large eggs
2 tablespoons water
bread crumbs
1 cup vegetable oil

ANCHOVY SAUCE:

8 anchovy fillets, mashed
2 tablespoons olive oil
2 tablespoons butter
2 tablespoons capers
⅔ cup dry white wine
1 tablespoon fresh lemon juice

For each spiedino, quarter each slice of the bread. Place 3 ⅛-inch-thick slices of the cheese, cut the same size as the bread pieces, between the 4 pieces of bread, and pierce the center through the bread and cheese with a 6-inch wooden skewer. Repeat for each spiedino. Dip each in the eggs beaten with 2 tablespoons of water, and coat with the bread crumbs. Heat the oil in a large skillet and fry the spiedinis until golden all over. Drain. Prepare the sauce by heating ingredients in a saucepan over high heat, constantly stirring, for 3 minutes. Spoon the sauce over each spiedino.

•

MENU

Three Cheese Fettuccine
Boston Lettuce Salad with Anchovy and
Garlic Dressing
Raspberry Sherbet with Strawberries in Rum

•

THREE CHEESE FETTUCCINE *20 minutes*

  1 tablespoon salt plus salt for seasoning
  1 pound fettuccine
  4 tablespoons butter, cut into pieces
  1 cup hot heavy cream
  ½ cup grated Fontina cheese
  ½ cup Bel Paese cheese
  ½ cup fresh grated Parmesan cheese
  ¼ pound thinly sliced prosciutto or ham, cut into thin strips
  freshly ground pepper

Bring 4½ quarts of water to a rolling boil in a large pot. Add
1 tablespoon salt, stir, and add the pasta. Stir once and cook
until tender, about 6 minutes. Drain well and turn into a large
bowl. Add the butter and cream and toss a few seconds. Add
the cheeses and prosciutto and toss. Taste for salt and
pepper.

BOSTON LETTUCE SALAD WITH ANCHOVY
AND GARLIC DRESSING *10 minutes*

  2 heads Boston lettuce, cleaned, dried, and torn into
    bite-size pieces

  ANCHOVY AND GARLIC DRESSING:

  ¼ cup olive oil
  ¼ cup vegetable oil
  4 anchovy fillets
  1 large garlic clove, minced
  1½ tablespoons red wine vinegar
  1 teaspoon Dijon mustard
  salt and freshly ground pepper

Place the lettuce in a salad bowl. In a small bowl combine
the dressing ingredients with a wire whisk. Pour the Anchovy and Garlic Dressing over the lettuce and toss just
before serving.

RASPBERRY SHERBET WITH
STRAWBERRIES IN RUM *5 minutes*

  1 pint strawberries, hulled and sliced
  ½ cup dark rum
  1½ pints raspberry sherbet

Place the sliced strawberries in a bowl and add the rum. Toss. Refrigerate until dessert is served. At that time place 1 scoop of the raspberry sherbet in each of 4 dessert bowls and spoon the strawberries and rum over the sherbet.

•

MENU

Caponata
Spaghetti Matriciana
Fresh Spinach and Endive Salad
Fresh Italian Whole Wheat Bread
Bel Paese Cheese with Pears

•

CAPONATA   *5 minutes*

    1 8-ounce can caponata
    1 8-ounce jar marinated artichoke hearts, drained
    1 8-ounce jar marinated whole mushrooms, drained
    8 Boston lettuce leaves, washed and dried

Combine all the ingredients, except for the lettuce. Place 2 lettuce leaves on each of 4 first course plates and spoon equal portions of the mixture over the lettuce.

SPAGHETTI MATRICIANA   *25 minutes*

    8 strips bacon
    ¼ cup olive oil
    1 cup chopped onions
    2 large garlic cloves, crushed
    1 20-ounce can crushed tomatoes
    1 6-ounce can tomato paste
    1 tablespoon fresh finely chopped basil or ½ teaspoon dried
      basil
    1 tablespoon fresh chopped parsley
    salt and freshly ground pepper
    1 pound spaghetti

Place 4½ quarts of water in a large pot and bring to a boil. Meanwhile, fry the bacon until crisp; heat the olive oil in a large saucepan and add the onion and garlic. Stir and cook for 5 minutes over medium-low heat. Drain the bacon and

155

crumble. Set aside. Add the crushed tomatoes, tomato paste, and herbs. Season with salt and pepper to taste and stir. Bring to a boil, reduce heat to a simmer and cook for 10 minutes. After the sauce has cooked a few minutes, add 1 tablespoon of salt to water, stir, and add the spaghetti. Stir and cook until just tender, about 6 minutes. Add the bacon to the sauce, and stir. Drain the cooked spaghetti and turn into a bowl. Pour the sauce over the spaghetti and toss.

FRESH SPINACH AND ENDIVE SALAD   *10 minutes*

  1/2 pound fresh spinach, washed, dried, stemmed, and torn
    into bite-size pieces
  3 Belgian endives, cut into 1/2-inch slices and separate
    leaves
  imported olive oil
  red wine vinegar
  salt and freshly ground pepper
  fresh grated Parmesan cheese

Place the spinach and endive leaves in a salad bowl and toss. Serve with the oil, vinegar, salt, pepper, and Parmesan cheese.

•

MENU

*Fried Italian Sausages with
Red Peppers and Onions
Linguini with String Beans and Garlic Butter
Crusty Italian Bread
Chocolate Ice Cream with Pine Nuts and
Tiny Chocolate Morsels*

•

FRIED ITALIAN SAUSAGES WITH
RED PEPPERS AND ONIONS   *30 minutes*

  5 tablespoons olive or vegetable oil
  8 sweet Italian sausages, each pricked in several places with
    a fork
  2 large red peppers, seeded and cut into thin strips
  3 medium onions, sliced
  1/2 teaspoon oregano

½ teaspoon rosemary
¼ cup chicken broth
¼ cup dry red wine

In a skillet heat 2 tablespoons of the oil and cook the sausages over medium heat until browned and evenly cooked. Meanwhile, heat the 3 remaining tablespoons of oil in a large saucepan and cook green peppers, onions, oregano, rosemary, broth, and wine for 10 minutes over medium-low heat, stirring often. Add the cooked and drained sausages to pan and top with the pepper mixture; cover and simmer for 5 minutes.

LINGUINI WITH STRING BEANS
AND GARLIC BUTTER
25 minutes

½ pound fresh string beans, ends trimmed
salt
1 pound linguini
5 tablespoons butter
2 tablespoons olive oil
2 large garlic cloves, minced
1 tablespoon fresh chopped parsley
freshly ground pepper
fresh grated Parmesan cheese

Place 3 cups of water in a saucepan and bring to a boil. Also place 4½ quarts of water in a large pot and bring it to a boil. Meanwhile, cut the green beans on the extreme diagonal every ½ inch. Season the boiling water in the saucepan with salt and drop in the green beans. Cook over medium heat for exactly 5 minutes. Drain. When the water boils in the large pot, add 1 tablespoon of salt, stir, add the pasta, stir, and cook until pasta is just tender, about 6 minutes. Meanwhile, heat the butter and oil in a skillet and add the garlic. Cook over low heat for 5 minutes. Drain the pasta and turn it into a large bowl. Immediately add the butter mixture and toss. Add the string beans and parsley. Toss and season with salt and pepper to taste. Serve with the Parmesan cheese.

CHAPTER SIX

1-Hour Meals

Seafood

•

MENU

Striped Bass with Cream Herb Sauce
Bouquet of Fresh Vegetables
Strawberry Pie

•

STRIPED BASS WITH
CREAM HERB SAUCE   *55 minutes*

2 large garlic cloves, crushed
½ cup imported olive oil
½ teaspoon rosemary
salt and freshly ground pepper
3½-pound whole striped bass, cleaned
2 cups dry white wine

CREAM HERB SAUCE:

6 tablespoons butter
½ cup flour
2½ cups heated milk
¼ teaspoon thyme
1 teaspoon tarragon
¼ cup fresh chopped parsley
½ teaspoon salt
freshly ground pepper

Preheat the oven to 450°F. Combine the garlic, oil, and
rosemary and season with salt and pepper. Cut the fish ½
inch deep, on the diagonal, at three 3-inch intervals on each
side. Place the bass in a roasting pan and sprinkle each side
of the fish with the seasoned oil. Add the wine and cook in
the oven for 45 minutes or until tender.

161

Ten minutes before serving, prepare the Cream Herb sauce. Heat the butter in a saucepan, whisk in the flour, and cook for 1 minute. Whisk in the heated milk, stirring constantly, until thickened. Add the herbs and season with salt and pepper. Simmer for a few minutes and serve with the bass.

STRAWBERRY PIE
10 minutes

    1 14-ounce can sweetened condensed milk
    2 tablespoons fresh lemon juice
    1 9-inch graham cracker crust
    1½ pints fresh strawberries, hulled and dried

In a bowl, combine the sweetened condensed milk and lemon juice. Stir a few minutes until the mixture thickens. Turn the mixture into a pie shell and smooth surface with a spatula. Place the strawberries in circles on the top of the pie. Refrigerate until served.

NOTE: Raspberries or blueberries can be substituted for the strawberries.

BOUQUET OF FRESH VEGETABLES
30 minutes

    1½ pounds small new potatoes, peeled
    1 pound carrots, peeled and cut into 1-inch lengths
    1 bunch fresh broccoli, trimmed and cut into 2-inch pieces

Thirty minutes before dinner, prepare the vegetables. Cook the potatoes in boiling water for about 18 minutes. Five minutes before dinner, cook the carrots and broccoli in separate saucepans in boiling water for 5 minutes each. Drain the vegetables and surround the fish in platter.

•

MARYANN LOPINTO'S SOLE DINNER FOR 4 MENU

*Fillet of Sole with Mushrooms and Cream
Rice Pilaf
Romaine, Orange, and Red Onion Salad with
Sweet and Sour Dressing
Snowballs*

•

ROMAINE, ORANGE, AND RED ONION SALAD
WITH SWEET AND SOUR DRESSING   *15 minutes*

1 medium romaine lettuce, washed, dried, and torn into
bite-size pieces
2 navel oranges, peeled and cut into segments
1 medium red onion, thinly sliced

SWEET AND SOUR DRESSING:

½ cup vegetable oil
2 tablespoons red wine vinegar
1 garlic clove, crushed
1 tablespoon ketchup
1 teaspoon sugar
salt and freshly ground pepper

Line a salad bowl with the lettuce and top with the orange
segments and onion rings. In a small bowl, beat together
Sweet and Sour Dressing ingredients. Refrigerate until serving time; combine and toss.

FILLET OF SOLE WITH
MUSHROOMS AND CREAM   *35 minutes*

4 small sole fillets
salt and freshly ground pepper
5 tablespoons butter
½ pound mushrooms, sliced
2 tablespoons flour
2 tablespoons dry white wine
1 cup heavy cream
1 cup bottled clam juice
fresh chopped parsley

Season the fish with salt and pepper and place in lightly
buttered shallow baking dish. Heat 3 tablespoons of the
butter in a skillet and sauté the mushrooms for 3 minutes
over high heat. Spoon the mushrooms over fish fillets in pan.
Preheat oven to 375°F. In a saucepan melt 2 remaining
tablespoons of the butter and add flour. Stir with a wire
whisk over medium heat for 1 minute. Add wine, cream, and
clam juice, constantly whisking. Bring to a boil, and cook,
stirring, until sauce thickens. Spoon sauce over fish and
cook in the oven for 20 minutes. Sprinkle with parsley.

RICE PILAF

30 minutes

2¼ cups chicken stock or broth
2 tablespoons butter
¼ cup minced shallots or onions
1 cup long-grain rice
1 pinch saffron
1 tablespoon fresh chopped parsley
salt and freshly ground pepper

Bring the chicken stock to a boil in a saucepan. Meanwhile, heat the butter in a small skillet and sauté the onions for 5 minutes, stirring occasionally. Add the butter and onions to the boiling stock and add rice and saffron. Stir once, cover, and simmer for 20 minutes. Turn off heat and leave lid on for 5 minutes. Add the parsley; toss rice lightly, then add salt and pepper according to taste.

NOTE: For variety, use beef stock instead of chicken stock and/or add ¼ cup of pine nuts, raisins, or diced tomatoes to rice with parsley when cooked.

SNOWBALLS

10 minutes

1 cup shredded coconut
1½ pints butter pecan ice cream

Preheat broiler. Spread the coconut on a baking sheet. Cook under broiler until lightly browned, about 2 minutes. Cool and place in a plate. Make 4 large even scoops of the ice cream. Roll each in the toasted coconut and serve immediately.

•

MENU

Clam and Sausage Brochettes
Ratatouille
Szechwan Noodles
Danish Butter Cheese with Plums

•

RATATOUILLE   *1 hour*

   3 tablespoons olive oil
   1 medium-large onion, thinly sliced
   1 large garlic clove, minced
   1/2 cup dry white wine
   1 medium eggplant, cubed
   2 medium zucchini, cubed
   2 medium green peppers, seeded and diced
   3 firm ripe tomatoes, peeled and cut into 6 wedges each*
   1/2 teaspoon oregano
   1/2 teaspoon thyme
   1 bay leaf
   salt and freshly ground pepper to taste

Heat the olive oil in a Dutch oven or large saucepan. Add the onion and garlic and sauté for 5 minutes. Pour in wine and bring to a boil. Immediately add remaining ingredients, reduce heat, cover, and simmer for 45 minutes, stirring twice during cooking time. Serve hot or cold.

CLAM AND SAUSAGE BROCHETTES   *35 minutes*

   2 cups dry white wine
   8 fresh cherrystone clams, shucked
   4 Italian sweet or hot sausages
   flour
   2 eggs, beaten
   1 1/2 cups fresh bread crumbs**
   2 cups vegetable oil

Pour the wine into a large saucepan and bring to a boil, reduce heat and add the clams. Poach for 4 minutes. Remove the clams with a slotted spoon to side dish. Add sausages to wine and simmer for 10 minutes, turning occasionally. Remove and drain. Cut sausages into thirds. Thread an 8-inch wooden skewer with a piece of sausage, a clam, sausage, clam, and end with a piece of sausage. Set aside and thread remaining 3 skewers in the same manner. Dust each with flour, coat with eggs, and roll in bread crumbs. Heat oil in a large skillet and fry the brochettes until golden brown on all

---

   * To peel tomatoes, immerse in enough boiling water to cover them for 8 seconds. Peel off the skins with the sharp point of a small knife.
   ** To make fresh bread crumbs, trim the crusts from 6 slices of day-old white bread. Tear pieces and place in bowl of a food processor fitted with steel blade. Turn on and run until the crumbs are smooth, about 20 seconds.

sides, about 6 minutes, total cooking time. Drain on absorbent paper.

SZECHWAN NOODLES

20 minutes

2 large garlic cloves, crushed
½ cup sesame oil
3 tablespoons soy sauce
¼ cup white wine vinegar
1 teaspoon hot pepper flakes
1 teaspoon Szechwan peppercorns, crushed* (optional)
1 teaspoon fresh grated ginger root
1 tablespoon salt
1 pound linguini
5 scallions, thinly sliced

Bring 4½ quarts of water to a rolling boil in a large pot. Meanwhile, in a bowl combine the garlic, sesame oil, soy sauce, vinegar, pepper flakes, Szechwan peppercorns, and ginger root and set aside. Add 1 tablespoon salt to boiling water, stir, and add the pasta. Cook for about 6 minutes until just tender. Drain well and immediately turn into a bowl and pour the sesame oil mixture over pasta. Toss with the scallions.

•

MENU

*Lemon and Orange Chicken Cocktail
in Cucumber Nest
Shrimp Scampi
Saffron Rice
Fresh Green Peas with Sage and Butter
Chocolate Ice Cream with Kahlua*

•

LEMON AND ORANGE CHICKEN COCKTAIL
IN CUCUMBER NEST

15 minutes

2 cups cooked chicken breast, cut into thin strips
½ cup mayonnaise
2 tablespoons thawed orange juice concentrate
2 tablespoons fresh lemon juice

* Szechwan peppercorns can be found in Chinese or specialty food shops.

1 medium ripe tomato, seeded, and finely diced
1 tablespoon grated onion
1 teaspoon horseradish
dash or two of nutmeg
salt and freshly ground pepper to taste
1 large cucumber

Gently combine all the ingredients, except for the cucumber.
Refrigerate. Peel the cucumber and cut in half lengthwise.
With a teaspoon, scoop out the seeds in the center of each
half. Shred the cucumber using the shredding disk in a food
processor or by hand grater. Place in a colander and sprinkle
lightly with salt. Pat dry and, using equal amounts of cucumber, make rings in the center of 4 plates. Spoon chicken
cocktail in center.

NOTE: Chicken cocktail mixture can be made in advance and
refrigerated until ready to finish preparing dish. Cucumber
must be prepared at the last minute.

SHRIMP SCAMPI   *45 minutes*

1½ pounds large shrimp, shelled and deveined
½ cup olive oil
2 garlic cloves, minced
1 tablespoon fresh chopped parsley
½ teaspoon oregano
½ teaspoon salt
freshly grated pepper to taste
2 lemons, halved and seeded

Combine all the ingredients except for the lemons in a bowl,
cover and refrigerate for 30 minutes. Preheat broiler. Remove shrimp from the marinade and arrange in rows in a
broiling pan. Cook under broiler for 5 minutes and brush
with the marinade. Cook 3 minutes longer. Garnish with the
lemon halves.

SAFFRON RICE   *30 minutes*

Cook 1 cup of long-grain rice according to the package
directions, but substitute chicken broth for water in the
recipe and add ¼ teaspoon of saffron.

FRESH GREEN PEAS WITH
SAGE AND BUTTER
20 minutes

1½ pounds fresh peas
3 tablespoons butter
1 teaspoon sage
salt and freshly ground pepper

Shell the peas and cook in a saucepan in boiling water until tender, about 12 minutes. Drain. Add the butter and sage and toss. Season lightly with salt and pepper to taste.

●

MENU

*Shrimp Creole
Rice
Boston Lettuce and Cucumber Salad
Fresh Raspberries in Pattie Shells with
Rum Whipped Cream*

●

SHRIMP CREOLE
1 hour

⅓ cup peanut or vegetable oil
2 cups chopped celery
2 cups chopped green pepper
2 cups chopped onion
2 large garlic cloves, crushed
¼ cup fresh chopped parsley
2 bay leaves
8 mustard seeds (optional)
1 teaspoon thyme
1 6-ounce can tomato paste
4 cups chicken broth
4 cups water
salt and freshly ground pepper
2 large ripe tomatoes, peeled and chopped*
3 pounds shrimp, shelled and deveined

Heat the oil in a large pot. Add the celery, peppers, onions, and garlic. Cook over medium heat for 10 minutes, stirring often. Add parsley, bay leaves, mustard seeds, thyme, and

_____
* To peel tomatoes immerse them in boiling water for 8 seconds, and peel them with the aid of a small sharp knife.

tomato paste; stir and pour in the broth and water. Season to taste with salt and pepper. Bring to a boil and simmer for 30 minutes. Add the tomatoes and shrimp and cook for 5 minutes.

RICE   *30 minutes*

Cook 1 cup of long-grain rice according to the package directions.

BOSTON LETTUCE AND
CUCUMBER SALAD   *10 minutes*

1 large head Boston lettuce, washed, dried, and torn into
  bite-size pieces
1 large cucumber, peeled and thinly sliced
½ cup vegetable oil
1 tablespoon red wine vinegar
½ teaspoon basil
salt and freshly ground pepper

Combine the lettuce and cucumber in a salad bowl. Mix together the remaining ingredients in a small bowl. Refrigerate until serving time; pour the dressing over the salad. Toss.

FRESH RASPBERRIES IN PATTIE SHELLS
WITH RUM WHIPPED CREAM   *35 minutes*

4 frozen pattie shells
1 pint fresh raspberries
1 cup heavy cream, whipped
¼ cup confectioners' sugar
1 teaspoon vanilla
2 tablespoons rum

Cook the pattie shells according to package directions. Cool. Spoon the raspberries into shells. Add confectioners' sugar, vanilla, and rum to the whipped cream and beat. Spoon the cream on top of the raspberries.

Poultry

•

MENU

Cream of Fennel Soup
Sautéed Chicken Breasts with Ham and
Melted Mozzarella
Romaine and Crouton Salad with Caesar Dressing
Nora's Baked Pears

•

ROMAINE AND CROUTON SALAD WITH
CAESAR DRESSING   *15 minutes*

   1 medium head romaine lettuce, washed, dried, and torn into
     bite-size pieces
   4 tablespoons butter
   1 tablespoon vegetable oil
   4 slices white bread, crusts trimmed, cubed
   ¼ cup fresh grated Parmesan cheese

CAESAR DRESSING:

   ½ cup vegetable oil
   1½ tablespoons fresh lemon juice
   1 teaspoon Dijon mustard
   2 anchovy fillets, mashed
   1 large garlic clove, crushed
   1 teaspoon Worcestershire sauce
   salt and freshly ground pepper

Prepare the lettuce and refrigerate it wrapped in a kitchen
towel until ready to serve. Combine the Caesar Dressing
ingredients in a small bowl with a wire whisk and let rest at

170

room temperature until ready to use. Heat the butter and oil in a skillet and brown the bread cubes. Just before serving the salad place the lettuce in a salad bowl, pour the dressing over salad, and toss. Add the croutons and cheese and toss again. Serve immediately.

CREAM OF FENNEL SOUP   45 *minutes*

 2 tablespoons butter
 1 medium onion, chopped
 3 cups chopped fennel
 4 cups chicken stock or broth
 2 egg yolks
 1 cup heavy cream
 salt and freshly ground pepper to taste
 fresh chopped parsley

Heat the butter in a large saucepan and cook the onion and fennel for 5 minutes, stirring often. Add the stock and bring to a boil; reduce heat, cover, and simmer for 30 minutes. In a blender puree mixture, a few cupsful at a time, and place in a clean saucepan. In a small bowl, beat the egg yolks and add the heavy cream and mix. Stir in ½ cup of the pureed soup then add the cream mixture to the soup. Heat the soup thoroughly, but do not boil. Taste for salt and pepper. Garnish with parsley.

SAUTÉED CHICKEN BREASTS WITH HAM
AND MELTED MOZZARELLA   40 *minutes*

 4 small chicken breasts, halved
 salt and freshly ground pepper
 flour
 4 tablespoons butter
 4 tablespoons vegetable oil
 8 thin slices of boiled or roast ham
 ½ pound mozzarella cheese, thinly sliced

Pat the chicken pieces dry. Season well with salt and pepper. Dust with flour. Heat the butter and oil in a large skillet and cook over medium-high heat until crisp and golden brown on each side, about 12 minutes per side. Heat broiler. Place the cooked chicken pieces in a shallow baking pan and top each with 1 slice of ham and mozzarella cheese. Cook under broiler until the cheese melts.

171

NORA'S BAKED PEARS   *45 minutes*

    8 fresh firm ripe pears
    6 tablespoons melted butter plus butter for pan
    ½ cup sugar
    1 cup heavy cream, at room temperature

Preheat oven to 425°F. Peel the whole pears with a vegetable
peeler, quarter them, and cut away cores. Arrange the pear
pieces, cut side up, on a lightly buttered shallow baking dish.
Sprinkle with sugar and butter. Cook in oven for 30 minutes
until brown and bubbly. Serve with the heavy cream.

•

MENU

Cream of Mushroom Soup
Lemon Chicken Sauté
Carrot Curls and Watercress Salad
Hot Almond Fudge Coffee Sundaes

•

LEMON CHICKEN SAUTÉ   *55 minutes*

    2 tablespoons butter
    1 tablespoon vegetable oil
    8 serving pieces of chicken
    salt and freshly ground pepper
    2 teaspoons fresh grated lemon rind
    2 tablespoons fresh lemon juice
    1 tablespoon fresh chopped parsley
    1 teaspoon tarragon
    ½ teaspoon thyme
    ¾ cup chicken broth
    1 tablespoon flour

Preheat oven to 375°F. Heat the butter and oil in a large
skillet. Season the chicken with salt and pepper, and brown
on each side. Transfer to a shallow baking dish. Sprinkle the
chicken with lemon rind. Combine lemon juice, parsley,
tarragon, thyme, and ½ cup broth. Pour over the chicken.
Bake in oven for 35 minutes. Remove the chicken to a

warmed serving platter. Combine the flour with the remaining broth and whisk into the liquid in the pan over high heat. Cook for 3 minutes, stirring, until thickened. Spoon over the chicken.

CREAM OF MUSHROOM SOUP   *30 minutes*

    6 tablespoons butter
    1 pound mushrooms, thinly sliced
    1 medium onion, chopped
    2 tablespoons flour
    2 cups chicken broth or stock
    2 cups milk
    salt and freshly ground pepper
    1/4 cup dry sherry
    1 cup heavy cream
    fresh chopped parsley

Heat 4 tablespoons of the butter in a large saucepan and add the mushrooms and onion. Cook over medium-low heat for 10 minutes, stirring often. Stir in the flour and cook for 2 minutes. Heat the combined broth and milk and pour over the mushroom mixture, stirring constantly. Season with salt and pepper and add the sherry. Cover and simmer for 10 minutes. Puree 2½ cups of the mixture in a blender and return it to the pan. Add remaining 2 tablespoons of the butter and heavy cream. Cook until thoroughly heated, stirring once or twice. Garnish with the parsley.

CARROT CURLS AND
WATERCRESS SALAD   *10 minutes*

    6 large carrots, peeled
    1 large bunch watercress, washed, dried, and stemmed

    BLUE CHEESE DRESSING:

    1/2 cup mayonnaise
    2 ounces blue cheese, crumbled
    1 tablespoon red wine vinegar
    2 tablespoons cream

Holding one end of each carrot, cut curls with a vegetable peeler. Place the carrot curls in a bowl with the watercress. Combine the Blue Cheese Dressing ingredients and spoon over the salad and toss.

HOT ALMOND FUDGE
COFFEE SUNDAES   *15 minutes*

1 quart coffee ice cream
1 cup chopped toasted almonds

ALMOND FUDGE SAUCE:

1 6-ounce package semisweet chocolate morsels
2 tablespoons butter
1 14-ounce can sweetened condensed milk
1/3 cup Amaretto

Prepare the sauce first by melting the chocolate morsels with
the butter in a saucepan over low heat. Stir in the sweetened
condensed milk and cook, stirring, about 5 minutes until the
mixture thickens. Stir in the Amaretto. Divide the ice cream
into 4 dessert bowls. Spoon the warm sauce over ice cream
and sprinkle with the nuts. (Place the remaining sauce in jar
with a cover and refrigerate until reheated and used another
time.)

•

MENU

*Cheese Stuffed Chicken Breasts Wrapped in Bacon
Poached Asparagus Spears
Top of the Stove Rice Pudding with
Dates and Raisins*

•

TOP OF THE STOVE RICE PUDDING
WITH DATES AND RAISINS   *35 minutes*

1 cup long-grain rice
1 cup heavy cream
1/4 cup sugar or to taste
1/2 teaspoon cinnamon
1/2 cup raisins
12 pitted dates

Cook the rice in 2 1/2 cups of boiling water, covered, over low
heat for 25 minutes. Remove from the heat. In a separate
saucepan bring the cream to a boil, stirring, and cook for
about 5 minutes until thickened. Stir into the rice the sugar,

cinnamon, and raisins. Cover and cool. Garnish with the dates.

CHEESE-STUFFED CHICKEN BREASTS
WRAPPED IN BACON   *45 minutes*

 4 medium chicken breasts, skinned and boned
 paprika
 freshly ground pepper
 ¾ cup shredded Cheddar cheese
 3 tablespoons plain dry bread crumbs
 ¼ cup thinly sliced scallions
 ½ teaspoon tarragon
 4 strips bacon
 vegetable oil

Preheat oven to 375°F. Flatten each breast between 2 sheets of wax paper to ¼-inch thickness. Remove the wax paper and sprinkle the chicken with paprika and pepper. Combine cheese, bread crumbs, tarragon, and scallions. Place equal amounts of the stuffing mixture across the center of each breast. Roll up each breast and wrap with the bacon in a spiral shape. Secure the bacon to chicken ends with toothpicks. Lightly grease a shallow baking dish with oil and place the prepared chicken breasts in the pan. Cook for 30 minutes and remove the toothpicks.

POACHED ASPARAGUS SPEARS   *20 minutes*

 16 medium asparagus, stem ends cut off, peeled with
    vegetable peeler
 2 tablespoons melted butter
 salt and freshly ground pepper

Place the asparagus in a skillet with 2 inches of boiling water. Simmer for 10 minutes. Drain and place in a serving dish. Pour the butter over the asparagus and season with salt and pepper to taste.

MENU

Poulet Plesser
Baked Glazed Acorn Squash
Buttered Asparagus
Goat Cheese with Seedless Green Grapes

•

POULET PLESSER   *1 hour*

8 serving pieces of chicken
salt and freshly ground pepper
4 tablespoons butter
1 tablespoon vegetable oil
1½ cups coarsely chopped celery
1½ cups coarsely chopped carrots
1½ cups coarsely chopped leeks or onions
1 large garlic clove, chopped
½ teaspoon thyme
2 bay leaves, crumbled
1 cup red wine
1 cup beef stock or broth
1 cup heavy cream
2 tablespoons flour
1 tablespoon fresh chopped parsley

Preheat the oven to 400°F. Season the chicken pieces well with salt and pepper. Heat 2 tablespoons of the butter with the oil in an ovenproof 4-inch sided casserole or pan. Brown the chicken on both sides. Transfer to a side dish. Add the celery, carrots, leeks, garlic, thyme, and bay leaves. Stir and cook for 1 minute. Add the wine and stock and bring to a boil. Place the chicken pieces, skin side up, on top of the vegetables. Cook in the oven for 40 minutes. Transfer the chicken to a warmed serving dish. Strain the mixture left in pan into saucepan and bring to a boil. Add the heavy cream and bring to a boil. Mash the remaining 2 tablespoons of butter with the flour and combine well. Whisk into the sauce and cook over high heat, stirring constantly with a wire whisk for 2 minutes, until the sauce thickens. Spoon the sauce over the chicken and sprinkle with parsley.

176

BAKED GLAZED ACORN SQUASH

40 minutes

2 medium acorn squash
2 tablespoons melted butter
cinnamon
2 tablespoons brown sugar

Cut each squash in half and remove the seeds. Place the halves, cut side up, in a baking pan. Brush each with equal amounts of butter. Cover with foil and bake for 30 minutes until the squash is tender. Remove the foil, sprinkle with equal amounts of cinnamon and brown sugar. Cook under the broiler for about 1 minute, until golden brown and sizzling.

BUTTERED ASPARAGUS

15 minutes

1 pound fresh asparagus, stalks peeled with vegetable
   peeler
salt
2 tablespoons butter
freshly ground pepper

Bring 3 cups of water to a boil in a skillet. Cut the asparagus into 1-inch lengths on the diagonal and drop into the lightly salted boiling water. Cook for exactly 5 minutes over medium heat. Drain and toss with the butter and season with salt and pepper.

•

MENU

Chicken and Leek Sauté
Artichoke and Tomato Salad
Fresh Cantaloupe Tart with Apricot and
Pepper Glaze

•

FRESH CANTALOUPE TART WITH APRICOT AND PEPPER GLAZE

1 hour

PASTRY:

1¼ cups sifted all-purpose flour
6 tablespoons chilled sweet butter
½ teaspoon salt
3 tablespoons ice cold water

TART:

2 small fresh ripe cantaloupes
1 10-ounce jar apricot preserves
1 tablespoon sugar
1 tablespoon water
½ cup finely chopped toasted almonds
fresh grated pepper

To prepare the pastry: Place flour and bits of the butter and salt into a food processor fitted with the steel blade. Run machine until mixture resembles coarse crumbs. Add the water through feed tube until dough begins to roll off sides of the container. Or, combine the flour, butter, and salt in bowl with a pastry blender until coarse crumb mixture is achieved. Add the water and mix. Remove, shape into a ball, cover with plastic wrap, and place in refrigerator.

Preheat oven to 400°F. Cut the cantaloupes in half, peel, and remove the seeds. Cut into ¼-inch-thick even slices and place on a clean kitchen towel. Cover with another towel. Roll out the dough on a lightly floured board and fit into 9-inch tart pan. Cut off the edges. Line tart pan with a sheet of aluminum foil and fill with dry beans or rice. Bake for 10 minutes. Remove the foil with beans or rice and continue cooking until golden and brown, about 15 minutes. Remove and cool thoroughly.

In a saucepan bring the apricot preserves to a boil with sugar and water, stirring. Cook for 5 minutes, remove from heat, and strain. Brush the cooled pastry shell lightly with apricot glaze. Sprinkle with the chopped almonds. Line the cantaloupe slices in an overlapping circle in the tart shell. Brush cantaloupe with apricot glaze, (reheat and stir, if necessary) and sprinkle with pepper. Chill until served.

CHICKEN AND LEEK SAUTÉ   *40 minutes*

    8 serving pieces of chicken
    4 tablespoons butter
    2 tablespoons vegetable oil
    4 leeks, white parts only, cut into ¼-inch-thick slices (use
        cleaned leek greens another time for stock making)
    1 lemon
    salt and freshly ground pepper
    1 teaspoon thyme
    ¼ cup chicken stock or broth
    ¼ cup dry white wine

Pat the chicken dry with paper towels or a clean kitchen
towel. Heat 3 tablespoons of the butter with the oil in a large
skillet. Brown the chicken on each side over medium-high
heat. Transfer the chicken to a side plate. Lower heat and
sauté the leek slices for 1 minute, stirring once. Return the
chicken to the pan, skin side down. Squeeze the lemon juice
over the chicken through a strainer. Season with salt, pepper, and thyme. Cover and cook over low heat for 15
minutes. Turn the chicken, partially re-cover, and cook for
10 minutes until the chicken is tender. Remove the chicken
to a warmed serving dish. Top with the leeks. Pour off all the
fat from pan, except for 1 tablespoon. Add the combined
stock and wine. Bring to a boil and cook over high heat for 2
minutes, stirring to release the food particles in bottom of
the pan. Whisk in the remaining tablespoon of butter, and
immediately pour sauce over the chicken and leeks.

ARTICHOKE AND TOMATO SALAD   *10 minutes*

    1 10-ounce package frozen artichoke hearts
    salt
    12 cherry tomatoes, halved
    ⅓ cup olive or vegetable oil
    1 tablespoon red wine vinegar
    2 teaspoons fresh chopped parsley
    1 teaspoon Dijon mustard
    freshly ground pepper

Cook the artichoke hearts in 1½ cups of lightly salted boiling
water just until thawed and hot. Immediately drain well.
Place in a salad bowl with the tomatoes. Mix together the
remaining ingredients in a small bowl with a wire whisk and
pour over the vegetables. Toss.

•

MENU

Chicken Pablo
Baked Whole Onions with Honey and Butter
Corn with Red Pepper
Oranges in Grand Marnier Sauce

•

CHICKEN PABLO   *40 minutes*

　　8 serving pieces of chicken
　　freshly ground pepper
　　3 tablespoons butter
　　6 strips bacon, cut into 1-inch lengths
　　2 garlic cloves, peeled and halved
　　½ teaspoon thyme
　　3 tablespoons Madeira
　　½ cup chicken stock

Pat the chicken pieces dry. Season with pepper. (No salt is necessary because of the salt in the bacon.) Heat 2 tablespoons of the butter in a large skillet. Brown the chicken on both sides. Add the bacon pieces, garlic, and thyme. Cook over medium-low heat for 15 minutes, turn the pieces and cook for 10 minutes or until tender. Transfer the chicken and bacon to a warmed serving dish. Discard the garlic. Pour out all but 1 tablespoon of the fat. Add the Madeira and boil for 2 minutes. Pour in the chicken stock and cook for 30 seconds. Whisk in the remaining tablespoon of butter and spoon the sauce over the chicken.

ORANGES IN GRAND MARNIER SAUCE   *10 minutes*

　　1 cup orange juice
　　1 tablespoon sugar
　　1 tablespoon cornstarch
　　2 tablespoons grated orange rind
　　3 tablespoons Grand Marnier
　　4 navel oranges, peeled, including white pith
　　bakery cookies (optional)

In a saucepan bring the orange juice, sugar, and cornstarch to a boil, stirring. Add the orange peel and Grand Marnier
180

and cook for 2 minutes. Place the oranges in a serving dish and pour the sauce over the oranges. Cool and refrigerate until served. Serve with bakery cookies.

BAKED WHOLE ONIONS WITH
HONEY AND BUTTER

30 minutes

2 tablespoons butter plus butter for pan
8 medium-small yellow onions, peeled but left whole, ends cut off ¼ inch
4 tablespoons honey
½ cup chicken broth
salt and freshly ground pepper to taste

Preheat the oven to 350°F. Lightly butter a small shallow baking dish. Place the onions in the dish and drizzle the honey over the onions. Dot with the butter and pour in the chicken broth. Season with salt and pepper. Bake for about 20 minutes until tender crisp. Pass under the broiler for 30 seconds to brown tops.

CORN WITH RED PEPPER

10 minutes

1 10-ounce package frozen whole kernel corn
2 tablespoons butter
1 tablespoon vegetable oil
1 large red pepper, seeded and cut into thin strips
1 small onion, thinly sliced
salt and freshly ground pepper

Cook the corn according to package directions. Meanwhile, heat the butter and oil in a saucepan and cook the pepper and onion for 5 minutes, over medium heat, stirring often. Drain the corn and add to the onion and pepper. Heat thoroughly, stirring. Season with salt and pepper to taste.

•

MENU

Sara's Chicken
Broiled Zucchini with Mushroom Stuffing
Grand Marnier Soufflé Omelet

•

SARA'S CHICKEN

40 minutes

    8 serving pieces of chicken
    salt and freshly ground pepper
    8 bacon strips
    2 tablespoons butter
    1 medium onion, thinly sliced
    1 garlic clove, crushed
    1 cup chopped canned tomatoes
    ½ teaspoon sage
    ½ teaspoon thyme
    3 tablespoons dry white wine

Season the chicken with salt and pepper. Fry the bacon until crisp. Remove and drain on paper towels. Brown the chicken on both sides in the bacon fat. Remove to a side dish. Pour out all the fat except for 1 tablespoon. Add the butter, onion, and garlic and stir. Top with the chicken pieces, cover, and simmer for 15 minutes. Turn the chicken pieces and add the tomatoes, sage, thyme, and wine. Re-cover and cook for about 10 minutes until the chicken is tender. Place the chicken in a warmed serving dish and sprinkle with the crumbled bacon.

BROILED ZUCCHINI WITH MUSHROOM STUFFING

25 minutes

    2 medium zucchini
    2 tablespoons butter
    1 small onion, minced
    ¼ pound mushrooms, finely chopped
    ⅓ cup fresh bread crumbs
    2 tablespoons fresh grated Parmesan cheese
    1 teaspoon fresh lemon juice
    ¼ teaspoon thyme
    salt and freshly ground pepper
    4 tablespoons grated mozzarella cheese

Bring 6 cups of water to a boil in a skillet. Add the zucchini and cook for 5 minutes, turning several times. Drain. Cut the zucchini in half lengthwise. With a teaspoon, scoop out the center pulp and place in a bowl. Take care not to break the shells. Heat the butter and sauté the onion and mushrooms for 5 minutes, stirring often. Place the onion and mushrooms in bowl with the zucchini pulp and add the bread crumbs, Parmesan cheese, lemon juice, and thyme. Mix thoroughly and season to taste with salt and pepper. Preheat the broiler. Fill zucchini shells with equal amounts of the mixture. Sprinkle 1 tablespoon of the mozzarella cheese on top of each piece of the filled zucchini. Place under medium broiler and cook for about 5 minutes until golden brown.

GRAND MARNIER SOUFFLÉ OMELET   *15 minutes*

    3 large eggs, separated
    2 tablespoons sugar
    2 tablespoons Grand Marnier
    1 tablespoon butter
    confectioners' sugar

Preheat the oven to 425°F. In a bowl beat together the egg yolks, sugar, and Grand Marnier. Set aside. In a large separate bowl beat the egg whites until stiff. Fold into the yolk mixture. Heat the butter in a large ovenproof omelet pan or skillet with curved sides, stickproof, if possible, and turn the egg mixture into it. Immediately place in the oven and cook for about 10 minutes until soft, but set. Slide the omelet onto a warm serving dish, folding it over in half, and sprinkle with sugar.

•

MENU

Avocado Soup
Garlic Chicken
Sautéed Zucchini and Corn
Fresh Gingerbread

•

FRESH GINGERBREAD
1 hour

2 cups sifted all-purpose flour
2 teaspoons ginger
½ teaspoon nutmeg
1 teaspoon cinnamon
1 teaspoon baking soda
½ teaspoon salt
6 tablespoons softened butter plus butter for pan
½ cup molasses
½ cup packed dark brown sugar
1 cup milk
2 eggs
heavy cream or ice cream

Preheat the oven to 375°F. Combine the flour, spices, baking soda, and salt. In a separate large bowl beat together the butter, molasses, and brown sugar. Add the milk and eggs and mix well. Combine with the flour mixture. Turn into a buttered 9-inch square baking pan and cook for about 45 minutes or until done. Serve with warmed heavy cream or ice cream.

GARLIC CHICKEN
35 minutes

8 serving pieces of chicken
salt and freshly ground pepper
flour
2 tablespoons butter
2 tablespoons vegetable oil
1 whole head garlic, each clove peeled and left whole
½ cup dry white wine
½ cup chicken broth
2 tablespoons cornstarch
3 tablespoons water
fresh chopped parsley

Season the chicken pieces with salt and pepper. Coat with flour. Heat the butter and oil in a large skillet and brown the chicken over high heat on each side. Add the garlic cloves, turn the chicken, and pour in the combined wine and broth. Simmer for 15 minutes, turn the chicken, and simmer 10 more minutes until tender. Transfer the chicken and garlic to a warmed serving dish. Stir the cornstarch dissolved in 3 tablespoons of water into the liquid in the pan, and cook over high heat for 2 minutes. Taste for salt and pepper. Spoon over the chicken and sprinkle with parsley.

SAUTÉED ZUCCHINI AND CORN   *20 minutes*

    2 tablespoons butter
    1 tablespoon vegetable oil
    1 medium onion, chopped
    ¼ cup chicken broth
    2 medium fresh zucchini, cubed
    1¼ cups fresh whole corn kernels, or 1 10-ounce package
        frozen corn, thawed
    ½ teaspoon thyme
    1 tablespoon freshly chopped parsley
    salt and freshly ground pepper

Heat the oil and butter in a skillet and add the onion. Sauté for 5 minutes, stirring often. Add broth and zucchini, cover, and simmer for 6 minutes. Add the corn, thyme, parsley, and season with salt and pepper to taste. Re-cover and simmer for 5 minutes.

AVOCADO SOUP   *10 minutes*

    1 large chilled avocado, peeled, pitted, and cubed
    1 13-ounce can chicken consommé, chilled
    1 small onion, grated
    juice of 1 lemon
    1 cup chilled light cream
    ½ cup sour cream
    salt and freshly ground white pepper to taste

Put the avocado, consommé, and onion in the blender and puree. Pour into a bowl and combine well with the remaining ingredients. Refrigerate until served.

·

MENU

Nancy's Sautéed Chicken with Vinegar Sauce
Wild Rice with Walnuts and Walnut Oil
Creamed Spinach with Mushrooms
Cantaloupe, Pineapple, and Bananas in
Rum Syrup

·

WILD RICE WITH WALNUTS
AND WALNUT OIL   *1 hour*

> ½ teaspoon salt plus salt for seasoning
> 1 cup wild rice
> 2 tablespoons vegetable oil
> ½ cup walnut halves
> 3 tablespoons walnut oil
> freshly ground pepper

In a saucepan bring 3½ cups of water to a boil. Add the salt
and rice. Cover and simmer for 50 minutes. Meanwhile, heat
vegetable oil in a skillet and lightly brown the walnuts over
medium-high heat, tossing often, about 5 minutes. Remove
the walnuts and drain. Drain the cooked rice in a colander
and place in a bowl. Add the walnuts and walnut oil. Toss,
and season with salt and pepper to taste.

CANTALOUPE, PINEAPPLE, AND BANANAS
IN RUM SYRUP   *50 minutes*

> 1 small ripe cantaloupe
> 1 small ripe pineapple
> 2 medium bananas

RUM SYRUP:

> ⅓ cup water
> ½ cup dark rum
> 3 tablespoons sugar

In a saucepan bring the water, rum, and sugar to a boil, and
cook for 3 minutes, until the sugar is completely dissolved.

186

Set aside. Peel the cantaloupe and cut it in half. Scoop out the seeds and cut into 1-inch cubes. Place in a large bowl. Cut off the top of the pineapple and cut the pineapple in half. Quarter each half and cut hard core away from each piece. Peel each piece and cut into 1-inch chunks. Place in bowl with cantaloupes. Peel the bananas and cut into ¼-inch slices; add to the other fruit. Pour the syrup over the fruit and gently toss, cover, and refrigerate for at least ½ hour.

NANCY'S SAUTÉED CHICKEN WITH VINEGAR SAUCE   *35 minutes*

      8 serving pieces of chicken
      salt and freshly ground pepper
      10 tablespoons butter at room temperature
      ½ cup dry white wine*
      ½ cup white wine vinegar*
      4 scallions, thinly sliced

Season the chicken pieces well with salt and pepper. Heat 8 tablespoons of the butter in a large skillet and brown the chicken over medium-high heat for about 5 minutes per side. Reduce heat, cover, and cook the chicken over low heat for 15 minutes. Turn the chicken, re-cover, and continue cooking until done, about 10 minutes. Transfer the chicken to a heatproof serving dish and keep warm in a low oven. Pour off all but 1 tablespoon of the fat from the pan. Add the wine and vinegar, bring to a boil, and reduce the mixture to half. Pour the juices that have accumulated in the serving dish into pan; add the scallions and whisk in the remaining 2 tablespoons of butter. Check seasoning. Spoon the sauce over the chicken.

CREAMED SPINACH WITH MUSHROOMS   *20 minutes*

      2 10-ounce packages chopped frozen spinach
      4 tablespoons butter
      1 medium onion, thinly sliced
      ¼ pound fresh mushrooms, thinly sliced
      1 cup heavy cream
      salt and freshly ground pepper

---

* Red wine and red wine vinegar can be substituted in place of the white wine and white wine vinegar.

Cook the spinach according to package directions. Drain well in a strainer by pressing spinach down with the back of a large spoon. Heat the butter in a large skillet and cook the onion over medium heat for 4 minutes, stirring often. Add the mushrooms and cook for 5 minutes, stirring occasionally. Meanwhile, in a saucepan, bring the heavy cream to a boil and cook it until it thickens, about 5 minutes, whisking often. Add the spinach and cream to the mushroom mixture in the skillet, and combine well. Season to taste with salt and pepper.

•

MENU

Fresh Greens Gazpacho
Chicken in Orange Sauce with Fresh Strawberries
Scalloped Potatoes and Onions
Mint Chocolate Ice Cream with
Chopped Pecans

•

SCALLOPED POTATOES AND ONIONS   *1 hour*

    4 baking potatoes, peeled, and thinly sliced
    4 tablespoons butter, plus butter for pan
    2 medium onions, thinly sliced
    salt and freshly ground pepper
    2 cups milk
    ½ cup heavy cream
    1 cup grated Gruyère or Swiss cheese

Preheat the oven to 400°F. Place half of the sliced potatoes in a buttered au gratin or shallow baking dish. Sprinkle the onions over the potatoes. Cover with the remaining potatoes. Season with salt and pepper to taste. Heat the combined milk and cream until hot, but not boiling. Pour over the potatoes and onions. Sprinkle with the cheese and dot with butter. Bake for 50 minutes until done.

CHICKEN IN ORANGE SAUCE WITH
FRESH STRAWBERRIES   *40 minutes*

    2 chicken breasts, boned, skinned, and cut into bite-size
      pieces

salt and freshly ground pepper
2 tablespoons butter
1 tablespoon vegetable oil
1 medium onion, chopped
1/2 teaspoon ginger
2 tablespoons dry sherry
2/3 cup orange juice
2 teaspoons fresh grated orange rind
1/4 cup chicken broth
1 tablespoon cornstarch
3 tablespoons water
1 1/2 cups fresh sliced strawberries

Pat the chicken pieces dry and season with salt and pepper. Heat the butter and oil in a large skillet and brown the chicken over medium heat for about 5 minutes. Add the onion, ginger, and sherry. Stir and add the remaining ingredients, except for the cornstarch and strawberries. Bring to a boil, reduce heat, and simmer for 25 minutes. Remove the chicken pieces to a serving dish. Dissolve the cornstarch in 3 tablespoons of water, stir into the sauce, and cook until the sauce thickens. Add the strawberries, gently toss, and spoon over the chicken.

FRESH GREENS GAZPACHO   *25 minutes*

2 medium cucumbers, peeled and chopped
1 large green pepper, seeded and chopped
1 bunch watercress, washed, stemmed, and chopped
2 scallions, sliced
1 large garlic clove, crushed
1/4 cup fresh chopped parsley
3 tablespoons olive oil
3 tablespoons red wine vinegar
1 cup chicken consommé
2 cups ice cold water
2 dashes Tabasco sauce
salt and freshly ground pepper
3 hard-cooked eggs, chopped*

Combine the ingredients, except for the eggs, in a large bowl. Place a few cupsful at a time in a blender and puree.

---

* Boil eggs in enough water to cover them for 10 minutes while chopping the vegetables. Cool them under cold running water for 1 minute; peel and chop them.

Pour the pureed mixture into a bowl or tureen. Taste for seasoning. Garnish each bowl with the chopped eggs.

●

MENU

Consommé with Mushrooms and Spinach
Covered Cooked Tender Fried Chicken
Black-Eyed Peas with Bacon
Cranberry Almond Upside Down Cake

●

CRANBERRY ALMOND
UPSIDE DOWN CAKE   *1 hour*

2 cups fresh cranberries
1¼ cups sugar
¼ teaspoon cinnamon
¼ teaspoon ginger
½ cup almond slivers
1 cup sifted all-purpose flour
2 eggs, beaten
¼ cup vegetable oil
½ cup melted butter

Preheat the oven to 325°F. Mix together the cranberries, sugar, cinnamon, ginger, and almond slivers. Place the mixture in a well-greased 9 × 9-inch cake pan. Combine the remaining ingredients well and pour over the cranberry mixture. Bake for about 50 minutes until the cake is done.

COVERED COOKED TENDER
FRIED CHICKEN   *55 minutes*

8 plump serving pieces of chicken
salt and freshly ground pepper
flour
2 cups vegetable oil

Season each piece of the chicken with salt and pepper. Coat the chicken with flour and shake off excess. Heat the oil in a large skillet and add the chicken. Reduce the heat to a simmer, cover, and cook for 30 minutes. Turn the chicken pieces and re-cover. Cook 10 minutes; turn the chicken, re-cover, and cook 10 more minutes.

NOTE: Substitute 2 sticks of butter for the oil in this recipe and cook exactly the same way. The result is a rich, crisp, butter-flavored chicken.

BLACK-EYED PEAS WITH BACON *15 minutes*

    2 10-ounce packages frozen black-eyed peas
    ⅓ pound thick slice of bacon, cut into small cubes
    pinch rosemary
    pinch thyme
    salt and freshly ground pepper to taste

Cook the black-eyed peas according to the package directions, just until tender. Meanwhile, fry the bacon cubes until crisp. Drain. Drain the peas and place in a bowl with the bacon and herbs. Season with salt and pepper and toss.

CONSOMMÉ WITH MUSHROOMS AND SPINACH *10 minutes*

    4 cups canned consommé
    ¼ pound fresh small mushrooms, thinly sliced
    1 cup coarsely chopped spinach
    2 tablespoons dry sherry

Bring the consommé to a boil in a saucepan. Add the mushrooms and spinach with the sherry. Stir, and cook the soup for 5 minutes, stirring occasionally.

•

MENU

Parmesan Chicken
Tomato, Mozzarella, and Basil Platter
Dilled Potato Salad
Cantaloupe with Lemon Sherbet

•

PARMESAN CHICKEN

1 hour

8 serving pieces of chicken
4 tablespoons melted butter
1 cup herbed bread crumbs
½ cup freshly grated Parmesan cheese
salt and freshly ground pepper to taste

Preheat the oven to 375°F. Brush the chicken pieces with the butter. Combine the bread crumbs and cheese and season with salt and pepper. Coat the chicken pieces evenly with the mixture. Place the chicken on a lightly greased baking sheet and cook in the oven for 50 minutes.

DILLED POTATO SALAD

30 minutes

2 pounds small new potatoes, halved
⅓ cup olive or vegetable oil
2 tablespoons white wine vinegar
2 teaspoons Dijon mustard
1 tablespoon fresh chopped dill, or ½ teaspoon dried dill
salt and freshly ground pepper to taste

In a saucepan bring 2 quarts of water to a boil. Add the potatoes and cook over medium heat for about 20 minutes, or until tender. Drain well and place in a large bowl. In a small bowl beat together the remaining ingredients and pour over the potatoes. Gently toss. Taste for seasoning.

TOMATO, MOZZARELLA, AND BASIL PLATTER

10 minutes

3 large fresh ripe tomatoes, thinly sliced
1 pound mozzarella, thinly sliced
2 dozen fresh coarsely chopped basil leaves
3 scallions, thinly sliced
⅓ cup imported olive oil
salt and freshly ground pepper to taste

Arrange alternating layers of the sliced tomatoes and cheese on a platter. Top with the chopped basil and sprinkle with the scallions, olive oil, salt, and pepper.

●

MENU

Sweet Potato Soup
Cindy Hubbard's Jamaican Chicken
Rice Cooked in Chicken Broth
Grilled Pineapple

●

CINDY HUBBARD'S
JAMAICAN CHICKEN

1 hour

12 serving pieces of chicken
1 large onion, grated
1 large green pepper, seeded and chopped
2 large cloves garlic, crushed
1 teaspoon thyme
1 teaspoon salt
½ teaspoon freshly ground pepper
4 tablespoons oil, or as needed
2 cups heated chicken broth
3 tablespoons butter

Place the chicken pieces in a large shallow baking pan. Sprinkle with the onion, green pepper, garlic, thyme, salt, and pepper. Turn several times to coat each piece of chicken evenly. Remove the chicken pieces and scrape off the vegetables and save. Preheat the oven to 400°F. Heat the oil in a large skillet and brown the chicken on both sides, a few pieces at a time. Place the browned chicken in a large roasting pan and cover with the vegetable marinade. Pour the stock over the chicken and dot with butter. Cover with foil and cook for 45 minutes until tender.

SWEET POTATO SOUP

40 minutes

2 tablespoons butter
1 tablespoon vegetable oil
1 cup chopped onion
2 stalks celery, chopped
1½ pounds sweet potatoes, peeled and thinly sliced
5 cups chicken stock or broth
few pinches of fresh nutmeg
½ teaspoon salt or to taste
freshly ground pepper
¾ cup heavy cream
1 cup toasted croutons

Heat the butter and oil in a large saucepan. Sauté the onion and celery for 5 minutes, stirring often. Add the remaining ingredients, except for the cream and croutons, and bring to a boil. Simmer for 25 minutes. Puree in a blender a few cupsful at a time. Return to a clean saucepan and stir in the cream. Heat thoroughly. Taste for salt and pepper. Garnish with the toasted croutons.

RICE COOKED IN CHICKEN BROTH

30 minutes

1 cup long-grain rice
chicken broth
fresh chopped parsley

Cook 1 cup of long-grain rice according to the package directions, substituting chicken broth for the water in the recipe. When cooked, sprinkle with 1 tablespoon fresh chopped parsley and toss.

GRILLED PINEAPPLE

15 minutes

1 fresh pineapple
thick natural honey

Peel the pineapple and core. Heat the broiler. Cut the pineapple into ½-inch-thick rings and brush with honey. Place in a shallow baking pan and cook under the broiler until browned.

MENU

Barbecued Chicken
Braised Onions with Rum
Vegetable Salad with Parsley and Garlic Vinaigrette Sauce
Strawberry Waffle Cakes

•

BARBECUED CHICKEN

12 serving pieces of chicken
1 lemon, thinly sliced

BARBECUE SAUCE:

1 medium onion, chopped
2 garlic cloves, crushed
2 stalks celery, chopped
2 bay leaves, crumbled
1 cup ketchup
1 teaspoon mustard
½ cup red wine vinegar
¼ cup Worcestershire sauce
1 cup water
1 tablespoon chili powder
1 teaspoon paprika
freshly ground pepper

Preheat the oven to 375°F. Combine the Barbecue Sauce ingredients in a saucepan and bring to a boil, reduce heat and simmer for 10 minutes. Strain the sauce. Place the chicken in a shallow baking dish and cover with the sauce. Cook for 40 minutes until browned and tender.

BRAISED ONIONS WITH RUM   *25 minutes*

2 tablespoons butter
1 tablespoon vegetable oil
1 large yellow onion, peeled and cut into 4 equally thick
   slices, kept intact
¼ cup dark rum
¼ cup chicken broth
2 tablespoons brown sugar

195

Heat the butter and oil in a large skillet with an ovenproof handle. Sauté the onion slices over medium-high heat until browned on one side. Carefully turn each slice. Pour in the rum and broth, cover, and simmer for 15 minutes. Heat the broiler. Sprinkle equal amounts of the brown sugar over the onions and pass under the broiler until golden brown and sizzling.

VEGETABLE SALAD WITH PARSLEY AND GARLIC VINAIGRETTE SAUCE   *15 minutes*

  ½ pound fresh green beans, ends trimmed, or 1 10-ounce
     package frozen green beans
  salt
  8 fresh mushrooms
  12 cherry tomatoes

  ### PARSLEY AND GARLIC VINAIGRETTE SAUCE:

  5 tablespoons olive or vegetable oil
  1½ tablespoons red wine vinegar
  1 teaspoon Dijon mustard
  ¼ teaspoon salt
  freshly ground pepper to taste
  1 clove garlic, quartered
  1 tablespoon fresh chopped parsley

Drop the green beans into 2 quarts of lightly salted boiling water and cook for 6 minutes until crisp but tender. (If using frozen green beans, cook them in lightly salted boiling water according to the package directions for half the time suggested on the package.) Meanwhile, cut the mushrooms into thin slices and halve the cherry tomatoes; set aside. Prepare Vinaigrette Sauce: Whisk together the ingredients in a medium-size bowl. Drain the green beans. Remove the pieces of garlic from the sauce and add the beans. Toss. Add the mushrooms and tomatoes.

STRAWBERRY WAFFLE CAKES   *10 minutes*

  2 pints fresh strawberries, hulled
  8 round individual frozen waffles
  1 cup heavy cream
  2 tablespoons sugar

Slice 1 pint of strawberries. Toast the waffles. Meanwhile,

whip the cream halfway and add the sugar. Continue whipping the cream until stiff but not dry. Top 4 of the waffles with a little whipped cream and equal portions of the sliced strawberries and place 1 waffle over each. Spoon a little of the whipped cream over each and top with equal amounts of the whole strawberries. Top with remaining whipped cream.

●

MENU

Cornish Hens with Fruit Stuffing and
Red Currant Glaze
Fried Potato Nests with Curried Vegetable Ragout
Mixed Green Salad
Vanilla Ice Cream with Semisweet Chocolate Shavings
and Almonds

●

CORNISH HENS WITH FRUIT STUFFING
AND RED CURRANT GLAZE   *1 hour*

6 Cornish game hens
salt and pepper
1 11-ounce package mixed dried fruit, chopped
1 orange, peeled, including white pith, seeded, and chopped
juice of 1 lemon
2 tablespoons melted butter

RED CURRANT GLAZE:

1 cup red currant jelly
2 tablespoons sugar
2 tablespoons Grand Marnier or water

Preheat the oven to 400°F. Season the hens inside and out with salt and pepper. Combine the chopped fruit and toss in the lemon juice. Stuff birds. Tie the legs together and fold the wings back. Place in a roasting pan and baste with the butter. Roast in the oven for 50 minutes or until tender. Five minutes before the hens are done, prepare the Red Currant Glaze by bringing the jelly, sugar, and Grand Marnier or water to a boil in a saucepan; cook, stirring, for 2 minutes. Cool the Cornish hens for 2 minutes and brush with the glaze.

Serves 6.

FRIED POTATO NESTS WITH CURRIED VEGETABLE RAGOUT   *25 minutes*

A bird's nest fryer is a specially designed cooking utensil which consists of two different sized, curved wire baskets, each having a long handle. The smaller basket fits into the larger one. Metal clamps hold the baskets together when not in use, but while frying the potato nests, the cook holds the baskets together. The fried potato nests can be filled with a variety of hot seafood, meat, or vegetable mixtures, and they can be served at lunch for a light meal, or as a first course, or with an entrée. Regardless of what course you select to serve them as, they make a spectacular presentation considering how easy it is to cook them.

FRIED POTATO NESTS:

4 medium Idaho baking potatoes, peeled and shredded
1 quart vegetable oil for deep frying

Heat the vegetable oil in a large heavy saucepan or fryer with 5-inch sides. Evenly place about ¾ cup of the shredded potatoes in the larger basket. Press the smaller basket, bottom side down, over the potatoes and hold firmly together. Lower the filled potato nest fryer into the oil and cook until the potatoes turn light brown. Lift out, drain on paper towels, and release the potato nest from the basket. Return the potato nest to the hot fat, holding it down with a large slotted spoon, until golden brown. Remove and drain. A few shreds of potatoes will be released from the fryer; skim them out with the slotted spoon. Repeat the same procedure for making 5 more nests. They can rest at room temperature for 30 minutes before serving them; reheat them in 325°F. oven for 5 minutes and fill them with Curried Vegetable Ragout. (See recipe below, after Mixed Green Salad.)

MIXED GREEN SALAD   *10 minutes*

1 large Boston lettuce, washed, dried, and broken into bite-size pieces
2 Bibb lettuce, washed, dried, and broken into bite-size pieces
½ cup vegetable oil
1 tablespoon red wine vinegar

198

1 teaspoon Dijon mustard
salt and freshly ground pepper

Place the lettuce in a salad bowl. Combine the remaining
ingredients and pour it over the salad and toss.

CURRIED VEGETABLE RAGOUT   *25 minutes*

2 carrots, peeled and thinly sliced
6 asparagus spears, cut diagonally into 1-inch lengths
salt
6 tablespoons butter
2 tablespoons flour
1½ cups light cream
freshly ground pepper
1 medium onion, finely chopped
½ pound sliced mushrooms
1 tablespoon curry powder
¼ cup dry white wine

Cook the carrots and asparagus in separate saucepans covered with lightly salted boiling water for 5 minutes each.
Drain and set aside. Heat 2 tablespoons of the butter in a
saucepan and stir in the flour with a wire whisk. Cook for 1
minute. Stir in the cream and cook until the sauce thickens
and is smooth. Season with salt and pepper and set aside. In
a skillet heat remaining 4 tablespoons of butter and add
onion. Cook over medium heat for 5 minutes, stirring often.
Add the mushrooms and curry powder, and cook for 5
minutes. Add wine and bring to a boil. Reheat the sauce and
add the mushroom mixture and the vegetables. Combine
well and taste for salt and pepper.

•

MENU

Cornish Game Hens Stuffed with Cabbage and Onion
Carrots with Marjoram
Romaine and Tomato Salad with Cucumber Dressing
Fruit Plate Cruz Bay

•

CORNISH GAME HENS STUFFED WITH CABBAGE AND ONION
1 hour

4 Cornish game hens
salt and freshly ground pepper
4 tablespoons butter
2 cups fresh chopped cabbage
1 medium onion, chopped
3 tablespoons dry white wine
½ teaspoon caraway seeds
4 slices white bread

Preheat the oven to 400°F. Season the hens inside liberally with salt and pepper. Heat 2½ tablespoons of the butter in a large skillet and sauté the chopped cabbage and onion for about 4 minutes, until just limp. Add the wine and cook for 1 minute. Stir in the caraway seeds and remove from the heat. Stuff the birds with equal amounts of stuffing. Tie each hen's legs together and fold the wings back. Rub the remaining 1½ tablespoons butter over hens. Place in oven and cook for 50 minutes.

ROMAINE AND TOMATO SALAD WITH CUCUMBER DRESSING
10 minutes

3 cups romaine lettuce pieces
2 medium tomatoes, thinly sliced

CUCUMBER DRESSING

1 cucumber
½ cup mayonnaise
1 teaspoon fresh lemon juice
1 tablespoon fresh chopped parsley
salt and freshly ground pepper

Peel cucumber and cut in half lengthwise. Scoop out seeds in center of each piece with a teaspoon. Grate cucumber and mix with remaining ingredients. Cover and refrigerate.

Line 4 individual salad bowls with equal amounts of the lettuce. Arrange the tomatoes over the lettuce. Refrigerate the salads until ready to serve. At that time, spoon equal amounts of the Cucumber Dressing over the tomatoes.

FRUIT PLATE CRUZ BAY

15 minutes

2 navel oranges
1 grapefruit
2 kiwi fruit, peeled and thinly sliced
1 pint vanilla ice cream
8 thin finger wafers

Peel the oranges with a sharp knife, including the white pith and the outer skins. Cut the oranges into ¼-inch slices crosswise. Remove any seeds. Peel the grapefruit in the same manner. With a small sharp knife remove the grapefruit sections by cutting along each side of section to the center of the fruit to release the sections. Discard any seeds. Refrigerate the kiwis, oranges, and grapefruit until serving dessert. Arrange equal amounts of the fruit slices and sections across 4 dessert plates. Add 2 small scoops of ice cream to each plate, along with 2 wafers.

CARROTS WITH MARJORAM

10 minutes

6 carrots, peeled and cut diagonally into ¼-inch slices
salt
2 tablespoons butter
freshly ground pepper
½ teaspoon marjoram

Drop the carrots into saucepan with 3 cups of lightly salted rapidly boiling water. Cook for 5 minutes. Drain. Heat the butter in a saucepan, add the carrots and season them with salt, pepper, and marjoram. Gently toss and cook over medium-low heat for 1 minute.

•

MENU

Creamy Fresh Potato Soup
Butter and Herb Roasted Cornish Game Hens
Zucchini, Carrots, and Onion
Canned Pear Halves with Pear Brandy and
Whipped Cream

•

BUTTER AND HERB ROASTED
CORNISH GAME HENS   *1 hour*

      4 Cornish game hens
      salt and freshly ground pepper
      1 medium onion, chopped
      1 garlic clove, crushed
      ¼ cup fresh chopped parsley
      1 teaspoon tarragon
      1 teaspoon sage
      4 tablespoons cold butter, plus ¼ cup melted butter

Preheat the oven to 400°F. Season the hens inside and out with salt and pepper. In a bowl combine the onion, garlic, and herbs. Spoon equal amounts into each hen cavity and add 1 tablespoon of the cold butter. Tie the legs together and fold the wings back. Place the hens in roasting pan and brush with the melted butter. Cook them in the oven for 50 minutes, basting with melted butter and the pan juices twice during cooking time.

CREAMY FRESH POTATO SOUP   *30 minutes*

      2 tablespoons butter, plus butter for garnish (optional)
      1 medium onion, chopped
      2 cups cubed potatoes
      1½ cups water
      2 cups chicken stock or broth
      salt and freshly ground pepper
      1 cup heavy cream
      fresh chopped parsley

Heat the butter in a saucepan and add the onion. Cook over medium heat for 4 minutes, stirring often. Add the potatoes, water, chicken stock, salt, and pepper and bring to a boil. Reduce the heat and simmer for 20 minutes until the potatoes are tender. Stir in the cream and heat thoroughly. Check the seasoning. Garnish with the parsley and, if desired, a dot of butter for each bowl of the soup.

ZUCCHINI, CARROTS, AND ONION   *15 minutes*

    2 tablespoons butter
    1 medium onion, chopped
    2 carrots, peeled and thinly sliced
    2 medium zucchini, cut into ⅛-inch slices
    1 tablespoon dry white wine
    ¼ cup chicken broth
    salt and freshly ground pepper to taste
    fresh chopped parsley

Heat the butter in a skillet. Sauté the onion for 5 minutes,
stirring often. Add the carrots, zucchini, wine, and broth.
Bring to a boil, reduce the heat, and season with salt and
pepper. Cover and simmer for 6 minutes. Uncover, add the
parsley, toss, and serve.

•

MENU

Cream of Watercress Soup
Lemon Roast Cornish Game Hens
Lyonnaise Potatoes
Fresh Pineapple Boats with Grand Marnier

•

LEMON ROAST CORNISH GAME HENS   *1 hour*

    4 Cornish game hens
    salt and freshly ground pepper
    4 teaspoons oregano
    4 large garlic cloves, peeled and halved
    1 lemon, quartered
    ¼ cup melted butter
    ¼ cup fresh lemon juice
    1 teaspoon paprika

Preheat the oven to 400°F. Season the hens inside and out
with salt and pepper. Place 1 teaspoon oregano, 2 halves of
the garlic, and 1 quarter of the lemon into each cavity. Tie
the legs together and fold the wings back. Place the hens in a
roasting pan and brush with combined melted butter, lemon
juice, and paprika. Cook in the oven for 15 minutes; reduce
the heat to 375°F. and baste. Cook for 30 minutes or until
tender, basting again after 15 minutes.

CREAM OF WATERCRESS SOUP   *25 minutes*

    1 bunch watercress, chopped
    1 small onion, minced
    1½ cups cubed potatoes
    3½ cups chicken broth or stock
    1 cup heavy cream
    salt and freshly ground pepper

Place the watercress, onion, and potatoes in a large saucepan. Add the broth and bring to a boil. Reduce the heat and simmer for 20 minutes. Puree the mixture, a few cupsful at a time, in a blender. Return to a clean pan and add the heavy cream. Bring to a boil and season with salt and pepper to taste.

LYONNAISE POTATOES   *30 minutes*

    2 pounds potatoes, peeled and cut into ¼-inch-thick slices
    9 tablespoons butter
    3 medium onions, thinly sliced
    paprika
    salt and freshly ground pepper
    1 tablespoon fresh chopped parsley

Boil the potatoes in enough water to cover them for 12 minutes and drain them well. Meanwhile, heat 4 tablespoons of the butter in a heavy skillet and cook the onions over medium heat for about 10 minutes, stirring often. Season with paprika, salt, and pepper to taste and remove from the pan to a side dish. Wipe the pan clean with paper towels. Add the 5 remaining tablespoons butter and sauté the potatoes over medium heat until evenly browned on both sides. Return the onions to the pan and gently toss them to combine well. Season to taste and sprinkle with the parsley.

FRESH PINEAPPLE BOATS WITH
GRAND MARNIER   *15 minutes*

    1 whole fresh ripe pineapple
    4 tablespoons Grand Marnier

With a sharp knife, cut through the pineapple and stalk lengthwise. Cut each half in half again, carefully cutting through the stalk. Cut away the tough core center from each piece. With a small sharp knife cut the pineapple meat away from the shell on each side of the individual pieces. Leave the released pineapple in the shell and cut it into 8 slices crosswise. With a finger, push one slice to the left beginning at one end, and the next slice to the right, and so on until a zigzag effect is created. Repeat with the 3 remaining pieces. Sprinkle each with 1 tablespoon of Grand Marnier.

•

MENU

Fresh Endive Leaves Stuffed with Curried Tuna
Sherried Cornish Hens au Gratin
Risi Bisi
Mixed Fruit Bowl

•

SHERRIED CORNISH HENS AU GRATIN   *1 hour*

4 Cornish game hens, halved and backbones removed
salt and freshly ground pepper
3 tablespoons butter
1 medium-large onion, thinly sliced
¾ cup grated Cheddar cheese
½ cup plain dry bread crumbs
1 teaspoon seasoned salt
½ cup chicken broth
½ cup dry sherry
2 tablespoons vegetable oil

Preheat the oven to 375°F. Season the hen halves with salt and pepper on both sides. Heat the butter in a skillet and cook the onion over medium heat for 5 minutes, stirring occasionally. Meanwhile, mix together the cheese, bread crumbs, and seasoned salt. Transfer the onion to the bottom of a large roasting pan. Place the hen halves over the onion, skin side up. Pour in the combined broth and sherry. Brush the birds with the oil and sprinkle with the cheese mixture. Cook in the oven for 45 minutes.

RISI BISI

30 minutes

½ teaspoon salt, plus salt for seasoning
1 cup long-grain rice
1 10-ounce package frozen peas, cooked and drained
1 tablespoon butter
freshly ground pepper

Bring 2½ cups of water to a boil in a saucepan. Season with ½ teaspoon of salt. Add the rice, stir, cover, and simmer approximately 25 minutes until tender. Stir in the peas and butter. Season with salt and pepper to taste.

FRESH ENDIVE LEAVES STUFFED WITH CURRIED TUNA

15 minutes

1 7-ounce can white meat tuna, drained
½ cup mayonnaise
1 teaspoon fresh lemon juice
1 teaspoon soy sauce
2 tablespoons sesame seeds
1 tablespoon fresh snipped chives
2 teaspoons curry powder
¼ teaspoon turmeric
salt and freshly ground pepper
16 whole fresh Belgian endive leaves
3 tablespoons fresh finely chopped parsley

Mix together all the ingredients in a bowl except for the endive leaves and parsley.* Place a rounded teaspoon of the mixture at the stem end of each endive and spread it slightly up the leaf. Fill all the leaves and sprinkle the curried tuna with parsley.

NOTE: Curried tuna is excellent for sandwiches or as a stuffing for tomatoes or avocados. For variety, add minced green pepper or celery.

---

* Mixture can be covered and refrigerated until used.

·

MENU

Fruit Gazpacho
Ginger and Rum Roasted Cornish Game Hens
Whipped Sweet Potatoes with Orange
Lemon and Lime Sherbet

·

GINGER AND RUM ROASTED
CORNISH GAME HENS   *1 hour*

    4 Cornish game hens
    salt and freshly ground pepper
    1 large garlic clove, crushed
    ¼ cup honey
    ¼ cup chicken stock
    ¼ cup soy sauce
    ¼ cup rum
    1 tablespoon peanut or vegetable oil
    1 teaspoon ground ginger

Preheat the oven to 375°F. Season the Cornish hens well
with salt and pepper inside and out. Combine the remaining
ingredients in bowl. Spoon 2 tablespoons of the mixture
inside each hen. Tie the legs together and fold the wings
back. Place the hens in a roasting pan. Brush each hen
liberally with the sauce. Roast for 55 minutes or until tender,
basting twice during cooking time with the sauce.

WHIPPED SWEET POTATOES
WITH ORANGE   *40 minutes*

    4 medium sweet potatoes, peeled and quartered
    2 oranges
    2 teaspoons grated orange rind
    5 tablespoons butter
    ¼ teaspoon cinnamon
    ¼ teaspoon nutmeg
    2 tablespoons heavy cream
    salt and freshly ground pepper to taste
    ¼ cup brown sugar

Boil the sweet potatoes until tender. Drain and mash or rice them in a large bowl. Stir in the juice of the oranges, orange rind, 3 tablespoons butter, spices, and cream. Season with salt and pepper. Combine well and turn into a lightly greased shallow baking dish. Smooth the top with back of a spoon. Sprinkle with brown sugar and dot with the remaining 2 tablespoons of butter. Bake for about 20 minutes until the top sizzles.

FRUIT GAZPACHO   *10 minutes*

    1 pint strawberries, stemmed, chopped, and chilled
    2 Delicious apples, cored, peeled, and chopped
    1 16-ounce can chilled pitted Bing cherries with liquid
    2 cups chilled cranberry juice
    1 cup chilled orange juice
    2 tablespoons red wine vinegar
    sugar to taste
    1 cup sour cream

Combine the strawberries, apples, and cherries with the liquid in a bowl and mix. Puree the mixture in a blender a few cupsful at a time. Pour into bowl and combine with the cranberry and orange juice, vinegar, and sugar to taste. Refrigerate until served. Garnish each bowl with a dollop of the sour cream.

•

MENU

Tarragon and Lemon Flavored Roast Chicken
Wild Rice with Mushrooms and Cream
Asparagus Parmesan
Fresh Pears Stuffed with Brie and Pecans

•

TARRAGON AND LEMON FLAVORED
ROAST CHICKEN   *1 hour*

    1 3-pound chicken
    salt and freshly ground pepper
    1 lemon, halved
    2 teaspoons tarragon

1 medium onion, chopped
¼ cup dry white wine or dry vermouth
1 tablespoon vegetable oil

Preheat the oven to 425°F. Place the chicken in a small roasting pan. Season the chicken inside and out with salt and pepper. Squeeze half of the lemon into the body cavity and fit the lemon half into the cavity, stem end in first. Sprinkle the inside with tarragon and add the onion. Pour the wine into the cavity. (Some of the wine will fall into the pan.) Combine the remaining juice of the lemon half with the vegetable oil and brush or rub over the chicken. Cook in the oven for 55 minutes.

WILD RICE WITH MUSHROOMS AND CREAM
55 minutes

½ teaspoon salt
1 cup wild rice
4 tablespoons butter
1 medium onion, chopped
¼ pound fresh mushrooms, chopped
½ cup heavy cream
freshly ground pepper

Bring 3½ cups of water to a boil in a saucepan. Add the salt and rice. Cover and simmer for 50 minutes. Meanwhile, heat the butter in a skillet and sauté the onion for 5 minutes, stirring occasionally. Add the mushrooms and cook for 5 minutes. Remove from the heat and set aside. When the rice has cooked 50 minutes, drain in a colander and return to the saucepan. Stir in the mushroom mixture, heavy cream, and season with pepper. Cook over low heat for 2 minutes, stirring twice during cooking time until thoroughly heated.

ASPARAGUS PARMESAN
20 minutes

20 stalks fresh asparagus
salt
⅓ cup fresh grated Parmesan cheese
freshly ground pepper
4 tablespoons butter
¼ cup chicken stock or broth

Bring 2½ quarts of water to a boil in a large pot. Meanwhile, cut off the asparagus stem ends and peel the asparagus stalks with a vegetable peeler. (This process will take about 10 minutes.) Drop the asparagus into the lightly salted boiling water and cook for exactly 5 minutes over medium-high heat. Drain. Place the asparagus in a shallow baking dish. Sprinkle with the cheese and pepper and dot with the butter. Pour the chicken stock into the side of the dish. Cook under the broiler for about 1 minute, until the top is golden.

FRESH PEARS STUFFED WITH BRIE AND PECANS

15 minutes

    4 firm ripe pears
    6 ounces softened ripe Brie
    3 tablespoons chopped pecans

Cut ¼ inch off bottom of each pear. With a small sharp knife, cut the core out, being careful not to cut through the skin. With a small spoon remove all the center pulp, leaving ½ inch attached to the skin. In a bowl beat the cheese and the pulp with a fork. Stir in the nuts until well blended. Immediately spoon equal amounts of the mixture inside the pears. Place the cut sides on a plate and refrigerate. When ready to serve, slice each pear crosswise into 4 slices and arrange on a dessert plate.

•

MENU

Cream of Zucchini Soup
Roast Chicken with Bacon
Fried Okra
Poached Peaches with Raspberry Puree

•

ROAST CHICKEN WITH BACON

1 hour

    1 3-pound roasting chicken
    salt and freshly ground pepper
    6 strips bacon

Preheat the oven to 425°F. Season the chicken inside with salt and pepper. Fold the chicken wings back and tie the legs together. Arrange the bacon strips over the chicken crosswise, tucking the ends under the chicken. Cook for 30 minutes. Reduce the heat to 350°F. and remove the bacon strips. Cook for about 20 minutes until golden and tender. Carve the chicken and garnish with the crisp cooked bacon.

CREAM OF ZUCCHINI SOUP   *15 minutes*

    4 tablespoons butter
    4 cups grated zucchini
    1 medium onion, grated
    3 cups chicken stock or broth
    3 tablespoons dry white wine
    1 cup heavy cream
    salt and freshly ground pepper
    fresh chopped parsley

Heat the butter in a large saucepan. Add the zucchini and onion and cook over low heat for 5 minutes. Add the chicken broth and wine. Bring to a boil; reduce heat and simmer for 5 minutes. Puree in a blender. Return to a clean pan and add the cream. Heat thoroughly, season to taste with salt and pepper, and garnish with parsley.

POACHED PEACHES WITH
RASPBERRY PUREE   *15 minutes*

    4 ripe firm peaches
    1 10-ounce package frozen raspberries, thawed
    2 tablespoons framboise (optional)
    3 tablespoons sugar

Fill a saucepan with 2 quarts of water and bring it to a boil. Simmer the peaches for 10 minutes. Remove the peaches with a slotted spoon and cool. Peel the peaches with the aid of a small sharp knife. Puree the raspberries with the framboise and sugar and spoon over the peaches. Refrigerate until served.

FRIED OKRA

1 pound fresh okra, trimmed and cut into ½-inch-thick slices
flour
1 egg
2 tablespoons water
cornmeal
½ cup vegetable oil
salt and freshly ground pepper

Dust the okra slices with flour and dip into the egg mixed with water. Coat with cornmeal. (This will be messy, so expect that.) Heat the oil in a large skillet and fry the okra until crisp on each side. Season with salt and pepper to taste.

●

MENU

Chicken Loaf
Creamy Mashed Potatoes
Italian Green Beans and Carrots
Cheddar Cheese and Apples

●

CHICKEN LOAF
1 hour

1½ pounds chicken breast, boned and ground
1 green pepper, seeded and diced
1 medium onion, finely chopped
12 saltines, crushed
2 eggs
4 tablespoons melted butter
½ teaspoon seasoned salt
freshly ground black pepper
½ teaspoon thyme
1 teaspoon paprika
1 teaspoon Dijon mustard
1 tablespoon vegetable oil

Preheat oven to 375°F. Combine all ingredients well except for the oil and 2 tablespoons of the butter. Grease a meatloaf pan with the oil and fill with the mixture; smooth top evenly with the back of a spoon. Sprinkle the remaining butter over top. Cover it with foil and place the loaf pan in a large pan with hot water coming halfway up the side of the pan. Bake in the oven for 30 minutes, remove the foil, and cook approximately 20 minutes more, until done. Let it rest 10 minutes before slicing.

NOTE: Chicken Loaf makes excellent hot or cold sandwiches. It also is a fine first course served over lettuce with gherkins or olives.

CREAMY MASHED POTATOES   *25 minutes*

    5 medium boiling potatoes, peeled and quartered
    3 tablespoons butter
    ½ cup milk
    salt and freshly ground pepper

Drop the potatoes into enough boiling water to cover them. Cook at a low boil for about 15 minutes, until tender. Mash the potatoes with a ricer. Place the potatoes in a large bowl and add the butter and milk. Beat vigorously until smooth and fluffy; season with salt and pepper to taste.

ITALIAN GREEN BEANS AND CARROTS   *15 minutes*

    1 pound carrots, peeled and thinly sliced
    1 10-ounce package frozen Italian green beans
    2 tablespoons melted butter
    salt and freshly ground pepper to taste
    ½ teaspoon thyme

Cook the carrots in boiling water for 5 minutes. Meanwhile, in a separate saucepan, cook the beans according to the package directions, just until tender. Drain both. Combine the vegetables in a bowl with the butter, salt, pepper, and thyme. Toss.

•

MENU

Catherine's Italian Onion Soup
Paisley Barbecue Chicken Wings
Sautéed Escarole
Vanilla Ice Cream with Brandied Bing Cherries

•

CATHERINE'S ITALIAN ONION SOUP   *1 hour*

    1 16-ounce can whole tomatoes, with liquid
    6 tablespoons butter
    2 tablespoons olive or vegetable oil
    2 large onions, thinly sliced
    2 garlic cloves, crushed
    2 tablespoons flour
    4 cups heated beef broth
    1/2 teaspoon oregano
    1 tablespoon fresh chopped parsley
    salt and freshly ground pepper
    6 1-inch-thick slices Italian bread
    1 cup shredded mozzarella cheese
    6 tablespoons fresh grated Parmesan cheese

Puree the tomatoes and liquid in a blender. Set aside. Heat
the butter and oil in a large pot and cook the onions and
garlic over medium heat until the onions are softened, about
20 minutes. Sprinkle the onions with the flour and stir often.
Cook 3 minutes. Stir in the broth, pureed tomatoes, oregano,
and parsley. Season to taste with salt and pepper. Bring to a
boil, reduce heat, and simmer for 20 minutes. Heat the
broiler and toast the bread under the broiler on one side.
Ladle the soup into 6 ovenproof soup crocks. Place the
bread on top of the soup, toasted side down. Sprinkle each
with equal amounts of the mozzarella and Parmesan cheese.
Pass under the broiler on a baking sheet until the cheese
sizzles and is golden. Serve immediately.

NOTE: Use the broiler after chicken has cooked.

PAISLEY BARBECUE CHICKEN WINGS   *50 minutes*

    12 chicken wings

    PAISLEY BARBECUE SAUCE:

    1/2 cup tomato sauce
    1/2 cup chili sauce
    1/4 cup red wine vinegar
    1 teaspoon Dijon mustard
    1 tablespoon chili powder
    1 teaspoon paprika
    1/4 cup brown sugar
    1 medium onion, grated

Preheat the oven to 350°F. Cut the chicken wings into 3

pieces each at the joints and discard the wing tips. Combine the ingredients for the Paisley Barbecue Sauce in a bowl and add the chicken wing pieces. Turn them to coat evenly. Place the wings in a greased roasting pan or on a baking sheet and cook in the oven for about 40 minutes, until tender.

SAUTÉED ESCAROLE   *20 minutes*

    1 large escarole, quartered lengthwise
    1 tablespoon butter
    2 tablespoons olive oil
    1 large garlic clove, quartered

Bring 2 quarts of water to a boil in a Dutch oven. Add the escarole and cook it over high heat for 4 minutes. Remove and drain. Cut off the tough stem ends. Fold each escarole quarter into a small packet about 4 × 4 inches. Heat the butter and oil in a skillet with the garlic and add the escarole. Cook, covered, for 8 minutes over low heat. Discard the garlic.

•

MENU

Ground Chicken and Broccoli Miniature Cutlets
Spinach and Cheese Soufflé
French Bread
Poached Pears

•

SPINACH AND CHEESE SOUFFLÉ   *1 hour*

    3 tablespoons butter, plus butter for pan
    2 tablespoons freshly grated Parmesan cheese
    4 tablespoons flour
    1½ cups milk
    2 10-ounce packages frozen chopped spinach, thawed and
      well drained
    1 cup grated Cheddar cheese
    ½ teaspoon salt
    freshly ground pepper
    2 tablespoons grated onion
    pinch of nutmeg
    6 eggs, separated

Preheat the oven to 350°F. Prepare the collar for the soufflé dish. Tear off a sheet of aluminum foil that will fit around a 2-quart soufflé dish. Fold the foil in half lengthwise and lightly butter one side of the foil. Butter the soufflé dish. With buttered side of foil facing in, fit the collar around the top of the soufflé dish and secure it with kitchen string. Place the Parmesan cheese in the dish and coat the inside of the dish and foil by turning in a circle and tilting dish. Knock out any extra cheese and set the dish in the refrigerator until ready to use it.

In a saucepan, heat the butter and whisk in the flour. Cook it over medium heat for 2 minutes, stirring. Gradually add the milk, stirring, and cook until the sauce is thick. Stir in the well-drained spinach, Cheddar cheese, salt, pepper, onion, and nutmeg. Cook for about 4 minutes and remove from the heat. Beat 5 egg yolks well. (Use the extra yolk for another recipe or discard.) Add a little of the spinach mixture to the yolks and beat. Add this mixture to spinach mixture and combine. Remove the prepared soufflé dish from the refrigerator and place it in an area where you are going to beat the egg whites. Beat the egg whites until stiff and immediately fold the spinach sauce into the whites. Pour into the soufflé dish. Bake in the oven for about 45 minutes.

GROUND CHICKEN AND BROCCOLI MINIATURE CUTLETS

30 minutes

1 10-ounce package frozen broccoli, cooked and drained
1½ pounds chicken breasts, ground
½ cup plain dry bread crumbs, plus bread crumbs for
   breading
3 eggs
¼ teaspoon fresh grated nutmeg
salt and freshly ground pepper
flour
3 tablespoons vegetable oil
3 tablespoons butter

Finely chop the cooked broccoli to coarse cut in a food processor fitted with the steel blade, or ½ a cup at a time in a blender. In a large bowl combine the chicken, broccoli, ½ cup bread crumbs, 1 egg, and nutmeg. Season with salt and pepper to taste. Divide the mixture in half and roll each half into 2 1-inch-thick sausage-shaped pieces. Dust each with flour and dip into the remaining 2 beaten eggs, coating them evenly. Roll in the bread crumbs. Heat the oil and butter in a large skillet. Cook the rolls until golden brown on all sides. Carefully remove them and drain. Let rolls rest 5 minutes before cutting them into ½-inch-thick pieces on the diagonal.

POACHED PEARS   *15 minutes*

½ cup sugar
1 teaspoon vanilla
1 teaspoon fresh lemon juice
4 whole pears, peeled with stems intact
1 cinnamon stick

Bring 7 cups of water to a boil and add the sugar, vanilla, lemon juice, and cinnamon stick. Add the pears and cook for 10 minutes, or until tender. Cover and let rest in pan at room temperature until served. Discard cinnamon stick.

Beef

•

MENU

Nachos Special
Roast Prime Rib Beef Bones
Mexican Rice
Romaine, Green Olive, Onion, and Tomato Salad
with Lorenzo Dressing
Mangoes and Lemon Sherbet

•

ROAST PRIME RIB BEEF BONES   *50 minutes*

1/4 cup Kitchen Bouquet
1/2 cup dry sherry
2 tablespoons Worcestershire sauce
12 prime rib meaty beef bones
1 garlic clove, crushed

Preheat the oven to 400°F. In a bowl combine all the ingredients except for the beef bones. Brush the ribs liberally with the mixture and place on a rack in a roasting pan and cook for 40 minutes, basting twice with the sauce during cooking time.

MEXICAN RICE   *30 minutes*

1 cup long-grain rice
1 tablespoon olive oil
1 1/4-ounce package taco mix
1 medium onion, chopped
1 tablespoon fresh chopped parsley

In a saucepan bring 2½ cups of water to a boil. Add the rice, oil, taco mix, and onion. Cover and simmer for about 25 minutes, until the rice is tender. Garnish with the parsley.

NACHOS SPECIAL

20 minutes

½ pound ground beef
1 small onion, minced
1 tablespoon chili powder
½ teaspoon cumin
1 3-ounce can Jalapeño chilies, seeded and diced
1 16-ounce package tortilla chips
½ pound thinly sliced mild or sharp Cheddar cheese

In a skillet cook the ground beef with the onion until lightly browned. Sprinkle with the chili powder and cumin and mix. Remove from the heat and stir in the chilies. Spread the tortilla chips in a large shallow ovenproof dish. Top the tortilla chips with the meat mixture and place slices of the cheese over the top. Cook under broiler for 5 minutes or until the cheese melts.

ROMAINE, GREEN OLIVE, ONION, AND TOMATO SALAD WITH LORENZO DRESSING

10 minutes

1 medium head romaine lettuce, washed, dried, and torn into bite-size pieces
½ cup sliced stuffed green olives
1 medium red onion, thinly sliced
2 medium tomatoes, cut into wedges

LORENZO DRESSING:

⅓ cup vegetable oil
1½ tablespoons vinegar
¼ cup chili sauce
salt and freshly ground pepper

Place the lettuce, olives, onions, and tomatoes into a salad bowl. Combine the Lorenzo Dressing ingredients in a separate bowl with a wire whisk. Pour the dressing over the salad and toss.

•

BOB GONKO'S ORIGINAL JOE'S BRUNO SPECIAL MENU

Original Joe's Bruno Special
French Fried Potatoes
Heated Sour Dough or French Bread
Port du Salut Cheese with
Seedless Green Grapes

•

ORIGINAL JOE'S BRUNO SPECIAL   *1 hour*

1 pound ground beef
1 small onion, chopped
1 10-ounce package frozen chopped spinach, cooked and
    well drained
8 eggs, beaten
salt and freshly ground pepper
butter for pan

Preheat the oven to 350°F. Brown the ground beef and onion in a large skillet. Drain off the fluid. Mix the meat with the cooked spinach and beaten eggs. Season to taste with salt and pepper. Put in a shallow buttered baking dish. Bake for 50 minutes, or until knife inserted in casserole comes out clean.

NOTE: In keeping with the spirit of the original, you can still fiddle around with the ingredients. Optional additions are sliced fresh mushrooms, mixed along with the onions, and seasonings such as oregano, garlic, or marjoram.

FRENCH FRIED POTATOES   *25 minutes*

4 medium Idaho potatoes, peeled and cut into ½-inch-thick
    sticks
oil for deep frying
salt

Wash the potatoes in cold water and pat them dry with a clean kitchen towel. Heat the oil in a fryer to about 360°F. and fry the potatoes, using frying basket, if possible, for 5 minutes. Remove and drain on paper towels. Reheat the oil to 375°F. and immerse the potatoes again in the oil. Cook them for a few minutes until golden. Drain and season with salt to taste.

●

MENU

Nachos
Chili
Hot Crusty Bread
Guacamole Salad
Easy Bread and Butter Pudding

●

CHILI

1 hour

1 pound sweet Italian sausage, removed from casings
3 tablespoons olive or vegetable oil
1 large onion, chopped
2 large garlic cloves, crushed
1 pound ground chuck
1 large green pepper, seeded and diced
1 16-ounce can Italian plum tomatoes and liquid
1 16-ounce can tomato sauce
2 cups water
1 6-ounce can tomato paste
1 12-ounce jar taco sauce
3 tablespoons chili powder
1 tablespoon cumin
1 teaspoon oregano
2 bay leaves, crushed
2 teaspoons salt or to taste
freshly ground pepper
1 ounce unsweetened chocolate
2 16-ounce cans chili beans and liquid in can

In a large pot cook the sausage over medium heat until it is lightly browned. Drain the sausage in a colander. Heat the oil in a pot, add the onion and garlic and sauté for 5 minutes, stirring often. Add the green pepper and sausage and simmer for 5 minutes. Meanwhile, puree the tomatoes with the liquid in the can in a blender. Add the pureed tomatoes to the pot along with the remaining ingredients, except for the chili

221

beans. Stir and simmer for 30 minutes, stirring twice during cooking time. Add the beans and simmer the chili for 15 minutes. Taste for seasoning.

Serves 6.

EASY BREAD AND BUTTER PUDDING   *35 minutes*

    butter, at room temperature
    12 slices of white bread, crusts trimmed
    1/4 cup raisins
    2 1/2 cups milk
    2 large eggs
    1 teaspoon vanilla
    1/4 cup sugar
    1/4 teaspoon cinnamon

Preheat the oven to 375°F. Lightly butter a shallow oblong-shaped baking dish. Spread butter on each slice of the bread. Cut the bread slices in half on a diagonal. Line the bread triangles in 2 rows in a baking dish and sprinkle with the raisins. Combine the milk, eggs, vanilla, sugar, and cinnamon in a bowl and pour over the bread. Bake for about 25 minutes, until golden and firm.

GUACAMOLE SALAD   *10 minutes*

    2 ripe avocados, peeled, pitted, and quartered
    1 small onion, coarsely chopped
    1 large garlic clove, peeled and halved
    1 tablespoon chili powder
    1 tablespoon fresh lemon juice
    2 or 3 dashes Tabasco sauce
    salt and freshly ground pepper
    6 medium tomatoes, thinly sliced
    salt and freshly ground pepper

Puree all the ingredients, except for the tomatoes, in a food processor fitted with steel blade, or in a blender. Taste for salt and pepper. Arrange 1 sliced tomato in a row in each of 6 salad plates and spoon the guacamole over the tomatoes.

NACHOS

10 minutes

> 1 16-ounce package tortilla chips
> ½ pound thinly sliced mild or sharp Cheddar Cheese

Preheat oven to 425°F. Arrange the tortilla chips on a large shallow ovenproof baking dish. Place the cheese slices over the chips and place in the oven for 5 minutes, or until the cheese melts.

●

MENU

New York Chef Salad
Croissant and Roast Beef Sandwiches
with Watercress

●

CROISSANT AND ROAST BEEF SANDWICHES WITH WATERCRESS

20 minutes

> 4 large bakery croissants
> softened butter
> ¾ pound thinly sliced roast beef
> 12 sprigs of fresh watercress, cleaned and dried

Carefully cut the croissants in half lengthwise. Spread inside with butter. Place equal amounts of the roast beef and watercress over bottom halves of the croissants and top with the top halves of the croissants.

NEW YORK CHEF SALAD

30 minutes

> 8 romaine lettuce leaves, washed and torn into bite-size
>   pieces
> 12 fresh mushrooms, thinly sliced
> 2 large stalks fresh broccoli, cut into bite-size pieces
> 1½ cups alfalfa sprouts
> 12 cherry tomatoes
> 1 avocado, halved, seeded, and thinly sliced
> 2 stalks celery, cut into 4 sticks
> 2 carrots, peeled and cut into 4 sticks
> ½ pound Swiss cheese, cut into ¼-inch-thick strips

CREAMY VINAIGRETTE SAUCE:

1 egg yolk
1 cup vegetable oil
1 teaspoon Dijon mustard
2 tablespoons white wine vinegar
salt and freshly ground pepper to taste

Arrange equal amounts of the lettuce pieces in 4 large individual salad bowls or plates. Top each with equal amounts of all the salad ingredients and prepare the Creamy Vinaigrette Sauce. Whisk the egg yolk in a medium bowl with the oil, a few drops at a time, until it thickens. Add the remaining oil in a slow steady stream. Beat in the mustard, vinegar, and season well with salt and pepper. Spoon the sauce over the salads and serve immediately.

NOTE: Vegetables can be added to, or substituted with any of the following: cauliflower, flowerets, cucumber spears, zucchini slices, chopped fennel, sliced scallions, green or black olives, hearts of palm, cooked asparagus, or artichoke hearts. Improvise.

Pork

•

MENU

*Sautéed Tournedos of Boneless Pork Roast
with Prunes
Carrots à l'Orange
Oven Crisp Potato Slices
Cinnamon and Walnut Ice Cream*

•

CINNAMON AND WALNUT ICE CREAM   *5 minutes*

1½ pints softened vanilla ice cream
1 tablespoon cinnamon
¾ cup chopped walnuts, plus 8 walnut halves

In a large bowl, beat the ice cream until creamy and smooth.
Stir in the cinnamon and chopped walnuts. Spoon the mixture into a square freezer container and refreeze. When
ready to serve the dessert, unmold ice cream by inserting a
knife between the container and the ice cream and tap it out
onto a plate. Slice the ice cream into 4 equal-size portions
and place each on a dessert plate. Garnish each with 2
walnut halves.

OVEN CRISP POTATO SLICES   *45 minutes*

4 medium baking potatoes, peeled and cut into thin slices
salt and freshly ground pepper
6 tablespoons melted butter

Preheat the oven to 400°F. Arrange dried potato slices across
a large baking sheet with sides, or in a roasting pan. Season
with salt and pepper. Drizzle the butter over the potatoes.
Cook in the oven until golden and crisp, about 35 minutes.

SAUTÉED TOURNEDOS OF BONELESS PORK ROAST WITH PRUNES

35 minutes

1 2½-pound boneless pork roast
salt and freshly ground pepper
paprika
flour
3 tablespoons butter
2 tablespoons olive or vegetable oil
3 tablespoons dry red wine
1 cup beef broth
1 tablespoon cornstarch
12 pitted prunes

Tie the rolled pork roast securely at equal intervals in six places. With a sharp knife, cut between pieces of each string, making six tournedos of pork. Season both sides with salt, pepper, and paprika; dust with flour. Heat 1½ table-spoons of the butter and the oil in a large skillet. Add the pork and cook over medium heat until browned; turn, lower heat slightly, and cook until browned and done, about 20 minutes. Transfer the meat to a warmed serving dish. Pour out all of the fat in the skillet except for 1 tablespoon, add the red wine and broth and cook until reduced by ¼ cup. Dissolve the cornstarch in a little of the broth and whisk it into the pan, stirring constantly, until thickened. Add the remaining 1½ tablespoons of butter and whisk until melted. Taste for seasoning. Spoon over the pork tournedos and top each with 2 prunes.

Serves 6.

CARROTS À L'ORANGE

15 minutes

1½ pounds carrots, peeled
salt
3 tablespoons butter
1 medium onion, chopped
¼ cup chicken broth
¼ cup Grand Marnier*
2 teaspoons fresh grated orange rind
1 tablespoon fresh chopped parsley
freshly ground pepper

---

* Grand Marnier can be substituted with Cointreau.

Bring 3½ cups of water to a boil in a saucepan. Cut the carrots into ¼-inch-thick slices on a diagonal. Drop the carrots into lightly salted boiling water and cook for exactly 6 minutes. Meanwhile, heat the butter in a skillet and cook the onion over medium heat for 5 minutes, stirring often. Drain the carrots well. Add to skillet along with the broth, Grand Marnier, and orange rind. Gently toss, and season to taste with salt and pepper. Sprinkle with the parsley.

•

MENU

Cream of Broccoli Soup
Earlyne's Sautéed Pork Chops
Baked Potatoes with Sauerkraut
Sliced Papayas and Honeydew Balls with
Rum and Toasted Walnuts

•

BAKED POTATOES WITH SAUERKRAUT   *55 minutes*

    4 medium Idaho potatoes
    4 tablespoons butter
    3 tablespoons vegetable oil
    1 8-ounce can sauerkraut, rinsed and well drained in
       colander
    1 teaspoon caraway seeds
    salt and freshly ground pepper

Preheat oven to 400°F. Wash and dry the potatoes. Prick each potato with a fork. Place on a rack in the oven and cook for approximately 40 minutes, or until tender. Five minutes before the potatoes are done, heat the butter and oil in a skillet and add the sauerkraut and caraway seeds and toss. Cover and set aside. Remove the potatoes and cut ½ inch off the top of each lengthwise. Remove the potato pulp from the shells with a teaspoon and combine with the sauerkraut mixture in a skillet. Season to taste with salt and pepper. Spoon the mixture back into the potato shells and serve immediately.

EARLYNE'S SAUTÉED PORK CHOPS   *50 minutes*

This delicious plain recipe is one my mother cooked often when I was a child. It smelled wonderful cooking and tasted just as good while eating it right down to chewing on the bone, which I heartily recommend.

    4 1-inch-thick pork chops
    salt and freshly ground pepper
    flour
    ½ cup vegetable oil

Season the chops with salt and pepper. Coat with flour and shake off any extra. Heat the oil in a skillet and add the pork chops. Cook over medium-low heat for 20 minutes. Turn and cook for 20 to 25 minutes until golden and tender.

CREAM OF BROCCOLI SOUP   *15 minutes*

    1 10-ounce package frozen chopped broccoli
    1 14-ounce can chicken broth
    1 small onion, chopped
    1 cup heavy cream
    salt and freshly ground pepper

In a saucepan cook the broccoli in the chicken broth with the onion over medium-high heat for 10 minutes. Puree in a blender and return to the pan. Add the heavy cream and season to taste with salt and pepper. Heat thoroughly.

SLICED PAPAYAS AND HONEYDEW BALLS
WITH RUM AND TOASTED WALNUTS   *15 minutes*

    2 tablespoons butter
    ⅔ cup walnut halves
    2 ripe medium papayas, peeled, seeded, and cut into thin
      slices
    1 small honeydew melon, peeled, seeded, and cut into balls
    1 cup heavy cream
    2 tablespoons sugar
    1 tablespoon rum

Heat the butter in a skillet and cook the walnuts over medium-high heat for 3 or 4 minutes until lightly toasted. Remove and place on paper towels. Arrange the papaya slices in a circle, in equal portions, on 4 dessert plates. Place

228

equal amounts of the melon balls in the center of the papaya circles. Whip the cream until it is thickened, but not stiff. Add the sugar and beat until stiff but not dry. Add the rum and beat in for a few seconds. Spoon the rum whipped cream over one area of the papayas and melons and sprinkle with the nuts.

•

MENU

Boiled Artichokes with Walnut Sauce
Pork Chops Creole-Style
Hot Cooked Rice
Eggplant Pancakes
Vanilla Almond Ice Cream with Kahlua

•

PORK CHOPS CREOLE-STYLE   *1 hour*

    2 tablespoons olive oil
    4 1-inch-thick pork chops
    ½ cup chopped onion
    1 garlic clove, crushed
    1 green pepper, seeded and chopped
    3 celery stalks, thinly sliced
    1 16-ounce can whole tomatoes, drained (reserving liquid)
      and chopped
    ½ teaspoon thyme
    salt and freshly ground pepper
    1 tablespoon fresh chopped parsley

Heat the oil in a large skillet and brown the pork chops on each side over medium-high heat. Remove and add the onion, garlic, pepper, and celery. Stir and cook for 5 minutes. Push the vegetables to one side in the pan and add the pork chops. Cover with the vegetables and add the tomatoes, liquid, and thyme. Season to taste with salt and pepper. Cover and simmer for 45 minutes. Sprinkle with the parsley.

HOT COOKED RICE

30 minutes

long-grain rice
fresh chopped parsley

Cook the long-grain rice according to the package directions for 4. Sprinkle with chopped parsley before serving with the Pork Chops Creole-Style.

BOILED ARTICHOKES WITH
WALNUT SAUCE

45 minutes

4 large artichokes
1 tablespoon salt

WALNUT SAUCE:

1 cup mayonnaise
2 tablespoons walnut oil
2 teaspoons fresh lemon juice
1 tablespoon fresh chopped parsley
salt and freshly ground pepper

Bring 4½ quarts of water to a boil. Meanwhile, cut off the stem ends and ½ inch from the top of each artichoke. Cut off the sharp points of each leaf with kitchen shears. Place the artichokes in boiling salted water, stem ends down, and simmer for 30 minutes. Turn the artichokes over and cook for 10 minutes. Artichokes are done when the sharp point of a knife is easily inserted into the stem end. Meanwhile, combine the Walnut Sauce ingredients and place in equal portions in 4 small bowls. Drain the artichokes well, stem ends up. Serve each artichoke with a small bowl of the sauce.

NOTE: Artichokes can be cooked the night before and served chilled with the same sauce.

EGGPLANT PANCAKES

15 minutes

2 cups grated eggplant
1 medium onion, grated
⅔ cup all-purpose flour
1 teaspoon baking powder
1 large egg, beaten
salt and freshly ground pepper

butter
vegetable oil
fresh grated Romano or Parmesan cheese

Combine the eggplant, onion, flour, baking powder, and egg
in a bowl. Season with salt and pepper. Heat 1 teaspoon of
the butter and 1 teaspoon of the oil in a large skillet (stickproof, if possible) and cook the pancakes, using about ¼ cup
of the batter for each pancake. Cook until golden on each
side. Add equal parts of butter and oil to skillet as needed.
Sprinkle with cheese.

•

MENU

Grilled Pork Chops with Apricot Orange Glaze
Orzo Salad
Sautéed Apples
Strawberry Ice Cream with Strawberry Liqueur and
Chopped Walnuts

•

ORZO SALAD   *15 minutes*

2 cups orzo (rice-shaped pasta)
2 teaspoons salt
½ cup vegetable oil
2 tablespoons white wine vinegar
½ teaspoon dill
½ teaspoon oregano
½ teaspoon thyme
2 tablespoons fresh chopped parsley
1 firm ripe tomato, diced
1 small green pepper, seeded and diced
freshly ground pepper

Bring 2½ quarts of water to a boil. Add the salt, stir, and add
the pasta and stir. Cook until the orzo is just tender, about 5
minutes. Meanwhile, combine the remaining ingredients in a
bowl with a wire whisk. Drain the pasta well and turn it into
a bowl. Pour the mixture over the orzo and toss. Taste for
seasonings. Cool, cover, and refrigerate until ready to serve.

GRILLED PORK CHOPS WITH
APRICOT ORANGE GLAZE   *35 minutes*

12 1-inch-thick large loin pork chops

APRICOT ORANGE GLAZE:

½ cup apricot preserves
½ cup marmalade
½ cup ketchup
1 tablespoon soy sauce
1 tablespoon red wine vinegar
1 teaspoon Dijon mustard
¼ cup grated onion

Over hot coals grill the pork chops for 8 to 10 minutes.
Meanwhile, combine the Apricot Orange Glaze ingredients
in a bowl. Turn the chops and brush with the glaze. Cook for
7 minutes. Turn and brush with glaze. Cook until done,
turning and brushing with the glaze one or two more times
until the pork is tender.

SAUTÉED APPLES   *15 minutes*

4 tablespoons butter
4 Delicious apples, peeled, cored, and cut into ½-inch-thick
   wedges
1 tablespoon sugar

Heat the butter in a skillet and add the apples. Cook over
medium-high heat until browned. Sprinkle with the sugar
and turn. Cook until browned on the other side.

•

MENU

*Scallops of Barbecued Boneless Pork Butt
Harlequin Stuffed Sweet and Baked Potatoes
Baby Lima Beans and Yellow Squash
Orange Sections and Raspberries with
Bakery Sponge Cake*

•

SCALLOPS OF BARBECUED
BONELESS PORK BUTT
1 hour

1 3½-pound boneless smoked pork shoulder butt
1½ cups Open Pit barbecue sauce

Soak the pork butt in warm water for 5 minutes and peel off
the cloth netting, if necessary. Bring 1 quart of water to a
boil and simmer the pork butt in the water, covered, for 30
minutes. Remove and drain the pork. Preheat oven to 400°F.
Cut the pork into ⅓-inch slices. Spoon ½ cup of the barbecue sauce over bottom of a shallow baking dish, brushing to
cover each piece of the pork. Cook for 20 minutes. Pass
under broiler for a minute, or 2 if further browning is
desired.

Serves 6.

HARLEQUIN STUFFED SWEET AND
BAKED POTATOES
55 minutes

4 medium-large baking potatoes
4 medium sweet potatoes
6 tablespoons butter, or as needed
6 tablespoons heavy cream
salt and freshly ground pepper
2 tablespoons rum

Preheat the oven to 400°F. Scrub and dry the potatoes. Prick
each baking potato with the sharp point of a knife and place
on a rack in the oven with the sweet potatoes. Cook for
approximately 40 minutes or until tender. Remove the potatoes from the oven and reduce heat to 325°F. Cut the baking
potatoes in half and scoop out the potato pulp into a bowl.
Mash the potatoes with 3 tablespoons of the butter and 4
tablespoons of the heavy cream. Season to taste with salt
and pepper. Cut the sweet potatoes in half and scoop out the
potato pulp into another bowl and mash the potatoes with 3
tablespoons of the butter, 2 tablespoons of the cream, and
rum. Season to taste with salt and pepper. In each baking
potato shell, spoon the baked potato mixture into one half of
the shell. Fill the other half of the shell with the sweet potato
mixture. Place the potatoes on a baking sheet and heat in the
oven for 5 minutes.

BABY LIMA BEANS AND
YELLOW SQUASH   *15 minutes*

1 10-ounce package frozen baby lima beans
2 yellow squash, cubed
3 tablespoons melted butter
1 tablespoon fresh chopped parsley
salt and freshly ground pepper

Cook the lima beans according to the package directions just
until tender. Meanwhile, cook the yellow squash in boiling
water in a separate saucepan for 5 minutes. Drain both of the
vegetables well. Combine vegetables in a bowl and add the
butter, parsley, and season to taste with salt and pepper.

•

MENU

Sib's Ribs
Baked Beans
Fried Onion Rings
Fruit Kebobs

•

SIB'S RIBS

3 pounds spareribs, cut into individual ribs
6 cups vegetable oil
3 cups Open Pit barbecue sauce

Drop the ribs into a large pot of boiling water and simmer for
25 minutes, skimming the surface of the water frequently.
Drain the ribs in a colander and then on a clean kitchen towel
until dried. Heat the oil in a large fryer and fry 8 ribs in
370°F. fat for 4 minutes. Remove and drain. Cook the
remaining ribs in the same manner. Heat the broiler. Place
the fried ribs in a large roasting pan and cover with the
barbecue sauce. Cook under the broiler (or over grill),
turning often, until browned and crispy, about 10 minutes.

Serves 6.

BAKED BEANS   *45 minutes*

8 strips bacon
1 medium-large onion, chopped
1 large garlic clove, crushed
2 16-ounce cans oven-baked beans
2 teaspoons Dijon mustard
¾ cup fresh bread crumbs
2 tablespoons melted butter
2 tablespoons brown sugar

Preheat the oven to 350°F. Fry the bacon in a skillet until crisp. Drain. Pour out all but 2 tablespoons of the fat from the skillet and cook the onion and garlic over medium-low heat for 8 minutes, stirring often. Transfer the onion mixture to a bowl and add the beans and mustard; gently combine. Turn into a lightly greased baking dish and sprinkle with the bread crumbs, butter, and brown sugar. Bake for 30 minutes.

FRUIT KEBOBS   *10 minutes*

1 cantaloupe, halved, seeded, and cut into 1½-inch cubes
1 pint strawberries, hulled
1 2-pound watermelon wedge, cut into 1½-inch cubes and seeded
3 navel oranges, cut into 8 wedges each

On each of 6 8-inch wooden skewers place alternating pieces of the fruit. Refrigerate until served.

FRIED ONION RINGS   *30 minutes*

2 large onions, peeled and cut into ⅓-inch-thick slices
1 egg yolk
1 cup flour
1 cup beer
½ teaspoon salt, plus salt for seasoning
vegetable oil for deep frying

Break the onion slices into rings. Heat the oil in a large 6-inch sided pan. Meanwhile, in a bowl, beat together the egg yolk, flour, and beer with the salt. Dip each onion ring into the batter and fry the rings, a few at a time, in the hot oil (about 370°F.) and cook until golden brown on each side. Drain on paper towels and keep warm on a hot dish. Season with salt and serve immediately.

•

MENU

Ribs and Sausages with Instant Barbecue Sauce
Mom P's Potato Salad
Vegetable and Bean Salad
Watermelon and Cantaloupe Wedges

•

RIBS AND SAUSAGES WITH INSTANT
BARBECUE SAUCE   *1 hour*

    8 Italian sweet sausages
    3 pounds meaty spareribs, cut into individual ribs

INSTANT BARBECUE SAUCE:

    3 cups Open Pit barbecue sauce
    2 teaspoons fresh lemon juice
    ½ cup apricot preserves
    2 dashes Tabasco sauce
    1 tablespoon Worcestershire sauce
    1 tablespoon Dijon mustard
    1 medium onion, grated

Preheat the oven to 375°F. In a large bowl combine the sauce
ingredients and add the ribs. Toss to coat them evenly and let
stand at room temperature. Bring 2 cups of water to a boil in
a skillet and add the sausages, which have been pricked with
the point of a knife. Simmer for 5 minutes, turn, and cook 5
minutes. Drain. Meanwhile, place the coated ribs in a roasting pan and cook for 15 minutes. While the ribs are cooking
add the sausages to the sauce in a bowl and toss to coat them
evenly. Add the sausages to the roasting pan and baste the
ribs with the sauce and cook for 30 minutes. Pass under the
broiler for a few moments until sizzling and golden brown.

MOM P'S POTATO SALAD   *30 minutes*

    2 pounds new potatoes, boiled until tender in their skins
    1 medium onion, thinly sliced
    1 small green pepper, seeded and cut into thin strips
    2 carrots, peeled and shredded
    2 celery stalks, thinly sliced

2 tablespoons fresh chopped parsley
mayonnaise
salt and freshly ground pepper to taste
2 eggs, hard-cooked and chopped

Peel and cut up all the boiled potatoes into a large bowl. Add the onion, green pepper, carrots, celery, and parsley. Add the mayonnaise, a little at a time, until the potato salad holds together. Season with salt and pepper. Just before serving, separate the cooked whites and yolks. Chop them separately and use them to decorate the top of the salad.

VEGETABLE AND BEAN SALAD   *20 minutes*

1 16-ounce can chick-peas, drained
1 16-ounce can kidney beans, drained
1 10-ounce package frozen lima beans, cooked and drained
1 10-ounce package frozen whole kernel corn, cooked and drained
1 medium-large onion, chopped
1 cup thinly sliced celery
¼ cup fresh chopped parsley
1 cup vegetable oil
¼ cup red wine vinegar
1 tablespoon Dijon mustard
1 teaspoon dill
salt and freshly ground pepper to taste

In a large bowl combine the chick-peas, beans, vegetables, and parsley. In a medium bowl or blender, mix the remaining ingredients. Pour over the vegetable mixture, toss, and taste for seasoning.

WATERMELON AND
CANTALOUPE WEDGES   *10 minutes*

1 2-pound slice of watermelon
1 small cantaloupe

Cut the watermelon and cantaloupe into individual wedges and serve on a platter.

Lamb

•

MENU

Vichyssoise
Lamb Brochettes with Rosemary
Greek Salad
Toasted Pound Cake with Ice Cream and
Honey Amaretto Topping

•

LAMB BROCHETTES WITH ROSEMARY

3 pounds shoulder cut leg of lamb, cut into 1½-inch cubes
¾ cup olive oil
¼ cup fresh lemon juice
1 teaspoon mustard
1 tablespoon fresh chopped rosemary, or 1½ teaspoons
   dried rosemary
2 bay leaves, crumbled
1 teaspoon seasoned salt
freshly ground pepper to taste
2 medium onions, halved and separated

Place the lamb cubes in a large bowl. Combine the oil, lemon juice, mustard, rosemary, bay leaves, seasoned salt, and pepper in a bowl. Pour over the lamb and toss. Let sit for 30 minutes. Preheat broiler. Prepare 6 metal skewers with alternating pieces of the lamb and onion in equal amounts. Cook them in a roasting pan under a hot broiler for about 6 minutes per side for pink, or to desired doneness. Brush the lamb with the marinade several times during cooking.

Serves 6.

VICHYSSOISE   *45 minutes*

    4 tablespoons butter
    2 cups thinly sliced leeks, white part only
    3 medium boiling potatoes, peeled and sliced
    1 quart chicken stock or broth
    salt and freshly ground white pepper
    1 cup heavy cream
    2 tablespoons fresh chopped chives

Heat the butter in a large saucepan or Dutch oven. Add the
leeks and sauté over medium-low heat for 8 minutes. In a
separate pot place the stock or broth. Add the potatoes and
bring to a boil. Reduce heat and simmer for 30 minutes.
Season to taste with salt and pepper. Puree in a blender a
few cupsful at a time. Since this soup may be served hot or
cold, place in either saucepan or bowl and stir in cream.
Heat thoroughly if served hot. Garnish with chives.

GREEK SALAD   *10 minutes*

    1 head romaine lettuce, washed, dried, and torn into
       bite-size pieces
    1 small green pepper, seeded and sliced
    1 red onion, thinly sliced and broken into rings
    1 medium-large tomato, cut into wedges
    1/4 pound feta cheese, cubed
    1/2 cup black Greek olives
    1 medium cucumber, scored with a fork and sliced
    1 teaspoon oregano

    DRESSING:

    olive oil
    red wine vinegar
    salt and freshly ground pepper

Arrange the lettuce pieces in 6 salad bowls. Top with the
green pepper slices, onion rings, tomato wedges, feta
cheese, olives, and cucumber. Sprinkle with the oregano and
serve with cruets of olive oil and vinegar, salt and pepper.

TOASTED POUND CAKE WITH ICE CREAM
AND HONEY AMARETTO TOPPING   *10 minutes*

    6 slices pound cake
    1½ pints vanilla ice cream
    6 tablespoons warm honey
    6 tablespoons Amaretto
    ¾ cup almond slices

Toast the pound cake slices. Top each with a small scoop of the ice cream. Combine the honey and Amaretto and spoon it over the ice cream and sprinkle with the almonds.

•

MENU

Crown of Roast Lamb
Crustless Onion Tart
Boston, Watercress, and Endive Salad with
Walnut Oil Vinaigrette Sauce
Chocolate-Dipped Strawberries with
Coffee Ice Cream

•

CROWN OF ROAST LAMB   *1 hour*

    1 crown of roast lamb (have butcher prepare it)
    salt and freshly ground pepper

Preheat the oven to 375°F. Sprinkle the lamb with salt and pepper. Place it on a rack in a roasting pan. Cook lamb in the oven for 55 minutes.

Serves 6.

CRUSTLESS ONION TART   *55 minutes*

    3 tablespoons butter
    2 tablespoons olive or vegetable oil
    4 cups thinly sliced onions
    salt and freshly ground pepper
    ½ teaspoon basil

2 tablespoons flour
3 large eggs, lightly beaten
2 cups heavy cream

Heat the butter and oil in a large skillet. Add the onions and cook over medium heat for 12 minutes, stirring often. Sprinkle with salt, pepper, basil, and flour, mixing well. Combine the eggs and heavy cream in a large bowl. Place the onions in a well-greased 9-inch round au gratin dish. Place in pan with water coming halfway up the side of the au gratin dish in the oven and cook for 35 minutes or until the tart is set. Cool for 10 minutes before serving.

CHOCOLATE-DIPPED STRAWBERRIES
WITH COFFEE ICE CREAM   *15 minutes*

2 tablespoons butter
2 tablespoons sugar
6 ounces semisweet chocolate
confectioners' sugar
12 large ripe strawberries, washed and dried, stems intact
1½ pints coffee ice cream

Melt the butter, sugar, and chocolate in the top of a double boiler over simmering water in the lower pan. Stir occasionally. Meanwhile, sprinkle a light layer of confectioners' sugar over a sheet of foil in a small baking sheet. Holding the stems of the strawberries, dip them in the melted chocolate mixture, tilting the pan when necessary. Place the chocolate-coated strawberries on the confectioners' sugar lined foil. Refrigerate until serving time. Serve 2 of the strawberries on each of 6 plates with a large scoop of the coffee ice cream.

BOSTON, WATERCRESS, AND ENDIVE
SALAD WITH WALNUT OIL
VINAIGRETTE SAUCE   *10 minutes*

1 large head Boston lettuce, cleaned, dried, and torn into
   bite-size pieces
1 bunch watercress, cleaned, dried, and broken into bite-size
   pieces
3 Belgian endives, cut into 1-inch lengths and separated

241

WALNUT OIL VINAIGRETTE SAUCE:

⅓ cup vegetable oil
¼ cup walnut oil
1 teaspoon Dijon mustard
2 tablespoons white wine vinegar
salt and freshly ground pepper to taste

Combine the Boston lettuce, watercress, and endives and place in a plastic bag and refrigerate until ready to serve. Combine ingredients for the Walnut Oil Vinaigrette Sauce in a bowl with a wire whisk. Set aside. At serving time, beat the sauce well and pour it over the salad greens in a bowl. Toss.

•

MENU

Dinie James Shrimp Bisque
Lamb Braised in White Wine with Cranberry Sauce
Broccoli Spears
Corn Pudding with Pimientos
Parfait of Raspberry Yogurt with Strawberries

•

LAMB BRAISED IN WHITE WINE WITH CRANBERRY SAUCE   *1 hour*

1 3½-pound boneless leg of lamb, rolled and tied (have
   butcher prepare it, removing as much fat as possible)
salt and freshly ground pepper
2 tablespoons butter
2 cups dry white wine
2 cups beef broth
2 garlic cloves, coarsely chopped
1 medium-large onion, quartered
½ teaspoon rosemary
½ teaspoon thyme
½ teaspoon marjoram
½ teaspoon oregano
1 bay leaf
6 peppercorns
1 14-ounce can whole cranberry sauce, at room temperature

Season the lamb with salt and pepper. In a heavy Dutch

oven heat butter and brown the lamb all over, over medium-high heat. Add the remaining ingredients, except for the cranberry sauce, and bring it to a boil. Reduce heat and simmer for 30 minutes, covered. Turn the lamb, re-cover, and cook for 25 minutes. Remove the lamb and cool a few minutes before slicing. Serve with the cranberry sauce.

CORN PUDDING WITH PIMIENTOS $\qquad$ *55 minutes*

> 2 10-ounce packages of frozen whole corn kernels
> 2 cups light cream
> 3 eggs, beaten
> 1 medium onion, grated
> 1/3 cup well-drained minced pimiento
> 1/2 teaspoon salt
> freshly ground pepper to taste
> butter for casserole

Preheat oven to 350°F. Bring 1 cup of water to a boil in a saucepan. Add the corn and break it apart into individual kernels. Cook for 2 minutes. Drain well. Place the corn into a large bowl with the cream and stir. Add the remaining ingredients. Turn the mixture into a lightly buttered 2-quart casserole. Place the casserole in a pan with hot water that reaches halfway up the side of the casserole. Bake in the oven for about 50 minutes.

PARFAIT OF RASPBERRY YOGURT WITH STRAWBERRIES $\qquad$ *10 minutes*

> 1 pint fresh strawberries, washed, dried, hulled, and sliced, reserving 4 whole strawberries
> 3 cups well-combined raspberry yogurt

In 4 parfait glasses or balloon wineglasses make 4 alternating equal-portioned layers of sliced strawberries and yogurt, ending with a layer of the yogurt. Top each dish with a strawberry. Refrigerate until served.

DINIE JAMES SHRIMP BISQUE

25 minutes

6 tablespoons butter
½ pound shrimp, shelled, deveined, and finely chopped
½ teaspoon paprika
2 tablespoons tomato paste
2 tablespoons Cognac or brandy
2 8-ounce bottles clam juice
4 tablespoons flour
1 cup heavy cream
salt and freshly ground pepper
1 tablespoon freshly chopped parsley

Heat 2 tablespoons of the butter in a large saucepan and add the shrimp. Cook over medium heat for 3 minutes, stirring often. Add the paprika, tomato paste, and Cognac. Stir and cook for 1 minute. Add the clam juice and simmer for 10 minutes. Combine the remaining 4 tablespoons of butter and flour with a fork and stir into the liquid. Stir until thickened over high heat. Add the cream and season with salt and pepper to taste. Heat thoroughly. Garnish with the parsley.

BROCCOLI SPEARS

15 minutes

4 fresh broccoli spears, trimmed and halved lengthwise
salt and freshly ground pepper
2 tablespoons melted butter

Bring 3½ cups of water to a rolling boil in a large saucepan. Add the broccoli and cook over medium heat for about 8 minutes, until just tender. Drain. Season the broccoli with salt and pepper and sprinkle with the butter.

•

MENU

Lamb Curry
Hot Cooked Rice
Sheila Ginsberg's Hot and Spicy Chinese Eggplant
Toasted Sesame Pita Bread
Sour Cream Coffee Cake

•

LAMB CURRY

1 hour

2 pounds lean lamb shoulder, cut into 1-inch cubes
salt and freshly ground pepper
2 tablespoons butter
1 tablespoon vegetable oil
2 garlic cloves, chopped
1 cup chopped onion
1 cup sliced celery
1 tablespoon curry powder
½ teaspoon turmeric
3 cups chicken broth
2 medium potatoes, peeled and quartered
½ cup heavy cream
1 tablespoon fresh chopped parsley

Season the lamb cubes with salt and pepper. In a Dutch oven heat the butter and oil and brown the lamb over medium-high heat, several pieces at a time, removing the browned lamb cubes as they are cooked. Reduce the heat to medium, add the garlic, onion, and celery; stir and cook for 5 minutes. Return the lamb to the pan with the juices and sprinkle with the curry powder and turmeric, stir, and add the chicken broth and potatoes. Bring to a boil, reduce heat, cover, and simmer for 40 minutes. Remove the potatoes and puree them in a blender with ¾ cup of broth from the pot. Stir the pureed potatoes into the pot and add the heavy cream. Taste for seasoning. Serve over the Hot Cooked Rice and garnish with the fresh chopped parsley.

Serves 6.

SOUR CREAM COFFEE CAKE

45 minutes

½ cup softened butter
1 cup sugar
1 egg, separated
1 cup sour cream
1½ cups sifted all-purpose flour
1½ teaspoons baking powder
1 teaspoon baking soda
1 teaspoon vanilla

CINNAMON NUT CRUMB MIXTURE:

½ cup loosely packed brown sugar
1 teaspoon cinnamon
½ cup chopped walnuts

Preheat oven to 350°F. Cream together the butter and sugar. Blend the egg yolk and sour cream and add to the butter mixture with flour, baking powder, and baking soda; mix well. Stir in the vanilla. Beat the egg white until frothy but not stiff and immediately fold into the mixture. In a bowl combine the ingredients for the Cinnamon Nut Crumb Mixture. Turn half of the cake batter into a greased 8- × 8-inch cake pan and sprinkle with half of the crumb mixture. Add the remaining batter and top with the remaining crumb mixture. Bake for 35 minutes, or until done.

HOT COOKED RICE   *25 minutes*

Cook 1 cup of long-grain rice according to the package directions.

SHEILA GINSBERG'S HOT AND SPICY
CHINESE EGGPLANT   *15 minutes*

2 medium-small eggplants
4 garlic cloves, crushed
2 tablespoons chili paste*
3 tablespoons dark soy sauce
2 tablespoons dark vinegar*
1 tablespoon sugar
1 tablespoon sesame oil
peanut or vegetable oil for deep frying
3 scallions, thinly sliced

Cut the unpeeled eggplant into ¾-inch × 2-inch sticks. Combine the garlic and chili paste in a small bowl. In another bowl combine the soy sauce, vinegar, sugar, and sesame oil. Set each bowl within close reach of the stove. Heat 3 cups of the oil to about 370°F. in a wok or in a fryer large enough for oil to be approximately 3 inches in depth. Fry the eggplant for about 4 minutes. Remove and drain.

---

* Ingredients are available in Chinese specialty food shops.

Remove all of the oil from the pan except for ¼ cup. Add the garlic mixture and cook, stirring constantly, for 1 minute over high heat. Add the eggplant, soy sauce mixture, and scallions. Toss and cook over high heat for 1 minute, stirring. Serve immediately.

Pasta

•

MENU

*Spaghetti with Chicken Meatballs and
Marinara Sauce
Avocado and Tomato Salad*

•

MARINARA SAUCE   *55 minutes*

⅓ cup olive oil
½ cup chopped onion
2 garlic cloves, crushed
1 1-pound 20-ounce can Italian plum tomatoes, pureed in
    blender with liquid
1 cup chicken broth
1 small can tomato paste
½ teaspoon oregano
½ teaspoon basil
1 pound fresh parsley, chopped
1 bay leaf
salt and freshly ground pepper to taste

Heat the oil in a large saucepan and sauté the onion and
garlic for 5 minutes, stirring often. Add the remaining ingredients to the pan and bring to a boil. Reduce the heat and
simmer for 45 minutes. Check seasoning.

CHICKEN MEATBALLS   *35 minutes*

8 slices day-old white bread
1 cup milk
1½ pounds ground chicken (white and dark meat combined)

248

4 tablespoons softened butter
2 eggs
½ teaspoon fennel seeds
1 tablespoon fresh chopped parsley
1 medium onion, minced
½ teaspoon salt
freshly ground pepper to taste
½ teaspoon oregano
½ cup fresh grated Parmesan cheese
vegetable oil

Tear the bread into pieces and place into a bowl. Add the milk and turn the pieces until the milk is absorbed. Squeeze out the extra milk. Combine the remaining ingredients except for vegetable oil. Shape into 1½-inch balls. Heat ¼ inch of oil in a large skillet and cook the chicken balls over medium heat, until browned all over.

AVOCADO AND TOMATO SALAD *10 minutes*

3 cups of shredded romaine or iceberg lettuce
1 medium onion, cut into slivers
1 ripe avocado, halved, pitted and cut into thin slices
1 medium-large ripe tomato, cut into wedges
1 small green pepper, seeded and cut into strips
olive oil
red wine vinegar
salt and freshly ground pepper

Toss the lettuce and onion in a bowl and divide into 4 salad bowls. Top the salad with equal amounts of the avocado, tomato and green pepper. Sprinkle each salad lightly with the oil and vinegar and season to taste with salt and pepper.

SPAGHETTI *15 minutes*

1 pound spaghetti
1 tablespoon salt

Cook the spaghetti in 4½ quarts vigorously boiling water with salt until tender, about 6 minutes. Drain and serve with Marinara Sauce and Chicken Meatballs.

•

MENU

Baked Ziti with Cheese and Sausage
Tossed Green Salad with Italian Dressing
Italian Bread with Sweet Butter
Cantaloupe with Blueberries

•

BAKED ZITI WITH CHEESE
AND SAUSAGE

1 hour

6 tablespoons butter
2 tablespoons flour
1 cup light cream
1¼ cups milk
1 cup grated Cheddar cheese
¾ cup plus 2 tablespoons fresh grated Parmesan cheese
salt and freshly ground pepper
6 Italian sweet sausages
1 pound ziti
1 medium-large onion, chopped
1 large garlic clove, crushed
½ pound fresh mushrooms, thinly sliced
½ teaspoon oregano
½ teaspoon basil
1 cup fresh ripe peeled and chopped tomatoes*

Place 4½ quarts of water in a large pot and bring it to a boil. Meanwhile, heat 2 tablespoons of the butter in a saucepan and add the flour, stirring with a wire whisk. Cook for 1 minute over medium-low heat. Pour in the cream and milk, stirring constantly until the sauce is smooth, creamy, and hot. Add the Cheddar and Parmesan cheeses, stirring until melted. Season well with salt and pepper. Remove from the heat and cover.

Remove the sausage meat from the casings and brown it in a skillet over medium heat. Drain. Add 1 tablespoon of salt to the rapidly boiling water in the pot, stir, and add the ziti. Stir once and cook for about 8 to 10 minutes, until just tender. Preheat oven to 350°F. While the pasta is cooking,

---

* To peel tomatoes, immerse them into rapidly boiling water for 8 seconds. Remove with a slotted spoon and peel off the skins with the aid of a small sharp knife.

heat the remaining 4 tablespoons of butter in a skillet and sauté the onion and garlic for 5 minutes, stirring often. Add the mushrooms and cook for 4 minutes, stirring occasionally. Remove from the heat and sprinkle with the oregano and basil. Drain the pasta well and turn it into a large bowl. Immediately pour the sauce over the pasta and toss. Add the sausage, mushroom mixture, and tomatoes. Combine and taste for seasoning. Turn the ziti into a lightly greased baking dish, sprinkle the top with 2 tablespoons grated Parmesan cheese and bake in oven for 30 minutes.

TOSSED GREEN SALAD WITH
ITALIAN DRESSING
10 minutes

large head romaine lettuce, washed and leaves torn into
   bite-size pieces
6 escarole leaves, washed and torn into bite-size pieces

ITALIAN DRESSING:

½ cup olive or vegetable oil
2 tablespoons red wine vinegar
1 garlic clove, crushed
salt and freshly ground pepper to taste

Combine the lettuces in a bowl. Mix together the Italian Dressing ingredients with a wire whisk. Strain over the salad and toss.

●

MENU

Twists with Palace Bolognese Sauce
Escarole and Watercress Salad with
Garlic and Herb Dressing
Italian Bread
Chocolate Meringue and Nut Cookies with
Ice Cream

●

TWISTS WITH PALACE
BOLOGNESE SAUCE   *50 minutes*

> 1 tablespoon salt
> 1 pound twists
> 1 cup fresh grated Parmesan cheese
>
> **PALACE BOLOGNESE SAUCE:**
>
> 2 16-ounce cans Italian plum tomatoes and liquid
> 6 strips bacon
> 1 tablespoon olive oil
> 1 cup chopped onions
> 1 garlic clove, crushed
> 1 pound ground chuck
> 3 tablespoons butter
> ⅓ pound mushrooms, sliced
> 1 6-ounce can tomato paste
> ½ cup beef broth
> ½ teaspoon oregano
> ½ teaspoon thyme
> 1 bay leaf, crumbled

Puree the tomatoes with the liquid, one can at a time, in a blender. Set aside. Fry the bacon in a large skillet until crisp. Drain. Add the olive oil to the bacon fat and sauté the onions and garlic for 5 minutes, stirring occasionally. Transfer the onions and garlic to a bowl using a slotted spoon. Add the beef and brown it over medium heat, stirring often. Transfer to a bowl with the onions. Wipe out the pan. Heat the butter and sauté the mushrooms for 3 minutes over medium-high heat. In a large saucepan or Dutch oven, place the tomato puree, bacon, and onion mixture. Add the tomato paste, broth, oregano, thyme, bay leaf, and mushrooms. Bring to a boil. Reduce the heat and simmer for 30 minutes. Meanwhile, bring 4½ quarts of water to a boil in a large pot. When ready to serve dinner, add salt and cook the twists for 7 minutes, or until tender. Drain pasta well and immediately spoon the sauce over the pasta and toss. Serve with fresh grated Parmesan cheese.

CHOCOLATE MERINGUE AND NUT COOKIES
WITH ICE CREAM   *35 minutes*

> 2 tablespoons butter, plus butter for pan
> 4 ounces semisweet chocolate morsels

252

3 egg whites
2 tablespoons sugar
½ cup ground hazelnuts or walnuts
1 pint ice cream

Preheat the oven to 325°F. Lightly butter a large baking sheet. Melt the 2 tablespoons butter in a saucepan and remove from the heat. Add the chocolate morsels and stir until melted. Set aside to cool. Beat the egg whites until foamy, but not stiff. Add the sugar and beat until stiff but not dry. Stir in the walnuts and cooled chocolate mixture. Fold together. Drop by the teaspoonsful onto a baking sheet. Bake in the oven for 30 minutes. Cool on a cookie rack. Serve with the ice cream of your choice.

Makes about 2 dozen cookies.

ESCAROLE AND WATERCRESS SALAD WITH GARLIC AND HERB DRESSING   *10 minutes*

1 small escarole, washed, dried, and torn into bite-size pieces
1 bunch watercress, washed and dried

GARLIC AND HERB DRESSING:

½ cup olive oil
1 tablespoon red wine vinegar
½ teaspoon basil
½ teaspoon oregano
½ teaspoon minced garlic
salt and freshly ground pepper to taste

Place the escarole and watercress in a bowl. Combine the Garlic and Herb Dressing ingredients and pour over the salad. Toss and serve.

•

MENU

Stracciatella
Linguini with Red Clam Sauce
Italian Bread
Nectarines and Grapefruit with
Grenadine and Cointreau

•

LINGUINI WITH RED CLAM SAUCE

45 minutes

1 tablespoon salt
2 pounds linguini
1½ cups fresh grated Parmesan cheese

RED CLAM SAUCE:

5 tablespoons olive oil
¾ cup chopped onions
2 garlic cloves, minced
1 16-ounce can Italian plum tomatoes with liquid
1 cup chicken broth
1 small can tomato paste
2 8-ounce bottles clam juice
½ teaspoon oregano
½ teaspoon basil
2 tablespoons fresh chopped parsley
salt and freshly ground pepper
2 cups minced fresh or canned clams

In a large heavy pot, heat the olive oil. Sauté the onions and garlic for 5 minutes, stirring occasionally. Add the remaining ingredients except for the clams; bring to a boil, reduce the heat, and simmer for 30 minutes. Meanwhile, heat 4½ quarts of water in a large pot for cooking the linguini. Add the clams to the sauce and continue simmering until ready to serve. Add salt to boiling water, add the linguini, and cook for about 6 minutes, until just tender. Drain pasta well and turn it into a large serving dish. Immediately pour the sauce over the pasta and toss. Serve with Parmesan cheese.

STRACCIATELLA

10 minutes

4 cups beef consommé
4 eggs, lightly beaten
½ cup fresh grated Parmesan cheese
1 teaspoon fresh lemon juice
2 tablespoons fresh bread crumbs
1 tablespoon fresh chopped parsley
salt and freshly ground pepper to taste

Bring the consommé to a boil in a saucepan. Meanwhile, beat the eggs, cheese, lemon juice, bread crumbs, and parsley together. Gradually add the egg mixture to the slow-boiling consommé, stirring constantly. Cook for about 2 minutes. Season with salt and pepper. Serve immediately.

NECTARINES AND GRAPEFRUIT WITH GRENADINE AND COINTREAU

10 minutes

  4 ripe nectarines, peeled, pitted, and sliced
  1 cup grapefruit sections
  1 teaspoon grenadine
  3 tablespoons Cointreau

Place the fruit in a bowl and gently toss. Combine the grenadine and Cointreau and pour over the fruit. Refrigerate until served.

CHAPTER SEVEN

Holiday Menus

Dinner Party Planning

1. Make the guest list, and send invitations.
2. Determine if dinner is to be sit-down or buffet. If sit-down, make seating chart.
3. Plan menu, including beverages and liquor.
4. Making shopping list and shop at a convenient time.
5. Before shopping make room in the refrigerator for beverages and food.
6. Prepare as much food the night before as you can. Ice cubes, too.
7. The day of the party, several hours before the dinner, arrange the flowers, set the table, and set up the bar.
8. Set out serving dishes and dessert plates, cups and saucers, et cetera.
9. Measure the coffee for the coffeepot so that it's ready to make when you need it.
10. Have garbage cans emptied and lined with plastic bags.
11. Empty dishwasher.
12. If playing music with tapes or records, have the music you wish to play lined up and ready to go.

Two Valentine's Day Menus for 2

•

MENU

Glaser Salad
Chicken and Sausage Brochettes with Sage
Roesti Potatoes
Pureed Carrots
Ripe Brie with Kiwi Fruit and Toasted Brioche Slices

•

CHICKEN AND SAUSAGE
BROCHETTES WITH SAGE

Begin preparations
a day ahead

½ pound sweet Italian sausages, cut into 2-inch lengths
2 chicken breasts, boned, halved lengthwise, then each half halved crosswise
8 whole sage leaves
½ cup olive oil
juice of 1 lemon
¼ cup dry white wine
1 garlic clove, crushed
8 peppercorns

Thread alternating pieces of the sausage (crosswise), chicken, and folded sage leaves in equal portions onto 2 10-inch skewers. Place the brochettes in a pan. In a bowl combine the oil, lemon juice, wine, garlic, and peppercorns. Pour the mixture over the brochettes, cover, and refrigerate overnight. Turn the brochettes in the morning, re-cover, and refrigerate. Twenty minutes before serving, remove the brochettes from the marinade and pat dry. Heat the broiler.

Cook the brochettes under the broiler in a broiler pan until golden brown on each side, about 8 minutes per side.

GLASER SALAD

8 fresh mushrooms, very thinly sliced
1 cup thinly sliced celery hearts
¾ cup grated Gruyère cheese
4 Boston lettuce leaves
1 large pimiento

GLASER DRESSING:

½ cup imported olive oil
1½ tablespoons white wine vinegar
½ teaspoon dry mustard
dash of nutmeg
½ teaspoon basil
1 garlic clove, halved
1 tablespoon fresh finely chopped parsley
salt and freshly ground pepper to taste

Place the mushrooms, celery hearts, and cheese in a bowl. Mix together the ingredients for Glaser Dressing with a wire whisk. Discard the garlic halves. Pour the dressing over the salad and toss well. Place the lettuce leaves on two salad plates and top with equal amounts of the salad. Cut the pimiento into 4 small heart shapes and garnish each salad with 2. Leave at room temperature until served.

RIPE BRIE WITH KIWI FRUIT AND TOASTED BRIOCHE SLICES

8 ounces ripe Brie
2 fresh kiwi fruit, peeled and thinly sliced
freshly grated pepper
2 bakery brioches, sliced and toasted

Carefully remove the rind from the Brie. Spread equal portions of the Brie over the bottom of 2 dessert plates. Arrange the kiwi slices in layers across center of the cheese. Serve with the toasted brioche.

PUREED CARROTS

½ pound fresh carrots, peeled and cut into ¼-inch-thick
   slices
2 tablespoons butter
1 tablespoon heavy cream
salt and freshly ground white pepper to taste

Cook the carrots in a saucepan in slowly boiling water for 10
minutes, until very tender. Puree in a food processor fitted
with the steel blade with the butter and heavy cream, or
force through a food mill. Season with salt and pepper.

ROESTI POTATOES

2 tablespoons butter
2 tablespoons vegetable oil
2 medium Idaho potatoes, peeled and grated
salt and freshly ground pepper to taste

Heat the butter and oil in a large skillet. Place ¼ of the
potatoes in 4 different areas of the pan. Mash the potatoes
down with the back of a fork to form 4 potato pancakes.
Cook over medium-high heat until browned on one side,
turn with a spatula and cook until brown. Season with salt
and pepper.

•

MENU

Hearts of Palm Salad
Boiled Lobster with Pernod Butter
Baked Potatoes with Sour Cream and
Red Salmon Caviar
Fresh Oranges in Raspberry Puree
Champagne

•

HEARTS OF PALM SALAD

*Begin preparations
a day ahead*

1 14-ounce can hearts of palm, drained
½ cup diced, peeled, and seeded cucumber
2 tablespoons minced shallots

½ cup olive oil
1½ tablespoons white wine vinegar
1 teaspoon Dijon mustard
salt and freshly ground pepper
4 Boston lettuce leaves
1 tablespoon fresh chopped parsley

Place the hearts of palm in a small dish. Combine the remaining ingredients, except for the lettuce and parsley, in a saucepan. Bring to a boil and immediately pour over the hearts of palm. Cool, cover, and refrigerate overnight. Just before serving line 2 salad plates with the lettuce leaves. Arrange the hearts of palm over the lettuce in equal portions and spoon the sauce over the tops. Sprinkle with the parsley.

BOILED LOBSTER WITH PERNOD BUTTER

Begin preparations a day ahead

2 1½-pound live lobsters
4 quarts water
1 cup dry white wine

PERNOD BUTTER:

8 ounces (2 sticks) butter
1 tablespoon Pernod
1 tablespoon fresh finely chopped parsley

The night before prepare clarified butter for Pernod Butter. Cut the butter into pieces and heat in a small saucepan. When the butter is melted, skim off the white substance which has risen to the top. Pour the clear butter into a jar, leaving the white sediment in the bottom of the pan. Cover and refrigerate overnight.

Bring the water and wine to a rolling boil in a large pot. Add the lobsters, cover, and cook for 18 to 20 minutes until the lobsters are bright red and done. Meanwhile, heat the clarified butter in a saucepan and add the Pernod and parsley; stir, and remove from the heat. Drain the cooked lobsters in a colander and serve immediately with equal parts of the Pernod Butter in 2 small bowls.

BAKED POTATOES WITH SOUR CREAM
AND RED SALMON CAVIAR

2 medium Idaho baking potatoes
salt and freshly ground pepper
⅔ cup sour cream
3 ounces red salmon caviar
1 tablespoon fresh snipped chives

Preheat the oven to 400°F. Scrub the potatoes and dry them. Pierce each potato with the sharp point of a knife. Place the potatoes on an oven rack and cook for 40 minutes or until tender. Cut crosses in the top of the potatoes and press potatoes open. Season with salt and pepper and spoon equal amounts of the sour cream and caviar over the potatoes and sprinkle with the chives.

FRESH ORANGES IN RASPBERRY PUREE
WITH ICE CREAM

2 large navel oranges, peeled, including white pith
1 10-ounce package frozen raspberries in syrup, thawed
½ pint vanilla ice cream

Cut the oranges into ¼-inch-thick slices. Place the slices in equal portions in 2 dessert bowls. Puree the raspberries and strain. Pour in equal amounts over the oranges. Just before serving, top each with 1 scoop of vanilla ice cream.

Easter Dinners for 6 and 8

•

MENU FOR 6

Fresh Endive Leaves Stuffed with
Smoked Salmon and Cream Cheese
Beef Tongue with Fruit Sweet and Sour Sauce
Oven Roast Potatoes
Green Beans and Carrot Sticks
Fresh Strawberries with Chocolate Crème Fraîche

•

BEEF TONGUE WITH FRUIT SWEET AND SOUR SAUCE

Begin preparations
a day ahead

    1 3-pound fresh beef tongue
    1 medium-large onion
    1 cup sliced celery
    2 carrots, sliced
    2 bay leaves
    6 sprigs parsley
    1 dozen peppercorns

FRUIT SWEET AND SOUR SAUCE:

    1/3 cup sugar
    3 tablespoons butter
    3 tablespoons flour
    3 cups water
    20 apricots
    1/2 teaspoon cinnamon or to taste
    salt
    1/3 cup brown sugar
    2 tablespoons fresh lemon juice
    3/4 cup raisins
    3/4 cup almond slivers

265

Place the tongue and remaining 6 ingredients in a Dutch oven or large pot and cover with water. Bring to a boil, reduce heat, and simmer for about 3 hours, until tender. Remove the tongue, drain, and cool. Cover and refrigerate overnight. Thirty minutes before dinner, remove the tongue from the refrigerator. Peel the tongue and cut it into thin slices. Place the slices in layers in a large serving dish, and cover. Prepare the Fruit Sweet and Sour Sauce.

In a saucepan, combine the sugar and butter and cook until it turns light brown. Whisk in the flour and cook for 3 or 4 minutes, whisking constantly, until the sauce turns brown. Remove the saucepan from the heat. In a separate saucepan place the water and apricots, and bring them to a boil; reduce the heat, and simmer for 5 minutes. Turn the heat on under the saucepan with the flour mixture, and slowly add the apricots and liquid, stirring constantly. Add the remaining ingredients. Taste for seasoning. Simmer for 10 minutes. Spoon the sauce over the tongue slices and serve immediately.

FRESH STRAWBERRIES WITH CHOCOLATE CRÈME FRAÎCHE

Begin preparations a day ahead

3 pints fresh ripe strawberries

CHOCOLATE CRÈME FRAÎCHE:

1 cup sour cream
1 cup heavy cream
4 tablespoons chocolate syrup
2 tablespoons superfine sugar

The night before, prepare the Crème Fraîche; combine the sour and heavy cream in a mason-type jar. Cover it tightly and shake vigorously. Let it stand at room temperature overnight. Shake Crème Fraîche vigorously the next morning and beat in the chocolate syrup and sugar. Cover and refrigerate. Fifteen minutes before serving time, hull the strawberries and place them in a bowl. Spoon the Chocolate Crème Fraîche into another bowl and serve.

FRESH ENDIVE LEAVES STUFFED WITH SMOKED SALMON AND CREAM CHEESE

May be prepared up to two days ahead

4 ounces smoked salmon, finely chopped

8 ounces cream cheese, softened
2 tablespoons mayonnaise
1 small onion, minced
2 teaspoons fresh lemon juice
16 Belgian endive leaves
freshly grated pepper

Mix together the smoked salmon, cream cheese, mayonnaise, onion, and lemon juice.* Place a rounded teaspoon of the mixture at the stem end of each endive leaf. Spread the mixture slightly up the leaf. Sprinkle the mixture with pepper.

NOTE: Smoked salmon and cream cheese spread also makes delicious canapés or open-face sandwiches.

OVEN ROAST POTATOES

6 medium Idaho potatoes, peeled and cut into 6 pieces each
4 tablespoons melted butter
2 tablespoons vegetable oil
salt

Preheat the oven to 375°F. Place the potato pieces in a bowl and pour the combined butter and oil over them. Toss to coat the potatoes evenly and place the potatoes in a shallow roasting pan. Cook in the oven for 20 minutes. Turn each piece and cook about 15 minutes, until done. Season lightly with salt.

GREEN BEANS AND CARROT STICKS

salt
1½ pounds green beans, trimmed and left whole
1½ pounds carrots, peeled and cut into sticks (about the
    same size as the beans)
2 tablespoons olive oil
3 tablespoons butter
freshly ground pepper
2 tablespoons fresh chopped parsley

Bring 1 quart of water to a boil in each of 2 saucepans. Season the water in each pan lightly with salt. Add the beans to one, and the carrots to the other. Cook for exactly 6

---

* Mixture can be covered and refrigerated until used; it will keep for 2 days in the refrigerator.

minutes and drain. Heat the oil and butter in a large skillet and add the vegetables. Lightly toss. Sprinkle with salt, pepper, and the parsley. Toss again and serve.

•

MENU FOR 8

Primavera Timbales
Marinated Butterflied Leg of Lamb
Victoria's Baked Cherry Tomatoes and
Herbed Mushrooms
Asparagus Mimosa
Cold Lemon Mousse

•

PRIMAVERA　　　　　　　　　　　*Begin preparations*
TIMBALES　　　　　　　　　　　　　*a day ahead*

1¼ cups diced, blanched, well-drained cauliflower
1¼ cups cooked well-drained peas
1¼ cups diced, blanched, well-drained carrots
1¼ cups diced cooked broccoli
2 packages plain gelatin
½ cup cold water
2 10-ounce cans clear chicken consommé
2 tablespoons dry white wine
1 bunch fresh watercress

TARRAGON MAYONNAISE SAUCE:

1½ cups mayonnaise
1 tablespoon tarragon wine vinegar
½ teaspoon tarragon
1 scallion, minced
3 tablespoons fresh chopped parsley

Cook and cut the vegetables as directed. Soften the gelatin in the water. Meanwhile, heat the consommé and wine in a saucepan, but do not boil. Remove from the heat and add the gelatin and stir until it dissolves. Set aside. Lightly oil 8 timbale molds, and place on a tray. Place 2 tablespoons of the vegetables in layers in each of the timbales in the following order: cauliflower, peas, carrots, and broccoli. Gently pour the consommé mixture to the top of each mold. Refrigerate overnight.

Prepare the Tarragon Mayonnaise Sauce by combining all the ingredients in a bowl, cover, and refrigerate overnight. At serving time, invert each timbale onto a first course plate and garnish with 3 sprigs of watercress. Spoon a dollop of sauce on top of each timbale and serve at once.

MARINATED BUTTERFLIED LEG OF LAMB

Begin preparations a day ahead

1 7½-pound leg of lamb, boned and butterflied (your butcher will do this for you)

MARINADE:

¾ cup vegetable oil
¼ cup red wine vinegar
1 tablespoon Dijon mustard
1 medium-large onion, coarsely chopped
2 bay leaves, crumbled
1 large garlic clove, crushed
1 teaspoon oregano
1 teaspoon rosemary
1 teaspoon salt
freshly ground black pepper

Place the lamb in a shallow pan, flesh side up. In a small bowl mix together the Marinade ingredients. Pour the mixture over the lamb. Cover and refrigerate overnight; turn the meat in the morning, re-cover, and refrigerate. Remove the lamb 1 hour before cooking and let it rest at room temperature. Heat the broiler and place the meat in a large broiling pan, fat side up, and cook for 10 minutes, 5 inches from heat. Turn the meat and broil 10 minutes. Heat the oven to 425°F. Remove the lamb in the pan to the oven and cook about 20 minutes. The meat should be pink. Transfer the lamb to a carving board and carve into thin slices.

VICTORIA'S BAKED CHERRY TOMATOES AND HERBED MUSHROOMS

Begin preparations a day ahead

    2 pints cherry tomatoes
    6 tablespoons butter
    1½ pounds fresh mushrooms, sliced
    salt and freshly ground pepper
    2 tablespoons dry white wine
    2 tablespoons fresh chopped parsley
    ½ teaspoon thyme
    ½ teaspoon tarragon

Lightly butter a 2-quart shallow baking dish. Place the cherry tomatoes in the dish. Heat 4 tablespoons of the butter in a large skillet and add the mushrooms. Season with salt and pepper and cook over high heat for 4 minutes, stirring. Add the wine and cook for 1 minute, stirring. Remove from the heat and sprinkle with the herbs. Spoon the mushroom mixture over the tomatoes. Dot with the remaining 2 tablespoons butter, cool, cover, and refrigerate overnight. One hour before dinner is served, remove the dish from the refrigerator and let it rest at room temperature. Ten minutes before serving time cook the tomatoes in the oven for 5 minutes.

COLD LEMON MOUSSE

Prepare a day ahead

    1 envelope plain gelatin
    ½ cup cold water
    4 large eggs, separated
    ¼ cup fresh lemon juice
    1 cup sugar
    1 teaspoon fresh grated lemon rind
    ice cubes
    1 cup whipped heavy cream

Place the gelatin in the cold water to soften. Meanwhile, in the top of the double boiler placed over simmering water in the lower pan, add the combined egg yolks, lemon juice, and ½ cup of the sugar. Cook, constantly beating with a wire whisk until the mixture thickens slightly. Stir in the softened gelatin and lemon rind and remove from the heat. Turn the mixture into a bowl and place in a larger bowl filled with ice cubes. Beat until cool. Set aside. Whip the cream. Beat the egg whites, gradually adding the remaining ½ cup of sugar.

270

Fold the egg whites into the lemon mixture. Fold the whipped cream into the combined mixture. Turn into a 2-quart soufflé dish or bowl and refrigerate overnight.

ASPARAGUS MIMOSA

> 2 pounds fresh asparagus, stalk ends trimmed
> salt
>
> **MIMOSA SAUCE:**
>
> 2 large eggs, at room temperature
> ¾ cup olive oil
> 2 tablespoons white wine vinegar
> 1½ teaspoons Dijon mustard
> 1 teaspoon tarragon
> salt and freshly ground pepper

Bring 3 cups of water to a rolling boil in a saucepan. Reduce the heat to medium and gently lower the eggs into the water and cook for 10 minutes. In a large pot bring 2 quarts of water to a boil. Meanwhile, peel the asparagus stalks with a vegetable peeler. Drain the eggs and immediately run cold water over them for 1 minute. Lower the peeled asparagus into the lightly salted boiling water and cook over medium heat for 6 minutes. Peel the eggs and finely chop them. Place the eggs into a bowl. In a separate bowl beat together the remaining Mimosa Sauce ingredients with a wire whisk. Add the eggs and mix. Drain the asparagus and place in equal numbers in serving plates. Spoon the sauce over the stalks.

Independence Day Menus for 6, 8, and 12

•

MENU FOR 6

Lobster Rolls
Cold Broccoli Sesame
Stanley's Tomato Aspic
Fresh Strawberries and Blueberries
Lemonade

•

STANLEY'S TOMATO ASPIC   *Prepare a day ahead*

2 packages lemon Jell-O
1 16-ounce can tomato sauce
3 tablespoons red wine vinegar
1 tablespoon Worcestershire sauce
1 tablespoon fresh lemon juice
2 dashes of Tabasco sauce
½ cup thinly sliced scallions
½ cup thinly sliced stuffed green olives
½ cup black olive slivers
Boston lettuce leaves

In a saucepan bring 2½ cups of water to a boil. Stir in the Jell-O and remove from the heat. Stir until it dissolves. Add the tomato sauce, vinegar, Worcestershire sauce, lemon juice, and Tabasco sauce. Refrigerate until partially set, about 45 minutes; stir in the remaining ingredients except the lettuce and turn into a 2-quart mold. Refrigerate, covered, overnight. Unmold and serve on Boston lettuce leaves.

COLD BROCCOLI SESAME   *Prepare a day ahead*

    1 large bunch fresh broccoli spears, cleaned, stem ends and
        leaves cut off
    salt
    ½ cup sesame oil
    1 large garlic clove, crushed
    2 tablespoons soy sauce
    1 teaspoon fresh lemon juice
    3 tablespoons sesame seeds

Cut the broccoli spears into bite-size pieces. In a large pot,
bring 2 cups of lightly salted water to a boil and add the
broccoli. Cover and cook over medium-high heat for exactly
5 minutes. Drain. Place in a shallow serving dish. Combine
the sesame oil, garlic, soy sauce, and lemon juice. Sprinkle
over the broccoli. Cool, cover, and refrigerate overnight.
Garnish with the sesame seeds before serving.

LOBSTER ROLLS   *Begin preparations a day ahead*

    4 cups chopped cooked lobster meat
    2 scallions, thinly sliced
    2 tablespoons fresh chopped parsley
    1 teaspoon tarragon
    ¾ cup mayonnaise, or as needed
    1 tablespoon fresh lemon juice
    salt and freshly ground pepper
    6 soft hero rolls
    paprika

The night before, combine the lobster meat, scallions, parsley, tarragon, mayonnaise, and lemon juice in a large bowl.
Season to taste with salt and pepper. Cover and refrigerate.
Just before the picnic, cut pockets in each hero roll and stuff
it with equal amounts of the lobster salad. Sprinkle with
paprika.

FRESH STRAWBERRIES AND BLUEBERRIES

*Begin preparations
a day ahead*

2 pints fresh strawberries, hulled
2 pints fresh blueberries, stemmed

CRÈME FRAÎCHE:

1 cup heavy cream
1 cup sour cream

Prepare the Crème Fraîche the night before: In a mason-type jar combine the heavy cream and the sour cream, put lid on tightly, and shake vigorously. Leave at room temperature overnight. Shake mixture again the next morning and refrigerate it until used. Just before serving time, place the strawberries in one side of a large serving bowl and the blueberries in the other half. Serve with the Crème Fraîche.

LEMONADE

5 tablespoons sugar, or to taste
½ cup water
¾ cup fresh lemon juice
1½ quarts club soda
ice cubes
6 ⅛-inch-thick fresh lemon slices, seeded

Combine the sugar and water in a small saucepan. Bring mixture to a boil, stirring, until the sugar dissolves. Immediately remove it from the heat. Pour the sugar syrup, lemon juice, and club soda into pitcher and stir. Pour Lemonade into glasses filled with ice cubes. Garnish each drink with a slice of lemon.

NOTE: Fresh limeade can be made with the same recipe, substituting fresh lime juice and lime slices for the lemon juice and the lemon slices.

•

BETTY PAPPAS'S OUTDOOR DINNER
FOR 8 MENU

Antipasto Salad
Marinated London Broil
Spinach Salad with Pappas Dressing
Greek Pasta Salad
Hot Crusty Bread
Easy 'n Elegant Strawberries Romanoff

•

SPINACH SALAD WITH PAPPAS DRESSING

*Begin preparation
the night before*

2 pounds fresh spinach, washed, dried, and torn into
   bite-size pieces
12 bacon slices
4 eggs, hard-cooked and chopped

PAPPAS DRESSING:

¼ cup sugar
¼ cup ketchup
¼ cup red wine vinegar
juice of ½ lemon
½ teaspoon salt (optional)
1 small grated onion
1 tablespoon Worcestershire sauce
½ cup bacon fat
½ cup vegetable oil
freshly ground pepper to taste

Place the dried spinach in a large plastic bag and refrigerate
it overnight. Prepare the Pappas Dressing 30 minutes before
serving. Cook the bacon until crisp, drain, reserving ½ cup
of the bacon fat. Crumble the bacon and set aside. In a bowl,
combine the dressing ingredients and beat well. Taste for
seasoning. At serving time place the spinach in a large salad
bowl. Sprinkle with the crumbled bacon and chopped eggs.
Stir the dressing well and pour desired amount over the salad
and toss.

GREEK PASTA SALAD   *May be prepared a day ahead*

    1 pound feta cheese
    2 large fresh ripe tomatoes
    1 large red onion
    2 large green peppers, seeded
    1 tablespoon salt, plus salt for seasoning
    2 pounds macaroni, twists, shells, or other bite-size-shaped
        pasta
    1¼ cups olive oil
    4 tablespoons red wine vinegar
    1 tablespoon Dijon mustard
    2 teaspoons oregano
    freshly ground pepper to taste
    2 cups Greek olives

In a large pot bring 6 quarts of water to a rolling boil. Meanwhile, cube the cheese and tomatoes and chop the other vegetables. When the water is boiling, add 1 tablespoon salt, stir, and add the pasta; stir again and cook until just tender. Combine the oil, vinegar, mustard, oregano, salt, and pepper in a bowl with a wire whisk. Drain the pasta well and turn it into a large bowl. Add the olive oil mixture, cheese, vegetables, and Greek olives. Toss and cool. Cover and refrigerate overnight.

MARINATED   *Begin preparations*
LONDON BROIL   *a day ahead*

    2 2½-pound London broil steaks

    MARINADE:

    ½ cup soy sauce
    ¼ cup brown sugar
    1 teaspoon ground ginger
    1 teaspoon dry mustard
    2 large garlic cloves, crushed
    fresh grated pepper

Mix together the Marinade ingredients well and pour over the meat. Cover and refrigerate overnight. Turn the meat in the marinade a few times during the marination. When ready to serve, cook the meat over hot coals on grill about 5 minutes per side for rare, or to desired doneness.* Slice the meat against the grain diagonally into thin slices.

* NOTE: Meat can also be cooked under a hot broiler about 8 minutes per side for rare.

EASY 'N ELEGANT STRAWBERRIES ROMANOFF

        4 pints ripe strawberries
        3 tablespoons confectioners' sugar
        ½ gallon strawberry ice cream
        ½ cup orange juice
        ½ cup Cointreau

Wash, hull, and dry the strawberries. Place them in an attractive serving bowl, sprinkle with the sugar, and chill. One hour before serving, place the ice cream in another bowl and let it soften in the refrigerator. Add the orange juice and Cointreau to the softened ice cream. Stir gently. Serve the strawberries and ice cream sauce in bowls and let the guests prepare their own dessert.

ANTIPASTO SALAD   *May be prepared a day ahead*

        2 7-ounce cans white meat tuna, drained
        ½ pound Italian salami, cubed
        4 stalks celery, thinly sliced
        ½ cup green stuffed olives
        ½ cup black pitted olives
        1 pint cherry tomatoes, halved
        2 10-ounce packages frozen artichoke hearts, cooked and
            drained
        ½ pound mozzarella cheese, cubed
        ½ pound mushrooms, quartered
        4 scallions, thinly sliced
        1 large green pepper, seeded and cut into thin strips
        1 16-ounce can chick-peas, drained
        1 8-ounce jar hot Italian peppers, drained

DRESSING:

        1 cup vegetable oil
        3 tablespoons red wine vinegar
        1 teaspoon oregano
        ½ teaspoon rosemary
        1 large garlic clove, crushed
        1 teaspoon salt
        freshly ground pepper

In a large bowl place all of the salad ingredients. Prepare the dressing by beating all the ingredients together in a bowl with a wire whisk. Pour the dressing over the salad, toss, cover, and refrigerate until ready to serve.

●

AMANDA URBAN AULETTA'S ELEGANT DINNER FOR 12 MENU

Chicken and Pine Nut Sates
Chinese Sliced Fillet of Beef Salad
Tomatoes Stuffed with Spinach
Caesar Potato Salad
Toasted Pita Bread with Herb Butter
July 4th Fruit Salad

●

CHINESE SLICED FILLET OF BEEF SALAD

Begin preparations a day ahead

1 5-pound trimmed and tied fillet of beef
1½ pounds fresh bean sprouts
4 scallions, thinly sliced
¼ cup fresh chopped parsley

CHINESE VINAIGRETTE SAUCE:

1¼ cups peanut or vegetable oil
4 tablespoons rice wine vinegar or 3 tablespoons red wine vinegar
¼ cup soy sauce
1 tablespoon Dijon mustard
1 teaspoon tarragon
salt and freshly ground pepper to taste

Preheat the oven to 425°F. Place the beef in a roasting pan and cook in the oven for 15 minutes. Turn the roast and cook 20 minutes longer to medium-rare. Cool, cover, and refrigerate overnight. To prepare the salad, cut the beef in half lengthwise with a sharp slicing knife. Cut each piece of the beef into thin slices and place in a large bowl. Add the bean sprouts, scallions, and parsley. Combine the Chinese Vinaigrette Sauce ingredients well in a bowl and pour over the salad. Toss and taste for seasoning.

CHICKEN AND
PINE NUT SATES

*Begin preparations
a day ahead*

2½ pounds breast of chicken, boned and ground
3 tablespoons melted butter plus 7 tablespoons unmelted
  butter
1 cup fresh bread crumbs
2 eggs, beaten
½ teaspoon coriander
½ teaspoon ginger
2 tablespoons fresh chopped parsley
¼ cup minced shallots
½ cup pine nuts
salt and freshly ground pepper
3 tablespoons vegetable oil

In a large bowl thoroughly combine all the ingredients, except for the unmelted butter and oil. Shape into small fingers, approximately 3 inches in length and ¾ inch in thickness. Mixture should yield about 36 sates. In a large skillet, heat 3 tablespoons of the butter and 3 tablespoons of the oil and lightly brown about a dozen sates at a time. Remove, drain, and cool each batch as cooked. When all are cooled, cover and refrigerate overnight. Thirty minutes before serving, remove sates from refrigerator. Heat 4 tablespoons of the butter in a large skillet. When foaming subsides, add the sates. Cook, covered, shaking pan for 1 minute over medium-high heat. Uncover and sauté for a few minutes, shaking pan often until the sates are golden brown and thoroughly heated. Remove and drain. Stick one end of a 6-inch wooden skewer into each sate and serve.

CAESAR POTATO SALAD

5 pounds boiling potatoes, washed, peeled and cut into
¼-inch-thick slices

CAESAR DRESSING:

salt
1½ cups olive oil
¼ cup fresh lemon juice
10 anchovy fillets, chopped
2 tablespoons fresh chopped parsley
2 large garlic cloves, crushed
2 tablespoons Worcestershire sauce
freshly ground pepper
¾ cup fresh grated Parmesan cheese

In a large pot boil the potatoes in lightly salted water until
tender, about 14 minutes. Meanwhile, place the oil, lemon
juice, anchovies, parsley, garlic, and Worcestershire sauce
in a blender and puree. Taste for seasoning. Set aside. Drain
the potatoes well and place in a large bowl. Pour the dressing
over the potatoes, add the Parmesan cheese, and toss.

JULY 4th FRUIT SALAD

3 pints fresh strawberries, stemmed, washed, and halved
3 pints fresh blueberries, stemmed and washed
2 11-ounce cans litchi nuts in syrup, drained
½ cup confectioners' sugar

Combine the fruit in a large bowl. Sprinkle with the sugar
and gently toss. Refrigerate until ready to serve.

TOMATOES STUFFED WITH SPINACH

3 tablespoons butter, plus 4 tablespoons melted butter
1 medium onion, minced
1 large garlic clove, crushed
2 10-ounce packages frozen spinach, cooked and well
drained
fresh grated nutmeg
salt and freshly ground pepper to taste
12 medium fresh ripe firm tomatoes
¾ cup herbed bread crumbs

Heat the 3 tablespoons butter in a skillet and sauté the onion and garlic over medium heat for 5 minutes, stirring often. Remove from the heat and stir in the well-drained spinach. Season with the nutmeg, salt, and pepper. Preheat the oven to 350°F. Cut ½ inch off the top of each tomato. Hollow each of the tomatoes with a spoon and reserve the tomato pulp in a bowl. Drain the pulp and discard the seeds. Chop the pulp and mix into the spinach mixture. Taste for seasoning. Stuff the tomatoes with the mixture. Sprinkle the tops with the bread crumbs and the melted butter. Place on a baking sheet and cook in the oven for 25 minutes.

TOASTED PITA BREAD WITH HERB BUTTER

12 small pita breads
6 tablespoons melted sweet butter
2 teaspoons fresh finely chopped parsley
salt and freshly ground pepper

Preheat the broiler. Separate each pita bread by cutting open edge in circle with a small sharp knife. Cut each piece in half. Brush each piece with the combined melted butter and parsley. Sprinkle lightly with salt and pepper and place on a large baking sheet. Cook under the broiler until lightly golden.

Election Day Menus for 6 and 12

•

MENU FOR 6

Armenian Twist Cheese
Italian Sausages, Mushrooms, and Artichokes in Wine Sauce
Seafood Lasagne
Hot Cooked Asparagus and Endive Salad with Bacon
Ambrosia Fruit Salad

•

AMBROSIA FRUIT SALAD   *Prepare a day ahead*

    1 16-ounce can pineapple chunks with ½ cup of liquid
    1 cup mandarin oranges, drained
    1½ cups cubed Delicious apples
    1½ cups seedless green grapes
    1 cup grapefruit sections
    1 cup shredded coconut
    2 tablespoons confectioners' sugar
    ¼ cup dry sherry

Combine the ingredients in a bowl, cover, and chill overnight.

SEAFOOD LASAGNE   *May be prepared a day ahead*

LASAGNE:

    1½ pounds medium shrimp
    1 pound sea scallops, quartered

1 tablespoon salt
1½ cups chopped fresh or canned clams
1 pound lasagne noodles
2 pounds ricotta cheese
1 pound mozzarella cheese
1 cup fresh grated Parmesan cheese

SAUCE:

¼ cup olive or vegetable oil
2 cups chopped onions
2 large garlic cloves, crushed
1 1-pound 12-ounce can Italian plum tomatoes, pureed with
  liquid in blender
2 6-ounce cans tomato paste
2 8-ounce bottles clam juice
1 cup water
1 bay leaf, crumbled
1 teaspoon salt
½ teaspoon oregano or to taste
½ teaspoon basil or to taste
freshly ground pepper
¼ cup fresh chopped parsley

Prepare the sauce first: Heat the oil in a Dutch oven or similar shaped pot. Add the onions and garlic and cook over medium-low heat for 8 minutes, stirring often. Add the remaining ingredients, stir, and simmer for 30 minutes. Meanwhile, shell, devein, and chop the shrimp and quarter scallops. Heat 5 quarts of water in a pot and bring to a boil. Add 1 tablespoon of salt to water and when the sauce has cooked for 30 minutes, add the lasagne noodles to the boiling water. Cook the noodles until just tender.

While the pasta is cooking add the shrimp, scallops, and clams to the sauce; stir and cook until the pasta is done. Drain the pasta in a colander and immediately return it to the pot with 1 quart of cold water to prevent the pasta from sticking together. Preheat the oven to 325°F. Line a rectangular-shaped baking dish, approximately 12 × 16 inches with a little of the sauce. Place 3 lasagne noodles lengthwise over the sauce. Spoon the sauce over the noodles and dot with ricotta cheese. Place thin slices of the mozzarella cheese over the top and sprinkle with Parmesan cheese. Repeat layers 2 more times, spoon sauce over the final layer of ricotta cheese, top with mozzarella slices and Parmesan cheese. Bake for 45 minutes. Cool, cover, and refrigerate. To reheat place in preheated 350°F. oven for 25 minutes.

ITALIAN SAUSAGES, MUSHROOMS, AND ARTICHOKES IN WINE SAUCE

Begin preparations a day ahead

2 pounds sweet Italian sausages
3 tablespoons olive oil
3 tablespoons butter
2 medium onions, chopped
1/2 pound mushrooms, thinly sliced
1 1/2 cups dry red wine
1 cup beef broth
1/2 teaspoon thyme
1/2 teaspoon rosemary
3 whole bay leaves
1 1/2 tablespoons cornstarch
2 tablespoons water
2 10-ounce packages frozen artichoke hearts

Sauté the sausage links in 2 tablespoons of the heated olive oil in a large frying pan over medium heat until well browned evenly. Drain and cool. Clean the pan and heat 1 tablespoon of the oil and butter and sauté the onions and mushrooms for 5 minutes, stirring often. Meanwhile, in a saucepan bring the wine and broth to a boil. Reduce the heat to a simmer and add the onions, mushrooms, thyme, rosemary, and bay leaves. Simmer for 5 minutes. Cut the sausages into 1/4-inch-thick slices on the diagonal. Dissolve the cornstarch in 2 tablespoons water and stir into the sauce. Cook until the sauce thickens slightly. Add the sausages, cool, cover, and refrigerate. Ten minutes before serving, heat the mixture in a saucepan and cook the artichoke hearts in a separate pan. Drain the artichoke hearts and add to the mixture.

ARMENIAN TWIST CHEESE

Armenian Twist cheese comes in the shape of a small braid. Unbraid it and cut it into 4-inch lengths. Tear into strips and serve in a bowl.

HOT COOKED ASPARAGUS AND ENDIVE WITH BACON

    8 strips bacon
    2 pounds fresh asparagus
    salt
    2 large Belgian endives
    1 tablespoon fresh chopped parsley

COOKED DRESSING:

    1/2 cup vegetable oil
    2 1/2 tablespoons white wine vinegar
    1 small onion, minced
    salt and freshly ground pepper
    2 teaspoons Dijon mustard

In a small enamel or glass saucepan combine the oil, vinegar, and onion; season with salt and pepper. Bring to a boil, reduce the heat, and simmer for 3 minutes. Remove from the heat, beat in the mustard, and cover. Let stand at room temperature for 45 minutes. Fry the bacon until crisp, drain, and crumble. Set aside.

Five minutes before serving, cut the asparagus into 1-inch lengths on the diagonal. Bring 2 quarts of lightly salted water to a boil, add the asparagus, and simmer for exactly 5 minutes. Meanwhile, cut the endives into 1/2-inch slices on the diagonal and separate the leaves. Place the leaves in a bowl with drained asparagus and add the bacon. Pour the Cooked Dressing over the ingredients and sprinkle with the parsley. Toss and serve immediately.

•

MENU FOR 12

Cold Shrimp with Emerald Sauce
Chicken Breasts Stuffed Under the Skin
Rice and Green Pea Ring Mold with
Whole Sautéed Mushrooms
Four Lettuce Salad Vinaigrette
Cheesecake

•

CHICKEN BREASTS STUFFED UNDER THE SKIN

*Begin preparations
a day ahead*

4 cups fresh bread crumbs
1/2 cup fresh chopped parsley
1 tablespoon tarragon
1/2 teaspoon thyme
1/4 cup minced shallots
9 tablespoons melted butter
salt and freshly ground pepper
12 medium chicken breasts, boned, skins intact, and left whole
3/4 cup dry white wine
3/4 cup chicken broth
2 cups heavy cream

The night before combine the bread crumbs, parsley, herbs, shallots, and 7 tablespoons of butter. Season to taste with salt and pepper. Preheat the oven to 350°F. With fingers release the skin from the flesh at each side of each chicken breast. Place several spoons of the mixture under each side of the skin and smooth the skin back in place. Fold each side of the breast under and secure with toothpicks. Place the breasts in a baking pan with the wine and broth and brush with the remaining butter, or as needed. Cook in the oven for 45 minutes. Remove from the oven and cool. Cover and refrigerate overnight.

Before serving, preheat the oven to 300°F. and bring the liquid in the pan to a boil and remove the stuffed chicken breasts to another pan and place in the oven. Meanwhile cook the liquid for 5 minutes, stirring often. Strain the liquid and place in a saucepan. Add the cream and bring to a boil, stirring for 5 minutes. Season to taste and pour around the heated chicken.

CHEESECAKE

Prepare a day ahead

Cheesecake is remarkably easy to prepare. Its flavor is at its best the day after, so it's a perfect party dessert. This rich creamy version easily serves 16, allowing seconds for several guests.

5 8-ounce packages cream cheese, at room temperature
1 8-ounce container sour cream
1 cup sugar
2 teaspoons vanilla

286

juice of 1 lemon
5 eggs, lightly beaten

GRAHAM CRACKER CRUST:

4 tablespoons melted butter, plus butter for pan
12 graham crackers

Preheat the oven to 350°F. Coat the sides of 9-inch springform pan with butter. Crumble the graham crackers and make crumbs in a food processor, using the steel blade, or a ½ cupful at a time in a blender. Mix the crumbs with the butter with a fork until each crumb is coated. Press the crumbs lightly to sides of springform pan and press evenly over the bottom of the pan, about ¼ inch thick. Set aside.

Beat the cream cheese with a wooden spoon until it is smooth and creamy. Add the sour cream and sugar and combine. Add the vanilla, lemon juice, and eggs. Mix well. Pour into the crumb-lined pan and bake in the center of the oven rack for 1 hour. Turn off the heat and leave in the oven for 1 hour more. Do not open the oven door during cooking time or during the hour in shut-off oven. Cool on a cake rack. Loosely cover and refrigerate cheesecake overnight.

COLD SHRIMP WITH EMERALD SAUCE

Begin preparations a day ahead

½ of 1 lemon
1 onion, halved
2 bay leaves
3 celery stalks, sliced
3 sprigs parsley
10 peppercorns
3 pounds medium shrimp, shelled and deveined

EMERALD SAUCE:

½ cup fresh chopped parsley
½ cup fresh chopped watercress
2 scallions, finely chopped
2 cups mayonnaise
2 dashes Tabasco sauce
1 tablespoon fresh lemon juice
1 teaspoon tarragon
freshly ground pepper to taste

In a large saucepan bring 2½ quarts of water to a boil with the juice of lemon, onion, bay leaves, celery, parsley, and peppercorns. Add the shrimp and cook over medium heat for exactly 6 minutes, stirring occasionally. Drain the shrimp and cool. Cover in a bowl and refrigerate overnight. One hour before serving, prepare the Emerald Sauce by combining the ingredients. Refrigerate the sauce until ready to serve. Place the sauce in a bowl on a serving dish and surround with the chilled shrimp. Accompany with toothpicks.

FOUR LETTUCE SALAD VINAIGRETTE

Begin preparations a day ahead

    1 large head romaine lettuce
    2 bunches watercress
    2 large heads Boston lettuce
    1 arugula

VINAIGRETTE SAUCE:

    1 cup olive oil
    2 tablespoons red wine vinegar
    1 garlic clove, crushed
    1/4 cup minced shallots
    salt and freshly ground pepper
    2 teaspoons Dijon mustard

Wash the lettuce leaves and dry them. Tear into bite-size pieces and place in a large plastic bag. Refrigerate overnight. In a saucepan, place the ingredients for the Vinaigrette Sauce, except for the mustard, and bring to a boil. Remove from the heat and beat in the mustard. Cool, cover, and refrigerate overnight. One hour before dinner remove the Vinaigrette Sauce and let rest at room temperature. Just before serving place the lettuce in a large serving bowl. Beat the Vinaigrette Sauce and strain it over the salad. Toss and serve.

RICE AND GREEN PEA RING MOLD WITH WHOLE SAUTÉED MUSHROOMS

    2 cups long-grain rice
    1 10-ounce package frozen peas
    2 tablespoons melted butter, plus 3 tablespoons butter
    oil for mold
    1½ pounds fresh mushrooms
    salt and freshly ground pepper

Cook the rice according to the package directions. While the rice is cooking, cook and drain the peas and set aside. When the rice is done, stir in the melted butter and peas. Oil a large ring mold and spoon the rice mixture into lightly oiled ring mold. Press the mixture down with the back of a spoon, and let rest for 5 minutes. Meanwhile, heat the remaining butter in a large skillet and sauté the mushrooms over high heat, shaking the pan frequently. Season to taste with salt and pepper. Place a round serving dish on the top of the ring mold. Holding each carefully, invert the dish and mold. Fill the center with half of the sautéed mushrooms and spoon the remaining mushrooms around the mold.

Thanksgiving Menus for 6 and 12

•

MENU FOR 6

Avocados Madeira
Roast Cornish Game Hens Burgundy
Turnip Puree
Spinach, Endive, and Walnut Salad with
Orange Vinaigrette Dressing
Pumpkin Cake
Irish Coffee

•

PUMPKIN CAKE   *Prepare a day ahead*

    1 cup vegetable oil
    ½ cup melted butter
    2 cups canned pumpkin
    4 eggs, beaten
    4 cups all-purpose flour
    2 cups sugar
    1 tablespoon baking powder
    1 tablespoon baking soda
    1 teaspoon salt
    2 teaspoons cinnamon
    ½ teaspoon ginger
    ¼ teaspoon fresh grated nutmeg
    1 cup chopped walnuts
    1 cup golden raisins
    ice cream (optional)

Preheat the oven to 350°F. In a large bowl mix the oil, butter, and pumpkin. Beat in the eggs. Sift all the dry ingredients

and add to the mixture. Mix well and fold in the walnuts and
raisins. Turn into a 10-inch tube pan and bake in the oven for
1 hour or until done. Cool. Remove the cake from pan and
keep under a cake cover overnight. Serve in slices with the
ice cream of your choice.

ROAST CORNISH GAME HENS BURGUNDY

*Begin preparations
a day ahead*

2 cups white burgundy wine
1 cup olive oil
1 teaspoon rosemary
1 teaspoon thyme
1 teaspoon marjoram
3 bay leaves, crumbled
1 large garlic clove, crushed
12 peppercorns
½ teaspoon salt
6 Cornish game hens

In a bowl combine wine, olive oil, herbs, bay leaves, garlic,
peppercorns, and salt. Place the Cornish hens in a large dish
and pour the mixture over the hens. Turn the hens, spooning
some of the marinade inside the birds. Cover and refrigerate
overnight. One hour and 15 minutes before serving remove
the hens from the refrigerator. Preheat the oven to 375°F.
Remove the hens from the marinade and pat them dry. Place
the hens in a roasting pan and cook for 1 hour or until tender,
basting with the pan juices twice during cooking time.

SPINACH, ENDIVE AND WALNUT SALAD WITH ORANGE VINAIGRETTE DRESSING

Begin preparations a day ahead

1 pound fresh spinach, washed, dried, and broken into bite-size pieces
4 Belgian endives, stem ends cut off and separated into individual leaves
1 cup chopped walnuts

ORANGE VINAIGRETTE DRESSING:

1 egg yolk
½ teaspoon Dijon mustard
1 cup vegetable oil
1 tablespoon red wine vinegar
1 teaspoon grated orange rind
2 tablespoons orange juice
½ teaspoon tarragon
salt and freshly ground pepper to taste

Place the spinach and endives in a plastic bag and refrigerate overnight. Make Orange Vinaigrette Dressing by beating the egg yolk and mustard with a wire whisk. Add the oil drop by drop until it is used. Beat in the remaining ingredients, cover, and refrigerate overnight. At serving time, divide the spinach onto 6 salad plates. Arrange the endive leaves in equal amounts across the spinach, turning curved sides of the leaves inward with the pointed ends toward the center of the salad. Sprinkle walnuts around border of the plates. Spoon the dressing over salad.

TURNIP PUREE

3 pounds turnips, peeled and quartered
4 tablespoons butter
⅓ cup milk, or as needed
salt and freshly ground white pepper to taste
2 tablespoons fresh chopped parsley

Boil the turnips in water to cover them, and cook until tender, about 15 minutes. Drain the turnips and mash. Add the butter and milk; combine well and season with salt and pepper. Place the turnip puree in a warmed serving dish and sprinkle with the parsley. Keep warm in low oven until served.

AVOCADOS MADEIRA

3 tablespoons butter
3 tablespoons vegetable oil
6 slices white bread, crusts trimmed
3 medium avocados, peeled, halved, and seeded
12 tablespoons Madeira

Heat the butter and oil in a skillet. Sauté 3 slices of the bread at a time, until golden brown on both sides. Drain. Place each slice of the bread on an individual serving dish. Slice an avocado half and place the slices over the toast. Sprinkle each with 2 tablespoons of Madeira. Serve immediately.

IRISH COFFEE

1 cup heavy cream
sugar
6 cups hot strong black coffee
6 ounces Irish whiskey

Whip the cream lightly, add sugar, then beat until light and fluffy. Pour 1 cup of the coffee into each Irish coffee glass or cup and add 1 ounce of whiskey to each. Spoon the whipped cream over each glass. Serve with sugar.

●

MENU FOR 12

*Roast and Broiled Duck Quarters with
Cranberry and Apricot Sauce
Candied Yams with Pecans and Maple Syrup
Hot Lentil Salad
Fresh Steamed String Beans
Mincemeat Cheesecake*

●

ROAST AND BROILED DUCK QUARTERS WITH CRANBERRY AND APRICOT SAUCE

*Begin preparations
a day ahead*

3 4½-pound ducks, quartered
salt and freshly ground pepper

CRANBERRY AND APRICOT SAUCE:

1 cup orange juice
1/2 teaspoon ginger
1 tablespoon cornstarch
1 16-ounce can whole cranberry sauce
1 10-ounce jar apricot preserves

The night before preheat the oven to 400°F. Cut off fat from ducks at the cavity openings. Prick the ducks in the lower thigh areas and season with salt and pepper. Place in 1 large or 2 smaller roasting pans and cook for 45 minutes. Remove the ducks and cool. Transfer to a clean pan and refrigerate overnight.

One hour before serving remove the ducks from the refrigerator. Thirty minutes before dinner place half of duck quarters in a large broiling pan, skin side down, heat broiler, and broil for 5 minutes. Turn and broil 5 minutes longer. Transfer the cooked ducks to another baking dish and place on a low rack. Broil the remaining ducks in the same manner. Meanwhile, prepare the Cranberry and Apricot Sauce. In a saucepan bring the orange juice, ginger, and cornstarch to a boil. Add the cranberry sauce and apricot preserves. Stir and bring to a boil. Turn off the heat and cover. Serve the duck with the sauce.

HOT LENTIL SALAD   *Begin preparations a day ahead*

2 cups dried lentils
1 cup chopped celery
1/2 cup chopped onion
1 large garlic clove, crushed
1/2 teaspoon thyme
2 bay leaves
2 teaspoons salt
freshly ground pepper
3 tablespoons softened butter

Place all the ingredients except for the butter in a Dutch oven and cover with water. Bring to a boil, reduce heat, and simmer for 1 1/2 hours. Stir occasionally, particularly near the end of cooking time to prevent the lentils from sticking to the bottom of the pan. Cool and refrigerate, covered, overnight. Heat before serving in sauce pan, adding a little water.

MINCEMEAT CHEESECAKE   *Prepare a day ahead*

2 8-ounce packages cream cheese, softened
1 14-ounce can sweetened condensed milk
¼ cup fresh lemon juice
1 envelope plain gelatin
1 cup mincemeat (None Such is an excellent brand)
2 teaspoons grated lemon rind
¾ cup chopped walnuts
1 cup heavy cream

GRAHAM CRACKER CRUST:

1 cup graham cracker crumbs
3 tablespoons melted butter
3 tablespoons sugar

Combine the ingredients for the graham cracker crust with a fork. Press the mixture firmly on the bottom of a 9-inch springform pan. Refrigerate. In a large mixing bowl beat the cream cheese until smooth and fluffy. Beat in the sweetened condensed milk. Place the lemon juice and gelatin in a small saucepan and cook over low heat until the gelatin dissolves. *Do not boil*. Add the mixture to the cream cheese mixture with the mincemeat, lemon rind, and ½ cup walnuts. Mix well. Beat the heavy cream until whipped and fold it into the cake mixture. Pour the mixture over the graham cracker crust in the bottom of a springform pan and sprinkle the remaining nuts around the border of the cake. Refrigerate overnight.

CANDIED YAMS WITH PECANS
AND MAPLE SYRUP

10 medium yams, quartered crosswise
1¾ cups orange juice
1 tablespoon fresh grated orange rind
3 tablespoons butter
2 tablespoons cornstarch
½ cup maple syrup
½ cup sugar
1 cup pecan halves

Boil the yams in a generous amount of water until just tender. Meanwhile, place the next 6 ingredients in a saucepan and bring to a boil, stirring with a wire whisk. Remove from the heat and preheat oven to 350°F. Drain and peel the yams and place in a lightly greased baking dish. Scatter the pecans over the yams and pour the sauce over the top. Bake in the oven for 25 minutes.

FRESH STEAMED STRING BEANS

> 3 pounds fresh string beans, ends trimmed and cut into
>   1-inch lengths
> 5 tablespoons butter
> salt and freshly ground pepper

Bring 1 inch of water to a boil in the bottom pan of a large vegetable steamer. Steam the beans for 15 minutes in a covered steamer. Toss beans in the butter and season with salt and pepper to taste.

Christmas Menus for 6 and 12

•

MENU FOR 6

Salmon Mousse
Marinated Broiled Rib Steaks
Batter-Fried Anchovies
Caesar Salad
Walnut Pie
Three Spice Ice Cream
Eggnog

•

WALNUT PIE   *Prepare a day ahead*

PIE DOUGH:

1½ cups sifted all-purpose flour
½ teaspoon salt
1 tablespoon sugar
6 tablespoons sweet butter
3 tablespoons ice cold water

WALNUT FILLING:

3 eggs, lightly beaten
1 cup dark corn syrup
3 tablespoons melted butter
pinch of salt
1 teaspoon vanilla
2 cups walnut halves

Prepare the pie dough. Place the flour, salt, sugar, and

butter, cut into pieces into a food processor fitted with the steel blade and turn on. When the mixture is a coarse crumb consistency, add the water through the feed tube and run the machine a few seconds until the dough forms a shape against the blade. Shape the dough into a ball, cover, and place in the freezer for 10 minutes.

Combine the ingredients for the pie filling. Preheat the oven to 375°F. Remove the pie dough and roll it out on a lightly floured board to 1/8-inch thickness. Fit it into a 9-inch pie pan and cut off the extra dough. Sprinkle lightly with flour. Add the stirred pie filling and place on a baking sheet. Cook in the oven for about 45 minutes until done. Cover and refrigerate.

MARINATED BROILED RIB STEAKS

Begin preparations a day ahead

1 cup dry sherry
1 cup water
1/3 cup olive oil
1 onion, chopped
1 garlic clove, crushed
2 bay leaves, crumbled
10 peppercorns
6 1-inch-thick boneless rib steaks

Place the sherry, water, oil, onion, garlic, bay leaves, and peppercorns in a shallow dish. Mix well and add the steaks, turning to make certain all the sides are coated with the mixture. Cover and refrigerate overnight. One hour before serving, remove the steaks from the refrigerator. Ten minutes before dinner, remove the steaks from the marinade, heat broiler, and broil in a large pan for 5 minutes per side for rare, or to desired doneness, basting when turned.

SALMON MOUSSE

Prepare a day ahead

1 1/2 envelopes plain gelatin
3 tablespoons fresh lemon juice
1 15-ounce can salmon, bones and skins removed
1 cup hot chicken broth
2 scallions, chopped
1 teaspoon tarragon
salt and freshly ground pepper
1 cup whipped heavy cream

In a small bowl soften the gelatin in the lemon juice. In a large bowl flake the salmon very fine with a fork. Stir the softened gelatin into the hot broth and pour into bowl with the salmon; add the scallions and tarragon. Mix well and season with salt and pepper. Fold in the whipped cream and turn into a lightly oiled 1-quart mold. Refrigerate overnight.

THREE SPICE ICE CREAM

May be prepared a day ahead

1 quart softened vanilla ice cream
1 teaspoon nutmeg
½ teaspoon ginger
2 teaspoons cinnamon

Combine the ice cream and the spices well and place back in the ice cream container or containers. Refreeze for several hours or overnight.

EGGNOG

Prepare a day ahead

2 quarts eggnog, well chilled
½ cup dark rum
½ cup bourbon
½ cup brandy
½ cup cream sherry
fresh grated nutmeg

Combine the ingredients except for the nutmeg in a large bowl. Refrigerate overnight. Stir and sprinkle with nutmeg when served.

BATTER-FRIED ANCHOVIES

12 anchovy fillets
1 cup milk
oil for deep frying
½ cup flour
½ cup beer

Soak the anchovy fillets in milk for 10 minutes. Remove and pat them dry. Heat the oil in a pan with 6-inch sides. Beat together the flour and beer with a wire whisk. When the oil is hot (about 370°F.), dip each anchovy fillet in the batter and fry until golden brown. Drain on paper towels.

CAESAR SALAD

5 slices firm white bread, crusts trimmed
5 tablespoons vegetable oil
2 tablespoons butter
1 large head romaine lettuce, washed, dried, and torn into bite-size pieces

DRESSING:

¾ cup olive oil
1 large garlic clove, crushed
6 anchovy fillets, mashed
1 teaspoon Dijon mustard
1 egg, boiled for 1 minute in shell
2 tablespoons fresh lemon juice
1 tablespoon Worcestershire sauce
½ cup fresh grated Parmesan cheese, or to taste

Cut the bread slices into ½-inch cubes. Heat the vegetable oil and butter in a large skillet. Add the bread cubes when the fat is hot but not smoking, and cook, stirring, for about 1 minute until golden brown. Drain on paper towels. Place the lettuce in a large salad bowl. In a small bowl beat together the olive oil, garlic, anchovies, and mustard. Pour the mixture over the salad and toss. Break the egg over the salad and toss. Sprinkle the lemon juice and Worcestershire sauce over the salad and toss again. Finally, sprinkle with the cheese and croutons and toss.

•

MENU FOR 12

Smoked Salmon Spread
Boneless Pork Roast Stuffed with Prunes
Brussels Sprouts with Walnuts
Christmas Cranberry Mold
Peach Mold
Fruit Cake
Date and Pecan Log Candy

•

FRUIT CAKE
Prepare at least four days ahead

½ pound (2 sticks) butter
1 cup sugar
5 large eggs
2 cups flour
2 teaspoons baking powder
½ teaspoon nutmeg
½ teaspoon cinnamon
½ teaspoon allspice
2 cups raisins
2 cups chopped candied citron
2 cups chopped dates
½ cup candied red cherries
2 cups chopped pecans or walnuts
¼ cup orange juice
½ cup dark rum

Cream together the butter and sugar until light and lemon colored. Beat in the eggs, one at a time. Sift the flour, baking powder, and spices into a mixing bowl. In a separate large mixing bowl combine the raisins, citron, dates, cherries, and nuts. Add ½ cup of the flour mixture to the fruit and nuts and toss well. Add the remaining flour mixture to the butter mixture along with the orange juice and rum. Mix well. Fold in the fruit mixture. Preheat the oven to 275°F. Grease 2 loaf pans and line them with strips of wax paper. Divide the mixture equally into the pans, packing it firmly. Place the pans in a large roasting pan filled with 1½ inches of hot water. Bake for about 2 hours, or until done. Cool. Turn out the cakes and wrap each in rum-soaked double layers of cheesecloth. Store in tightly closed containers or aluminum foil at room temperature for at least four days before serving.

DATE AND PECAN LOG CANDY
Prepare at least two days ahead

1 16-ounce can evaporated milk
4 cups sugar
4 tablespoons butter
1 8-ounce package pitted dates
1 8-ounce bottle maraschino cherries, drained and chopped
2 cups chopped pecans
1 teaspoon vanilla
confectioners' sugar

In a heavy saucepan add the evaporated milk and sugar. Cook over medium-high heat, stirring for 5 minutes. Add the remaining ingredients and cook at a low boil for about 20 minutes, stirring often, until the mixture reaches the hard ball stage. Cool and beat with a wooden spoon for 2 minutes. In a clean, wet and squeezed out, kitchen towel pour the mixture lengthwise, about 16 inches. Roll up and tie the ends. The candy should be about 1½ inches in diameter. Wrap the towel in foil and refrigerate. Just before serving, unwrap, dust with confectioners' sugar, and slice into ¼-inch-thick slices. Keep the unused log wrapped in foil in the refrigerator.

BONELESS PORK ROAST STUFFED WITH PRUNES

Begin preparations a day ahead

1 6-pound loin of pork
10 ounces pitted whole prunes
salt and freshly ground pepper
½ teaspoon ginger
2 tablespoons dry sherry

Ask your butcher to bone the pork and cut out a 1-inch hole in the center of the pork lengthwise. Preheat the oven to 350°F. Place the prunes in a bowl and pour 3 cups of boiling water over them. Let soak for 5 minutes, drain, and reserve the juice. Stuff the prunes into the hole with the aid of the end of a wooden spoon. Tie the roast with kitchen string at 1-inch intervals. Season with salt and pepper. In a large roasting pan, brown the pork roast on all sides over high heat on top of stove. Cook roast in the oven for about 2½ hours, basting with the combined prune juice, ginger, and sherry, every half hour. Remove roast from the oven and cool. Cover and refrigerate overnight. One hour before serving, remove the roast from the refrigerator and let rest at room temperature. Preheat the oven to 350°F. and place in the oven for 20 minutes. Slice thinly and serve.

CHRISTMAS CRANBERRY MOLD

Prepare a day ahead

2 envelopes plain gelatin
½ cup water
2 cups cranberry juice
2 cups fresh whole cranberries

¼ cup sugar
1½ cups crushed pineapple and liquid
½ cup thinly sliced celery
½ cup chopped walnuts

Soften the gelatin in the water. In a large saucepan bring the cranberry juice to a boil. Add the cranberries and cook over medium heat for about 5 minutes, until the cranberries begin to pop open. Remove from the heat and stir in the softened gelatin, sugar, pineapple, celery, and walnuts. Place the mixture into a lightly greased 2-quart mold or dish and refrigerate overnight. Unmold.

PEACH MOLD   *Prepare a day ahead*

2 20-ounce cans peach halves
2 packages orange-flavored Jell-O
2 3-ounce packages softened cream cheese
½ cup peach brandy
½ cup toasted almond slivers

Drain the peaches, reserving the liquid. Measure the liquid and add enough water to make 3 cups of liquid. Bring the liquid to a boil in a saucepan and add the Jell-O. Remove from the heat and stir until Jell-O dissolves. Pour half of the mixture into a blender with half of the peaches, 3 ounces of the cream cheese, and brandy. Puree. Pour the mixture into a large bowl and puree the remaining ingredients. Pour into the bowl and combine well. Turn the mixture into a lightly greased 3-quart Jell-O mold. Refrigerate overnight. Unmold and decorate the top with almond slivers.

SMOKED SALMON SPREAD   *Prepare a day ahead*

½ pound sliced smoked salmon
1 pound cream cheese, softened
2 cups sour cream
2 tablespoons fresh lemon juice
2 scallions, thinly sliced
4 ounces red salmon caviar
pepper
French bread, pumpernickel, and/or crackers

Grind the smoked salmon in a food processor fitted with the steel blade, or in a meat grinder. Beat the cream cheese until light and fluffy. Add the smoked salmon, sour cream, lemon

303

juice, and scallions. Mix well. Turn into a serving bowl and smooth the top. (Use glass bowl, if possible.) Cover and refrigerate overnight. At serving time make a border around top edge of the surface of the mixture with the red caviar. Grate fresh pepper over the top. Serve with sliced bread and/or crackers.

BRUSSELS SPROUTS WITH WALNUTS

    6 tablespoons butter
    1 cup chicken broth
    1 medium onion, minced
    3 pints fresh Brussels sprouts, stalk ends trimmed if
        necessary
    ¾ cup chopped walnuts
    salt and freshly ground pepper

Bring the butter and broth to a boil in a Dutch oven. Add the onion and Brussels sprouts. Reduce the heat and simmer for about 20 minutes, until tender. Toss the Brussels sprouts twice during cooking time. Sprinkle the sprouts with the walnuts and season with salt and pepper to taste. Gently toss.

New Year's Eve Menus
for 6 and 8

•

MENU FOR 6

Raclette
Bouillabaisse with Rouille
Arugula and Endive Salad with French Dressing
Raspberry Crepe Cake

•

RASPBERRY
CREPE CAKE

Begin preparations
a day ahead

CREPE BATTER:

¾ cup milk
¾ cup water
¾ cup flour
2 tablespoons sugar
3 eggs
2 tablespoons vegetable oil
½ teaspoon salt
4 tablespoons melted butter, or as needed
whipped cream or vanilla ice cream (optional)

RASPBERRY SAUCE:

1½ cups raspberry preserves
1 tablespoon sugar
2 tablespoons kirsch

In a large bowl combine the ingredients for the crepe batter, except for the butter, and beat with a whisk until thoroughly blended. In a 7- to 8-inch crepe pan heat 2 teaspoons of the butter and wipe out with a paper towel. Heat ½ teaspoon of butter and coat pan with it. Ladle about ¼ cup of the crepe batter into the hot pan and tilt it in a circle to distribute the batter evenly. When the crepe turns light brown around the edges, turn it with a spatula and cook for about 30 seconds until it is lightly browned on the other side. Transfer the crepe to a plate and repeat cooking process until all the batter is used; it should make about 16 crepes. Cover and refrigerate crepes overnight.

One hour before serving heat the raspberry preserves in a saucepan with the sugar and kirsch for 5 minutes. Puree in a blender. Place one crepe on a cake plate and brush with the Raspberry Sauce, top with another crepe, and brush with the sauce. Repeat this process until all the crepes are used. Spoon the remaining sauce over top and refrigerate. When ready to serve, cut into wedges. Serve with whipped cream or vanilla ice crea.

BOUILLABAISE WITH ROUILLE

Begin preparations a day ahead

4 tablespoons olive oil
1 large onion, chopped
2 garlic cloves, crushed
1 16-ounce can whole tomatoes and liquid
2 tablespoons tomato paste
2 bay leaves
½ teaspoon thyme
¼ teaspoon saffron
1½ quarts bottled clam juice
2 cups water
1 cup chopped fresh clams
salt and freshly ground pepper to taste
1 pound bay scallops
1 pound shrimp, shelled and deveined
½ pound haddock or bass fillets, cut into 2-inch pieces
½ pound halibut or snapper fillets, cut into 2-inch pieces

ROUILLE:

1 dried chili pepper, crushed
1 pimiento, chopped
2 large garlic cloves, crushed
2 tablespoons fresh bread crumbs
¾ cup olive oil

CROUTONS:

4 tablespoons butter
4 tablespoons vegetable oil
12 1-inch-thick slices French bread

The night before in a large pot heat the oil and sauté the onion and garlic for 10 minutes, stirring, over medium-low heat. Add the next 8 ingredients and stir. Season with salt and pepper. Bring to a boil, reduce heat, and simmer for 10 minutes. Remove from the heat and cool. Cover and refrigerate overnight.

Prepare the Rouille 45 minutes before dinner. Mash the chili pepper, pimiento, garlic, and bread crumbs in a plate and slowly beat in the olive oil until thickened. Place in a bowl and cover.

Prepare the Croutons. Heat the butter and oil in a large skillet and brown the bread slices on each side. Remove and drain on paper towels. Thirty minutes before serving dinner, remove the clam juice mixture from the refrigerator. Bring the mixture to a boil, reduce heat, and simmer for 10 minutes. Add the seafood and simmer for about 8 minutes. To serve, place 2 croutons into each of 6 large soup bowls and ladle the soup over the bread. Serve with the rouille.

ARUGULA AND ENDIVE SALAD WITH FRENCH DRESSING

4 Belgian endives, root ends trimmed
2 bunches arugula, washed, dried, and stems trimmed

FRENCH DRESSING:

½ cup olive oil
1 tablespoon red wine vinegar
½ teaspoon dry mustard
salt and freshly ground pepper to taste

Cut the endives into 1-inch pieces and separate. Place the endive leaves in a salad bowl with the arugula. Combine the French Dressing ingredients in a small bowl with a wire whisk. Pour over the greens and toss.

RACLETTE

1 pound Bagnes, Appenzeller, or Gruyère cheese
butter
freshly ground pepper
1 cup cornichon pickles
1 cup pickled cocktail onions
sliced French bread
sweet butter

Cut the cheese into ¼-inch-thick slices. Lightly butter 8 individual ramekins or ovenproof shallow dishes. Line bottom of each dish with equal amounts of the cheese. Heat the broiler and place the dishes on a baking sheet under the broiler, until the cheese melts, but don't let it brown. Sprinkle with pepper. Serve immediately, garnished with pickles, onions, French bread, and butter.

NOTE: Small hot new boiled potatoes can also be served.

•

MENU FOR 8

Peking Chicken Wings with Hoisin Sauce
Filet Mignon Kebobs
Fresh Vegetable Salad
Holiday Wild Rice
Chocolate Mousse

•

CHOCOLATE MOUSSE   *Prepare a day ahead*

2 14-ounce cans sweetened condensed milk
6 ounces semisweet chocolate morsels
1 tablespoon instant coffee powder
3 tablespoons Grand Marnier
2 cups heavy cream
4 egg whites

In a heavy saucepan combine the sweetened condensed milk, chocolate morsels, and coffee. Cook over medium heat, stirring constantly, until the chocolate melts and the sauce begins to thicken. Stir in the Grand Marnier and remove from the heat. Stir until the sauce thickens. Turn into a bowl and cool to room temperature. Meanwhile, whip

308

the heavy cream. When the chocolate mixture is cool, beat it vigorously and fold in the whipped cream. Beat the egg whites until stiff but not dry and fold into the mousse. Turn the mousse into a crystal or other serving bowl. Refrigerate overnight.

NOTE: Whipped cream can be used to garnish the mousse either piped on through a pastry bag fitted with a rose tube or spooned on. Grated semisweet chocolate can also be used to decorate the mousse.

BROILED FILET MIGNON KEBOBS

Begin preparations a day ahead

3 tablespoons olive oil
3 medium onions, halved and separated into pieces
1/4 cup dry red wine
1 pound fresh mushrooms, stems removed
1 3-pound filet mignon, cut into 1 1/2-inch cubes
3 medium firm ripe tomatoes, cut into 8 wedges each

MARINADE:

3/4 cup vegetable oil
1/4 cup red wine vinegar
1/4 cup dry red wine
2 bay leaves, crumbled
1 teaspoon basil
1 large garlic clove, crushed
1 dozen black peppercorns
salt and freshly ground pepper

In a large skillet heat the olive oil and add the onions. Cover and simmer for 5 minutes, shaking the pan frequently. Add the wine and mushrooms and cook, covered, for 2 minutes. Thread 8 8-inch wooden skewers with alternating pieces of the mushroom, beef, onion, and tomato. Push the ingredients snugly together on the skewers. Place the skewers in a large pan. Combine the marinade ingredients and pour over the kebobs and turn to coat them evenly. Cover and refrigerate overnight.

Thirty minutes before serving dinner, remove the kebobs from the refrigerator and let rest at room temperature. Heat the broiler. Cook in a large broiling pan 5 inches from the heat for 5 minutes on each side for rare, or according to desired doneness.

FRESH VEGETABLE SALAD   *Prepare a day ahead*

>1 bunch fresh broccoli, cut into bite-size pieces
>1 head cauliflower, cut into flowerets
>2 large green peppers, seeded and cut into squares
>3 carrots, cut diagonally into ¼-inch-thick slices
>2 large zucchini, cut into sticks
>4 stalks celery, cut into ¼-inch-thick slices
>4 scallions, cut into 1½-inch lengths
>½ pound snow pea pods, trimmed
>¾ cup vegetable oil
>2 tablespoons fresh lemon juice
>1 tablespoon soy sauce
>2 tablespoons fresh chopped parsley
>salt and freshly ground pepper to taste

Steam the vegetables, except for the snow pea pods, in a large steamer for 5 minutes over boiling water. Cook in 2 batches if the steamer isn't large enough. Transfer the vegetables to a large platter with the snow pea pods. Combine the remaining ingredients and pour over the vegetables and toss well. Cool, cover, and refrigerate overnight. Toss well before serving, and taste for the seasoning.

HOLIDAY WILD RICE

>3 cups chicken broth or stock
>½ cup dry sherry
>1 cup wild rice
>1 tablespoon butter
>½ cup chopped onions
>½ cup sliced almonds

Bring the broth and sherry to a boil in a saucepan. Add the rice, butter, and onions. Cook and simmer for 50 minutes. Drain in a colander. Return to the saucepan and stir in the almonds. Keep warm in the oven until served.

PEKING CHICKEN WINGS
WITH HOISIN SAUCE

>6 cups water
>½ cup honey
>16 chicken wings, cut into 3 pieces at joints (discard wing tips)

1 12-ounce can hoisin sauce, at room temperature*
8 scallions, trimmed

Preheat the oven to 400°F. Bring the water to a boil in a Dutch oven or similar size pot. Add the honey and stir. Immerse the chicken wings in the boiling mixture for 15 seconds. Immediately remove with a slotted spoon. Drain well. Place on a greased baking sheet and cook for approximately 30 minutes until crisp and brown. Place 4 wings in each of the 8 serving dishes in a star shape. Spoon 2 tablespoons of the hoisin sauce at the center and top with a scallion.

---

* Hoisin sauce is found in Chinese or specialty food shops.

CHAPTER EIGHT

Cocktail Parties

The Bar

Preparing the bar for a cocktail party, whether the party is to be small or large, is very similar; it's the quantities that differ enormously. Wine and spirits, beer, soda, and tonic, pitcher of water, ice, ice cubes, cocktail olives and onions, lemons and limes, highball and tall glasses, wine glasses, and cocktail napkins are all required. Space needs to be created in the refrigerator for white wine and beer.

The good thing about having too much is that nothing will spoil, and it is always better to have more than you need.

A drink just doesn't taste the same in a plastic glass. Dime store glasses are inexpensive and serve the purpose well. For a party of 50, it is possible to rent glasses, and if that is too costly, then borrow glasses from friends, but avoid plastic glasses.

For a cocktail party for 50 people set up the bar where it is convenient, but out of the kitchen. A card table in a hall or any open area of the living room is best. If it is summer and the guests will spend most of the party time outdoors, set up the bar on the deck or in the back yard.

For small gatherings, a tray on a coffee table, if large enough, is convenient.

A bar for 50 people is difficult unless you know all your guests' drinking habits. Today more and more people are drinking wine, but that's not always predictable.

The following bar was given to me by a bartender whose philosophy is that it is always better to be safe. If you know that none of your guests will drink bourbon or beer, plan accordingly.

THE BAR FOR 50

LIQUOR

1 bottle dry vermouth
1 bottle sweet vermouth
3 bottles vodka (if summer, 5 bottles)
3 bottles gin (if summer, 5 bottles)
3 bottles scotch (if summer, only 1 bottle)

2 bottles dark rum
1 bottle bourbon
1 bottle blended whiskey
1½ cases of dry white wine, chilled
6 bottles dry red wine
24 bottles beer, chilled
1 bottle dry sherry

SETUPS

1 case club soda
6 quarts tonic (if summer, 1 case)
4 quarts ginger ale
12 cokes

2 quarts each tomato juice and orange juice
1 large pitcher water
5 10-pound bags of ice

ACCOMPANIMENTS

4 lemons
4 limes (if summer, 8 lemons and 8 limes)
Cocktail onions and olives

Maraschino cherries
Tabasco sauce
Worcestershire sauce
Angostura bitters

GLASSES AND IMPLEMENTS

40 old-fashion glasses
40 highball glasses
40 wine glasses
Corkscrew
Bottle opener

Jigger
Zester and small paring knife
Wooden cutting board
100 cocktail napkins

Summer: Informal Cocktail Party for 12

•

MENU

Hummus
Curried Deviled Eggs
Steak Tartare Finger Sandwiches
Unsalted Cashews

•

HUMMUS   *May be prepared a day ahead*

   2 16-ounce cans chick-peas, drained and mashed
   2 large garlic cloves, crushed
   2 tablespoons fresh lemon juice
   1 cup tahini (sesame seed paste)
   6 tablespoons olive oil, or as needed
   salt and freshly ground pepper
   6 black olives, halved

In a large bowl combine all the ingredients. The consistency should be thick but easily spreadable. Place the mixture in a serving bowl just large enough to hold it. Garnish with olives. Refrigerate overnight. Serve Hummus with toasted pita bread, crackers or butter-fried thin slices of French bread.

CURRIED DEVILED EGGS

   1 dozen eggs, hard-cooked
   1/2 cup mayonnaise
   1 teaspoon Dijon mustard
   1 tablespoon white wine vinegar
   2 teaspoons curry powder
   2 tablespoons fresh chopped parsley
   salt and freshly ground pepper
   1 small onion, minced
   1/4 cup raisins
   paprika

Cut the eggs in half lengthwise. Scoop out the yolks into a bowl and add the mayonnaise, mustard, vinegar, curry powder, parsley, salt, pepper, and onion. Mix well and fold in the raisins. Fill the egg whites with the mixture using a teaspoon or place the mixture into a pastry bag fitted with a rose tube and press into the whites. Sprinkle with paprika.

STEAK TARTARE FINGER SANDWICHES

   1 pound ground lean sirloin
   1 egg yolk
   1 tablespoon Worcestershire sauce
   1/4 teaspoon Tabasco sauce
   3 tablespoons grated onion
   1/2 teaspoon salt, or to taste
   1/2 teaspoon freshly ground pepper
   3 tablespoons drained capers
   2 tablespoons fresh chopped parsley
   24 small finger rolls, or 24 1/4-inch-thick slices French bread
      or pumpernickel

Fifteen minutes before serving combine all the ingredients except the bread in a mixing bowl. Spread equal amounts in the center of the finger rolls or between 2 pieces of French or pumpernickel bread. Serve immediately.

Summer: Formal Cocktail Party for 24

•

MENU

Chicken Wings Tandoori
Croque Monsieur Finger Sandwiches with
Cherry Preserves
Mozzarella and Marinated Mushroom Tidbits
Macadamia Nuts

•

CHICKEN WINGS TANDOORI

*Begin preparations
a day ahead*

36 chicken wings
salt and freshly ground pepper
2 cups plain yogurt
4 large garlic cloves, crushed
4 teaspoons coriander
2 teaspoons cumin
2 teaspoons turmeric
2 teaspoons ginger
1 teaspoon cinnamon
1 teaspoon nutmeg
1/4 teaspoon of cayenne pepper
juice of 4 fresh limes
6 tablespoons melted butter
4 fresh limes, cut into 6 wedges each

Cut the chicken wings into three pieces at the joints. Discard the wing tips. Season the chicken with salt and pepper. Prick the chicken pieces with a sharp fork or the sharp point of a knife in several places. In a large bowl

319

combine the remaining ingredients except for the butter and lime wedges. Add the chicken wings to the mixture and turn to coat evenly. Cover and refrigerate overnight.

Preheat the oven to 375°F. Place the chicken pieces on a greased shallow baking pan and sprinkle with the butter. Cook in the oven for 35 minutes or until the chicken is golden brown and tender. Serve with the lime wedges.

CROQUE MONSIEUR FINGER SANDWICHES WITH CHERRY PRESERVES

12 slices firm white bread, crusts trimmed
12 thin slices Swiss cheese
6 thin slices ham, baked or boiled
3 eggs, beaten
2 tablespoons water
salt and freshly ground pepper to taste
4 tablespoons butter, or as needed
1½ cups cherry preserves*

Place 6 slices of the bread in a row. Top each with 1 slice of the cheese, 1 slice of the ham and another slice of the cheese. Place 1 slice of the bread over each. Beat the eggs with the water in a bowl and season with salt and pepper. Heat 1 tablespoon of the butter in a large skillet. Dip 1 sandwich into the eggs, coating each side, and sauté in the pan (cook 2 at a time). When browned on each side, remove and repeat, dipping the sandwiches in the egg mixture and sautéing until all are cooked. Cut each sautéed sandwich into quarters on the diagonal. Serve on a warmed platter with a bowl of the preserves.

MOZZARELLA AND MARINATED MUSHROOM TIDBITS

2 pounds mozzarella cheese, cut into 1-inch cubes
2 16-ounce jars small marinated mushroom caps

Pierce 1 mushroom cap through the middle with a toothpick and stick it into 1 cube of the cheese. Place on a serving tray. Repeat until ingredients are used.

Makes about 48 tidbits.

---

* Cherry preserves may be substituted with strawberry, raspberry, or blueberry preserves.

Winter: Informal Cocktail Party for 12

•

MENU

Appetizer Cheese Loaves
Smoked Cocktail Sausages with Wine Mustard
Sautéed Almonds

•

APPETIZER CHEESE LOAVES

8 strips bacon, cooked crisp
1 loaf fresh bakery French bread
4 tablespoons softened butter
1/2 cup chopped stuffed green olives
3 scallions, thinly sliced
2 cups shredded Cheddar cheese
1 cup fresh diced tomatoes
freshly ground pepper
paprika

While cooking the bacon, cut the bread loaf in half lengthwise, and then cut it in half crosswise. Spread 1 tablespoon of the butter on each piece of the bread. Crumble the cooked bacon and combine with the olives, scallions, cheese and tomatoes. Heat the broiler. Sprinkle the mixture evenly over the pieces of the bread and place under a hot broiler until the cheese melts and is golden. Sprinkle with pepper and paprika and cut each loaf into 6 pieces on a diagonal.

SMOKED COCKTAIL SAUSAGES WITH WINE MUSTARD

> 4 tablespoons butter
> 4 dozen smoked cocktail sausages

WINE MUSTARD:

> 1 cup Dijon mustard
> 3 tablespoons dry white or red wine

Combine the mustard and wine with a wire whisk. Place in a small jar or bowl. Just before serving heat the butter in a large skillet. Add the sausages and cook over medium-high heat, shaking the pan often for 4 or 5 minutes, until the sausages are lightly browned. Serve in a warmed dish with the Wine Mustard.

SAUTÉED ALMONDS

> 3 tablespoons butter
> 1 pound whole blanched peeled almonds (available canned)
> salt

Heat the butter in a large skillet and add the almonds. Cook over medium heat, shaking the pan often, until the almonds are light brown on both sides. Drain on paper towels and immediately sprinkle lightly with salt. Serve warm or at room temperature.

Winter: Formal Cocktail Party for 24

•

MENU

Red Salmon Caviar Dip
Onion Party Rounds
Warmed Brie with Toasted Coconut

•

RED SALMON CAVIAR DIP   *Prepare a day ahead*

    6 ounces cream cheese, softened
    1½ cups sour cream
    2 scallions, thinly sliced
    1 tablespoon fresh lemon juice
    1 4-ounce jar red salmon caviar
    freshly ground pepper

Beat the cream cheese until light and fluffy. Add the sour cream, scallions, and lemon juice. Mix well and fold in the caviar and season with pepper. Cover and refrigerate overnight. Stir before serving.

NOTE: Serve with toast triangles, toasted French bread, crackers, or fresh cut raw vegetables such as cucumbers, zucchini, carrots, celery, or fennel.

ONION PARTY ROUNDS

    mayonnaise
    1 loaf pumpernickel party rounds
    8–10 small yellow onions, sliced very thin
    paprika

Spread mayonnaise on one side of each slice of the bread. Top each with one slice of the onion and sprinkle lightly with paprika. Heat the broiler. Place on a large baking sheet. Cook under the broiler until the onions are golden.

WARMED BRIE WITH TOASTED COCONUT

1 3-pound Brie
1 cup flaked coconut
raisin bread, toasted

Place the Brie on an ovenproof serving dish. Heat the broiler. Place the coconut on a baking sheet and toast under the broiler for a few minutes. Stir the coconut and toast for 30 seconds. Remove and cool. Heat the oven to 325°F. and place the Brie in the oven for 10 minutes. Remove the Brie and sprinkle with the coconut. Serve with toasted raisin bread.

Year-Round Cocktail Party for 50

•

MENU

Marinated Mushrooms
Chicken Tarragon Finger Sandwiches
Crudités with Sour Cream and Herb Dip
and Russian Tuna Dip
Boiled Shrimp with Curried Dill Sauce
Salami with Herbed Ricotta

•

MARINATED MUSHROOMS   *Prepare a day ahead*

2 pounds small fresh mushrooms, stemmed
1 cup olive oil
4 tablespoons water
5 tablespoons fresh lemon juice
2 scallions, thinly sliced
1 garlic clove, quartered
½ teaspoon thyme
½ teaspoon rosemary
½ teaspoon oregano
1 bay leaf, crumbled
1 tablespoon Dijon mustard
2 tablespoons fresh chopped parsley
salt and freshly ground pepper to taste

Place the mushrooms in a bowl. In a saucepan bring the olive oil, water, lemon juice, scallions, and garlic to a boil. Immediately remove from the heat and whisk in the remaining ingredients. Pour over the mushrooms and gently toss with spoons. Cool, cover, and refrigerate overnight. Toss again before serving. Serve with toothpicks.

CHICKEN TARRAGON
FINGER SANDWICHES

Begin preparations
a day ahead

5 cups shredded cooked chicken breast
1 medium onion, grated
1½ cups mayonnaise
½ cup sour cream
1 tablespoon tarragon
¼ cup fresh chopped parsley, plus parsley for garnish
1½ tablespoons fresh lemon juice
salt and freshly ground pepper
2 long thin loaves of bakery French bread
1 lemon, halved

Combine well all the ingredients except for the bread and lemon. Cut the loaves of bread in half lengthwise. Scoop out the soft bread in both pieces of both loaves. Fill the bottom half of each loaf of bread with the salad mixture and place the tops on. Wrap each tightly in plastic wrap, and refrigerate overnight. Ten minutes before serving, slice the loaves into thin finger sandwiches and arrange on a platter garnished with the lemon halves sprinkled with parsley. (Cut the ends off the lemon halves so that they will stand up.)

CRUDITÉS WITH SOUR CREAM AND
HERB DIP AND RUSSIAN TUNA DIP

Prepare
a day ahead

3 pounds carrots, peeled and cut into sticks
3 whole stalks celery, cut into sticks
2 bunches fresh broccoli, cut into flowerets
3 pounds asparagus spears, ends trimmed
2 heads cauliflower, cut into flowerets
2 large green peppers, seeded and cut into strips
2 bunches radishes, ends trimmed
3 large cucumbers, cut into ¼-inch slices
4 medium zucchini, cut into ¼-inch slices
4 pints cherry tomatoes, stemmed
4 bunches scallions, root ends trimmed

SOUR CREAM AND HERB DIP:

2 cups sour cream
1 8-ounce package cream cheese, softened

½ cup fresh chopped parsley
2 teaspoons dill
2 teaspoons tarragon
3 scallions, thinly sliced
2 tablespoons fresh lemon juice
salt and freshly ground pepper to taste

RUSSIAN TUNA DIP:

2 7-ounce cans white meat tuna, drained
2 cups bottled Russian dressing
1 tablespoon fresh lemon juice
1 cup mayonnaise
2 tablespoons capers

Prepare the vegetables and place each in an individual plastic bag and close. Refrigerate overnight.

Combine the ingredients for the Sour Cream and Herb Dip well and cover. Refrigerate overnight.

Flake the tuna with a fork in a bowl and combine well with the remaining Russian Tuna Dip ingredients. Puree in a food processor fitted with the steel blade, or in a blender. Cover and refrigerate overnight.

At serving time, divide the vegetables between 2 large bowls or platters. Place one bowl of the vegetables and one dip at each end of the room, or wherever entertaining.

BOILED SHRIMP WITH CURRIED DILL SAUCE

Prepare a day ahead

5 pounds medium shrimp, shelled and deveined

CURRIED DILL SAUCE:

2 cups mayonnaise
1 cup sour cream
1½ tablespoons fresh lemon juice
1 tablespoon curry powder
1 tablespoon fresh chopped dillweed, or 1 teaspoon dried
    dillweed

Cook the shrimp in a large pot in slowly boiling water for exactly 6 minutes, stirring occasionally. Drain and cool. Place in a bowl, cover, and refrigerate overnight. Combine the ingredients for the Curried Dill Sauce in a small bowl, cover, and refrigerate overnight.

SALAMI WITH HERBED RICOTTA

Begin preparations a day ahead

2 pounds thinly sliced Italian salami
fresh parsley bouquet

HERBED RICOTTA:

1 pound ricotta cheese
1 8-ounce package cream cheese, softened
¼ cup minced shallots
3 tablespoons fresh snipped chives
1 teaspoon tarragon
½ teaspoon thyme
2 tablespoons fresh chopped parsley
½ teaspoon freshly ground pepper
salt to taste

Beat together the ricotta and cream cheese with an electric mixer or a wire whisk until smooth. Stir in the remaining ingredients for the Herbed Ricotta and combine well. Place into a bowl and refrigerate overnight. One hour before party, spread a full teaspoon of Herbed Ricotta on the center of each slice of the salami and fold it over. Place the stuffed salami on a large platter and garnish with the parsley bouquet. Cover and refrigerate until served.

CHAPTER NINE

Children's Birthday Parties

Children's birthday parties are often approached with resignation and a long sigh, and McDonald's specials. However, I believe that children's birthdays are an excellent opportunity for parents to introduce good home-cooked food to their child and the children attending the party. I'll never forget making butterscotch for sundaes for a friend's child and how she was amazed because she thought a butterscotch grew on trees. On another occasion, while cooking fresh potato chips for a nephew, I was told by a surprised child that he thought only machines could make potato chips. Cooking the foods that children love makes them feel special.

A French couple I know gave an omelet and crepe party for their five-year-old daughter, but, alas, most of the children ate very little of the food. It was simply too exotic for them, so it is best to stick to variations of safe children's fare.

Much of the preparation can be done the night before. Meantime, at the party, keep the children entertained with the help of another mother and the piñata game, a candy hunt in the house or apartment, or a long roll of craft paper and individual sets of crayons or paint sets for each child.

Summer Birthday Party for 12

•

MENU

Oven-Fried Chicken Legs
Fresh Potato Chips
Watermelon Half Filled with Fresh Fruit
Make Your Own Sundaes
Fresh Orange Juice
Milk

•

OVEN-FRIED CHICKEN LEGS

Begin preparations a day ahead

1 tablespoon seasoned salt
3 cups water
24 chicken legs
flour
3 eggs, beaten
plain dry bread crumbs

The night before, combine the seasoned salt and water. Place the chicken legs in a dish and pour the mixture over the legs. Cover and refrigerate overnight. One hour and 15 minutes before serving, remove the chicken legs from the marinade. Preheat oven to 350°F. Pat the chicken legs dry and roll in flour. Dip in the beaten eggs and coat with bread crumbs. Place on a lightly greased baking sheet and cook in the oven for 1 hour.

FRESH POTATO CHIPS

>4 pounds Idaho potatoes, peeled and very thinly sliced
>oil for deep frying
>salt

Plunge the potato slices into cold water and remove. Pat them dry in kitchen towels. Heat the oil in a fryer to 370°F. and cook a handful of the potatoes in the fryer basket at a time, for about 3 minutes, until golden. Drain and season lightly with salt. Continue frying the potatoes in batches until all are cooked. Serve in a large shallow tray lined with cloth napkins.

WATERMELON HALF FILLED WITH FRESH FRUIT

>1 large watermelon, halved
>1 large cantaloupe, seeded and cut into balls with melon-ball cutter
>2 pints blueberries, stemmed
>2 pints strawberries, hulled
>curly chickory leaves

Remove the watermelon from each half and discard one shell. Cut the watermelon into bite-size cubes and remove the seeds. Place in a large bowl with the remaining fruit and gently toss. Transfer the fruit to the hollowed-out melon shell. Surround the melon with chickory leaves.

MAKE YOUR OWN SUNDAES

>12 dessert bowls
>½ gallon vanilla ice cream
>½ gallon chocolate ice cream
>½ gallon strawberry ice cream
>8 bananas, sliced
>2 cups heavy cream, whipped and sweetened with 4 tablespoons sugar
>3 cups fudge sauce
>1½ cups chopped nuts
>1½ cups maraschino cherries

Place all the ingredients in a row in the order given on a low table with scoops and spoons where needed. Let each child prepare his or her own sundae, with assistance if necessary.

Winter Birthday Party for 12

•

MENU

Sloppy Joe Burgers
Fresh Potato Salad
Fresh Zucchini Cake with Cream Cheese Frosting
Vanilla and Chocolate Milk Shakes

•

FRESH ZUCCHINI CAKE WITH CREAM CHEESE FROSTING

*Prepare
a day ahead*

¾ cup vegetable oil
½ cup melted butter
4 eggs, lightly beaten
1¾ cups sugar
2 cups shredded zucchini
2 cups sifted all-purpose flour
1 tablespoon baking soda
2 teaspoons baking powder
1 teaspoon salt
½ teaspoon cinnamon
¼ teaspoon nutmeg
1 teaspoon vanilla
1 cup chopped pitted dates
1 cup chopped walnuts

CREAM CHEESE FROSTING:

1 8-ounce package cream cheese, at room temperature
8 tablespoons (1 stick) butter, softened

8 ounces confectioners' sugar
1 teaspoon vanilla

Preheat the oven to 350°F. Combine the vegetable oil, butter, eggs, and sugar well. Add the remaining ingredients except for the dates and walnuts. Mix well. Toss the dates with a little flour and add to the mixture with the walnuts and mix. Turn the mixture into a 9- × 13-inch cake pan and bake in the oven for about 35 minutes, until done. Let the cake cool before frosting.

With an electric mixer, beat the cream cheese with the butter until smooth and creamy, at medium speed. Gradually add the confectioners' sugar a little at a time until used. Finally, add the vanilla and mix well. Spread over the cooled zucchini cake with a frosting spatula. Refrigerate overnight.

NOTE: For variations on the frosting, sprinkle with toasted coconut or walnuts.

FRESH POTATO SALAD   *Prepare a day ahead*

4 pounds potatoes, peeled and sliced
1 cup mayonnaise, or as needed
¼ cup sour cream, or as needed
1 cup thinly sliced celery
1 cup fresh grated carrots
¼ cup fresh chopped parsley
1 small onion, grated
salt and freshly ground pepper

Boil the potatoes until tender, about 15 minutes, and drain well. Meanwhile, combine the remaining ingredients except the seasoning in a bowl. Add the potatoes and toss. Season to taste with salt and pepper, cover, and refrigerate overnight.

SLOPPY JOE
BURGERS

Begin preparations
a day ahead

3 tablespoons butter, plus softened butter for bread
1 cup chopped onions
1 cup chopped green pepper
1 garlic clove, crushed
3 pounds ground beef
1½ tablespoons chili powder
3 tablespoons tomato paste
2 cups tomato sauce
¼ cup chili sauce, or as needed
salt and freshly ground pepper
12 hamburger buns

Heat the 3 tablespoons butter in a large Dutch oven. Add the onions and green pepper. Cook over medium heat for 10 minutes, stirring often. Add the garlic and ground beef and cook until the pink color is gone. Stir in the chili powder, tomato paste, tomato sauce, and chili sauce. Season to taste with salt and pepper and simmer for 10 minutes. Cool, cover, and refrigerate overnight. Fifteen minutes before serving, reheat the beef mixture. Heat the broiler. Butter the insides of the buns and toast them under the broiler. Spoon the beef mixture onto the buns.

VANILLA AND CHOCOLATE MILK SHAKES

FOR EACH VANILLA MILK SHAKE:

1 large scoop vanilla ice cream
1 cup milk
1 ice cube
1 teaspoon malt (optional)

Combine the ingredients in a blender.

For each Chocolate Milk Shake use chocolate ice cream and add 2 tablespoons chocolate syrup to mixture. Combine in blender.

Index

342

345

354

FREE

THE DAILEY NEWSLETTER

Would you like to know more
about Janet Dailey and her newest novels?
The Janet Dailey Newsletter is filled
with information about Janet's life, her
travels and appearances with her
husband Bill, and advance information on
her upcoming books—plus comments
from Janet's readers, and a personal letter
from Janet in each issue. The Janet
Dailey Newsletter will be sent to you <u>free</u>.
Just fill out and mail the coupon
below. If you're already a subscriber,
send in the coupon for a friend!